CONVERSATIONS WITH WALLACE STEGNER

Conversations with Wallace Stegner on Western History and Literature

Wallace Stegner
and
Richard W. Etulain

Revised Edition

UNIVERSITY OF UTAH PRESS   SALT LAKE CITY

Library of Congress Cataloging-in-Publication Data
Stegner, Wallace Earle, 1909–
    Conversations with Wallace Stegner on Western history and
literature / Wallace Stegner and Richard W. Etulain. — Rev. ed.
        p.   cm.
    Includes bibliographical references.
    ISBN 0–87480–353–5 (alk. paper)
    1. Stegner, Wallace Earle, 1909–   —Interviews,   2. Authors,
American—20th century—Interviews.   3. West (U.S.)—Historiography.
4. West (U.S.) in literature.   I. Etulain, Richard W.   II. Title.
PS3537.T316Z465   1990
813'.52—dc20
                                                    90–12326
                                                    CIP

All the photographs in this book are the work of Leo Holub of San Francisco, California.

Contents

Photographs by Leo Holub

Books by Wallace Stegner

Remembering Laughter, 1937

The Potter's House, 1938

On a Darkling Plain, 1940

Fire and Ice, 1941

Mormon Country, 1942

The Big Rock Candy Mountain, 1943

One Nation, 1945 (with the editors of *Look*)

Second Growth, 1947

The Women on the Wall, 1950

The Preacher and the Slave, 1950
Reprinted as *Joe Hill: A Biographical Novel,* 1969

*Beyond the Hundredth Meridian: John Wesley Powell and the
Second Opening of the West,* 1954

This Is Dinosaur: Echo Park Country and Its Magic Rivers, 1956 (editor)

The City of the Living, and Other Stories, 1956

Great American Short Stories, 1957 (editor, with Mary Stegner)

A Shooting Star, 1961

*Wolf Willow: A History, a Story, and a Memory of
the Last Plains Frontier,* 1962

The Gathering of Zion: The Story of the Mormon Trail, 1964

*The American Novel: From James Fenimore Cooper to
William Faulkner,* 1965 (editor)

Twenty Years of Stanford Stories, 1966 (editor, with others)

All the Little Live Things, 1967

The Sound of Mountain Water, 1969

Angle of Repose, 1971

Discovery! The Search for Arabian Oil, 1971

The Uneasy Chair: A Biography of Bernard DeVoto, 1974

The Letters of Bernard DeVoto, 1975 (editor)

The Spectator Bird, 1976

Recapitulation, 1979

American Places, 1981 (with Page Stegner and Eliot Porter)

One Way to Spell Man, 1982

Crossing to Safety, 1987

The American West as Living Space, 1987

Collected Stories, 1990

Foreword

By NORMAN COUSINS

What is most remarkable about Wallace Stegner's development as a major American literary figure is the absence of sudden thrusts or skyrockets. He has added to his reputation year by year and book by book. Whether as novelist, biographer, historian, essayist, literary critic, or teacher, he has produced a body of work of cumulative substance and stature. Even more significant than the Pulitzer Prize or National Book Award he has received is the steady development of his artistry, reflected in his consistently distinguished work over four decades. When viewed in total perspective, these contributions admit no doubt of Stegner's high station in the community of American letters.

What gives his work its essential character is a deep familiarity with American historical, cultural, and political terrain. Few writers in the recent past have been able to summon as much knowledge of the main strands of our national life.

Conversations with Wallace Stegner is many things. It is personal history most of all, but it is also a large slice of Americana. There are pieces here that take in the intellectual and ideological campus scene of the thirties, affected as it was by the Spanish Civil War; the literary and publishing world, especially as experienced by a young writer outside the Eastern literary establishment; the unhinging social and political issues of the sixties and seventies; the relationships with writers and students in many places and on varying levels. Stegner's personal pantheon includes names like Vardis Fisher, Scott Nearing, Bernard DeVoto, Robert Frost, Robinson Jeffers— names of men with robust lives with thoughts and words to match.

Stegner properly takes exception to the careless tendency to pin geographic tags on writers outside the Northeast, where authors are regarded as authors and not regional oddities. For example, Saul Bellow is labeled an "American writer," not an Eastern writer, even though his books may be about East Coast life. Yet other writers who happen to live west of the Mississippi are tagged regionally, whatever their themes, as though it is necessary to warn readers about being in the company of writers who are somehow short of the mark. In my years at the *Saturday Review*, I deliberately tried to keep the magazine out of the swirls and eddies that characterized at least part of the New York intellectual life and that tended to reflect a certain provincialism. We consciously tried to take soundings from all over the country—not just in writing but in music, drama, and the other fine arts. This gave us the reputation of being "middle-brow," whatever that meant. What was most significant about the label was not its precise meaning but the obvious fact that it was intended invidiously.

In any event, whatever the correct location of the "brows" we were said to write for, we tried to recognize the existence of writers of genuine talent wherever they might be. What appealed to us most about Wallace Stegner was the integrity of the man, the identifiability of his values, the high quality of his scholarship, his undoubted craftsmanship as a writer, and the fact that his books added greatly to an understanding of the subjects he chose to write about.

Access to his wide-ranging observations and philosophy, made possible by these interviews, represents a long-overdue service—not just to those with primary literary interests but to anyone fascinated with the phenomenon of America. The book carries with it the happy prospect that readers who have not yet savored the full flavor of Wallace Stegner's work and thought will be moved in that direction.

After Ten Years:
Another Conversation with
Wallace Stegner

Etulain: What do you think have been the most notable changes in the American West during the last decade? Have the continuities been more significant than the changes?

Stegner: Actually change may have been part of the continuity. The old boom-and-bust routine still goes on. I suppose Dallas, Denver, and a lot of places are less prosperous now than they were ten years ago—was it ten years ago that we talked?

Yes.

Those ten years have gone by pretty fast. Billings has not become as big as Denver, as it was talking about becoming ten years ago. Denver itself is in a slump. Texas is in a slump. It seems to be almost like a continuous, repetitive act of God that the western resources should be mined in that fashion, that populations should rush in and have to rush out again, or trickle out again. I don't suppose they have trickled out of the Southwest, where sunshine is a relatively renewable commodity, but water is not, and I suspect sooner or later there is going to be a problem there. They're getting over-populated for what they can support.

No, I would guess that changes in the West are just another blip on that long curve. A big boom, prosperity, and population growth followed by a

This conversation took place in Wallace Stegner's home in California on 27 December 1989.

[ix]

bust, which in different places was of different proportions, but which was a bust or a decline. Some places, like Montana, don't seem to have the same kind of boom because they haven't got that much sunshine for one thing. The weather is rougher. I think Montana is relatively safe from the kinds of things that the Southwest is not so safe from just because it takes an awful lot to live there and there isn't a lot to make a living by. It's a helluva good life but a poor living. That's one of the reasons why Montana seems to me to get more and more characteristically western—it survives in the old fashion.

There's more literary acknowledgment, I think, of the West. Several people from the Southwest have come on pretty well since we talked. Leslie Silko, and people like that have made it pretty solidly. The bunch around Missoula, I suppose, is the latest and in some ways the most noticeable crowd because they're all pretty good. Rather insular, but they've made their impact, which is what a regional literary movement tries to do. Stay itself but get itself noted. I think that's a hopeful sign that in a town as small as Missoula there should be three or four writers of considerable importance. Not important to the *New York Times Book Review*, maybe, but important in the whole scheme of things. That's been going on there for quite a long time; that isn't a change either. It's just a kind of growth. A good many years ago, what's his name . . . ?

Richard Hugo or Leslie Fiedler?

Before them. He wrote a book about the *métis*, and the Louis Riel rebellion. . . . Joseph Kinsey Howard. He had a literary circle going in the 1940s. And H. G. Merriam published the *Frontier* up in Missoula before that. There was a kind of persistent, small literary germ growing there. It has not changed in its general emphasis, but it's got better and bigger as time has gone on. And the people who were there, though some of them died and some of them left, left their influence behind. Even Fiedler's influence, I think, was an enriching one in the way he stirred up the waters. He made an awful lot of people mad. I don't know that he learned much from his experience there, but people learned something from him just by seeing that particular eastern type.

I'm interested that the people who predict the future argue that California will stop growing, and yet it continues to expand.

California is, as we've said before, not fully part of the West. It's west of the West, as somebody in California recently said. And it has the water and the climate and the soil to support a population like Japan, if it has to. I wouldn't want to live here when it was going on that way, but I guess that's the way it's going to go. It'll be conurbial all the way from Santa Rosa to San Diego, and almost is now. Except, you can still drive down to Santa

Cruz along the coast—the lovely empty coast—and see a few guys wind surfing, and very little else except nature. California is a very, very special case because it's big and it's blessed. It's got a great deal of variety. Moreover, it is on the Pacific Rim, which makes an enormous difference. Utah may be shipping coal to Japan, but it ships it through California.

So it's still Carey McWilliams's Great Exception, and when you talk about the West, California is different.

I think the whole coast is different, actually, partly because of its Pacific Rim location, but also because of more adequate rainfall. At least west of the Sierra-Cascades. Eastern Oregon and eastern Washington are West in our sense, but Portland and Seattle are not; they bleed toward Alaska or Japan. The West is insular in the sense that it's stuck between the coasts, and there is that mix which Walter Webb described as a near desert with a desert heart. That always seemed to me not quite the right metaphor because it's circular, and it ought to be longitudinal. Reality has to do with mountain ranges more than it does with basins. But it's close. Now I'm not, as you probably know, terribly *au courant* on what's happening in the West because I've been spending about a third of my time, at least, in Vermont and elsewhere. I haven't been writing anything like western history, and I've been involved in environmental squabbles which have to do with other things. I'm certainly not up on it the way you are. I should ask you that question, and learn from the answer.

Doris Grumbach's very positive review of your recent novel Crossing to Safety *[1987] must have been satisfying to you. She really liked your novel. How did you come to write that book? Did it originate in people you had known over time?*

Oh sure. I suppose that's my native habit. Actually I didn't even write it as a novel. I wrote it as a sort of memoir more for Mary and myself than for anything else, and I wasn't at all sure I was ever going to publish it. These people were our very close friends, and at the same time they had some problems which were very personal; and an honest portrait of them, as honest as I could make it, I thought might be offensive to the family. Before I ever sent it to any publisher I sent it around to all the children, and they all said, "Yes, publish it." So, if it wasn't offensive, I thought, okay. But it was, really, in a way that no book of mine ever has been, an attempt to tell the absolute, unvarnished truth about other people and myself. Not in a sense of what is fitting for the novel, but how they literally were in life. Inevitably I found myself inventing scenes and suppressing things, and bringing things forward in order to make the story work because I guess my habits are incorrigible; but my intention, at least, was the utter, unvarnished truth. And there was nothing very dramatic in those lives either, so that I was taking risks, I was quite aware. The contemporary novel deals commonly in sensation, but there was not much sensation in this story to deal with. Academic life—publish or perish—it's hard to make that a matter of life or death. And I suppose the only reason it struck me as a potential something that I had to write was that I was puzzled about the relationships of those two very different personalities and the ambiguities within both of them. I loved them both and saw them breaking their hearts and their heads until they died. And also, I suppose, I had the muleheaded notion that it *ought* to be possible to make books out of something less than loud sensation. I was trying to make very small noises and to make them thoughtful, but to do that you have to make people listen. That was the hard part in this book, and that's where I suppose I made the biggest changes, in fact, occasionally to heighten something. Just in effect to say, oh, something's coming.

I didn't change much of anything really. I got Larry Morgan fired in Wisconsin, which didn't happen to me. I went to Harvard instead. But dismissal was happening to all my friends, and I knew all about it. I think it would have happened to me if I had stayed around Wisconsin long enough. They weren't promoting, so that everybody there—a very good, quite a distinguished bunch of young instructors, five or six of us—wound up having to go somewhere else at the end of two or three years. Because I wanted to tell it just as it happened, I didn't fictionalize places. I started the action in Wisconsin, took it to Vermont. I left out a whole wandering period when this friend I was writing about went to the Humanities School in Chicago, which was an academic graveyard in those years, and got buried ultimately, and finally wound up at Scripps, very much loved, a great teacher. He had a bad academic time just because he didn't publish—and the pressure to publish only made him unhappy. It made his wife *very* unhappy, because she was ambitious for him, and she was a managing woman. But all kinds of events in there, such as the shipwreck on Lake Mendota, were pretty much literally just as they happened. The walking trip in Vermont is also pretty much just as it happened. The episode in Italy I wrote the very last thing, because I had left a gap in the book that was too much. I had created a very intense relationship there in the beginning, up to the polio, and then it got rather summary, so I threw in the Florence chapter in order to help fill that later period out. There, too, I used real events, but the reality hadn't involved these people. The book's a mix. Nearly all of it can be tracked to real events, but it doesn't deal with the real events quite as literally as I set out to.

You and I have talked quite often about the ways you use passageways between the past and present. Does this emphasis result primarily from

*your search for a novelistic technique to tell the story, or does it result
from the way you see past impinging on present? A technique or a part
of your world view?*

Well, it is certainly a technical problem. But it's probably also a philosophical preoccupation that has just grown on me. The older you get, the
more the relation of past and present grows on you, because you have more
history to look at. Also, I felt a lack, because having grown up without any
history I kept hunting for some. Sometimes, when you don't have enough,
you may generate it, just like cholesterol. So I suppose the past-present
linkage does spring out of an intellectual preoccupation, but it gives me
problems, as in *Angle of Repose*, ducking back and forth all the time. In this
one.... This is pretty much a straightforward look back. A return to remote
Vermont and this deathbed. The whole novel takes one day. Nothing new
or very difficult about that. Just have to watch where you are. That's one
reason why it is told in first-person singular; it's easier to condense time in the
first person—at least for me. You can comment on it as it passes and it seems
to have passed, but if you're doing it in third-person, you somehow have to
have more textual duration to convince people that time has really gone by.

In this case, too, I was looking back inevitably over a good chunk of my
own life, fifty years or so. No matter how old you get, you don't feel old.
You're still the same guy inside, and so there is a continuity there, within
yourself. You can't ignore it. It seems to me that it is built into everybody
individually, and in some Spenserian way it may be built into societies
as well. Ideas go on ahead, at the same time that *regressus historicus* is taking
them on back into the dark.... Should I say something more on that?

*No, I'm getting an inkling of your personal philosophy, as well as an
insight into the problems a novelist faces in dealing with the past.*

In the American West as Living Space *[1957] you argue that the
typical westerner likely owes more to his or her experiences in a small or
mid-sized town or city rather than to those in a large urban area. That
idea intrigues me. Could you elaborate on that?*

Did I say it quite that way?

*You said that a person is more likely to find the typical westerner coming
from Billings or Boise or Missoula than from a Los Angeles or a ...*

We can check this. It's perfectly possible to go to the documents.
I thought I had said something like the West is more *visible* in the small
towns and cities than in the big urban centers.... I think when I wrote
that I had been reading Least Heat Moon. He agrees with me that the West
is most characterized by its *space*—the space between the oases, whatever

holds the towns apart. Even though the West is more urban than the rest of the United States—a larger proportion of its people live in cities—that fact doesn't say anything about that space. The urban West, it seems to me, is like urbanism anywhere else. There's not that much difference between Seattle and L. A., or Seattle and Denver, or Denver and Wichita, or Wichita and Omaha, or Omaha and Des Moines. But there is a lot of difference in the empty part of the country. It's what always strikes me coming home, whenever I drive back into it. It's what strikes newcomers most when they come west. You find it in everything from pioneer journals to a recent book like Frazier's [*Great Plains*, 1989] too.

So when I speak of the West . . . I guess I am thinking of the West I wish would grow up and get stable and develop some kind of continuous, sustainable life—an economic life that would keep a stable population. I am thinking of towns like Missoula, Bozeman, Boise, and so on, where there is a steady living for a modest population without the fevers and collapses of boom-and-bust. And there is likewise something absolutely essential, to leaven the lump, an academy of some kind, a college or university. My favorite places in the West are, I suppose, relatively small university towns. Villages are simply unkempt, half savage, and often impermanent. The cities are characterless, or relatively so. But those towns have their own quality, and the future of the West seems to me to lie in them.

> *I was struck with the third chapter of* The West as Living Space, *where you raised the questions of who is the westerner, what has the West produced? In thirty pages or so, you did what no other writer has done: you described what that westerner and his culture are.*

Well, I had to say everything I knew about the West in three fifty-minute lectures. That one went on for an hour, I think, but even so, it was an impossible job. Still, the first two lectures didn't seem to mean anything unless I could at least take a crack at the society and character the West had created. If there are such things as regional or national characteristics, you have to try to define them. They're always slippery. They may not exist at all. Maybe in the eye of the beholder.

I believe that the awesome space of the West, which is not a fiction, is not going to go away, no matter how badly we abuse it. It is always going to be holding the oases apart because nobody can live there. We can ruin it, tear it up with draglines and bulldozers and ORV's, but there is still going to be space. Whether that has any effect on human character or not I don't know. I think it probably does in some way. Looking a long way is not a social experience; it's an aesthetic or even religious one. And it happens outdoors.

I'm struggling with writing a book about culture in the modern West and trying to decide whether I'll put the emphasis on western *culture or* culture *in the West. Is there a difference between those two?*

Well, I don't know. I don't envy you. It's obvious there's a mix, much more of a mix than it would have been if the West hadn't been settled by the time of fast communication. When was the first telegraph?

About 1860.

In the 1860s, before the first transcontinental railroad, right? So that essentially a lot of the West was settled when you could get word to and from the East in a few minutes, if you had to. Isolation with all the space is not quite the same kind of isolation as you've got, let us say, in the Tennessee mountains, or Georgia somewhere. Those mountain boys lived in their own hollows and on their own knobs and didn't see much from outside and had very little communication with outside, so Elizabethan English and balladry and a whole peck of things lasted there. There isn't really a discernible western dialect of English—at least I don't think there is—distinguishable from the Midwest, or standard American; it seems to me in that case the West is part of the mainstream, whereas New England and the South are offshoots of it. Anybody who says "ideer" is not part of the mainstream.

The West has always been in communication, but it has always been various, and it didn't have the unity of the cotton South, or the corn Midwest, or small-farm New England. And variousness makes, I suppose—now I'm beginning to get a wild hair—variousness makes the social life less shaping. Variousness and space probably do promote the individual view rather than the social view. I wouldn't push that too far, however. It seems to me a possibility.

I've been struggling with a conception, one that doesn't work very well, and yet I'm using it. An oxymoron, a fragmented unity. Sometimes in the West we really want—in fact the human mind wants—to conclude that in the 1920s and 1930s we were such and such, in the 1940s and 1950s we were such and such, and in the 1960s we were something else. Yet there are so many continuities crossing over those time lines, and so much diversity coming in from outside, that the warp and woof of all these mixed things is a fragmented unity.

Yeah, maybe so. You know this recent book about the West?

Which one is that?

The Legacy of Conquest.

Oh yes, yes.

Patty Limerick is definitely talking continuities, all the way. The frontier still exists. Turner was wrong. She has a point. There's no question that, at least, self-image tends to remain somewhat the same. And the economic boom-and-bust cycle continues over and over. Well, fragmented unity is a perfectly good way to put it. Passionately at peace.

You mentioned Patricia Nelson Limerick. What other western writers, novelists or historians, have come to your attention in the last few years?

Actually the historians I have read most are Patty Limerick and . . .

Donald Worster?

. . . Donald Worster, yes. *The Dust Bowl* and *Rivers of Empire*. A good man. And a lot of books on western water. [Marc Reisner's] *Cadillac Desert* and [Philip A. Fradkin's] *River No More* and so on. My history is very, very limited. Tunnel vision as well as limited reading time. I get a chance, I must say, to read an awful lot of things in manuscript. Everybody that has anything to say about deserts in the West, publishers send to me. I have had to have some little cards printed saying Wallace Stegner can no longer comment on manuscripts or read books for blurbs. I hate it, because a lot of it I would like to read. But I've also got about 500 ex-students out there, all of whom it seems to me, write three books a year. I could really spend a very busy life doing *nothing* but attending to other peoples' books. I have a hard time selecting my own reading.

What about novelists?

Some of them I have read for double reasons—they're good, and they're former students, Stegner Fellows at Stanford. Larry McMurtry, Ed Abbey, Bill Kittredge, Tom McGuane, Robert Stone, Ken Kesey, Harriet Doerr, and others. And of course Scott Momaday, also a former Stegner Fellow. And James Welch, Ivan Doig, Leslie Marmon Silko, not former students but people whose work I admire.

About four or five months ago, I argued that of all the new western novelists, the one that followed most closely in your tradition was Ivan Doig. Strong sense of history, that northern West . . .

Yes, well, I never noticed that he followed in my . . . I never wrote in a Scottish brogue! But he's a very animated fellow, good eye, lots of energy. I have liked the general quality of his books even when it seemed to me, as in both *English Creek* and *Dancing at the Rascal Fair*, that there was a little bit more there than there needed to be. But better a feast than a famine.

To return for a minute to that first question of yours. It seems to me that what has been happening in the West in the way of continuity is the same strong tendency to exceed its limitations that the West always had. Rush in and trickle out. Get in, get rich, get out. It's always been a treasure hunt—and never a settlement. That may be inevitable. It may be that this country won't settle much. It will only support towns which are bound to become ghost towns of one kind or another. The exceeding of limitations, the limitation being imposed by water, more or less, or altitude, or a combination, is one of the West's abiding characteristics.

I think that we need a new Turner to write an essay not about "The Significance of the Frontier in American History" but about "The Significance of the Subregion in the West" because of the varied parts of the section. For example, consider the varieties of literary experiences in the West. Look at Missoula, which has helped put together that monumental anthology, The Last Best Place *[1958], reviewed so well and suggesting the rich literary tradition of Montana. Yet in a state nearby with many similarities, Idaho, there has never been the literary activity compared to that in Montana. Here's just one example of the subregional diversity in the West.*

No, and it's hard to know why. Because parts of Idaho are just as sparsely settled as Montana, and it's just as wild, and there's just as much wilderness left. Maybe because southeastern Idaho is all Mormon and western Idaho and the panhandle something else. But Idaho fiction, as far as I know, is esentially Vardis Fisher. Utah has never had such a literary movement. It had a few Mormon voices speaking up back in the time of Maurine Whipple and Virginia Sorenson, a generation or two ago. If there are comparable voices now, I don't know them. There should be—that's the most *settled* part of the West. Maybe something hindering in the Mormon tradition. It's so separate a culture that you could only write from within it, for the people within it—unless you adopted the old Mormon-baiting stance, which is, thank God, dead.

Even in that Montana literary culture, here's Richard Brautigan, Tom McGuane, so different from Kittredge, Doig, and James Welch. They're all there in Montana, but some are Montanan and some are not.

Montana, after all, acquired a rather special number of new migrants during the time when everybody was saying don't Californicate the rest of the West. Brautigan was here. He was from Oregon, but he came to San Francisco in the first instance and then—perhaps because of Tom McGuane —went up and was part of the crowd at McGuane's up in Paradise Valley on the Yellowstone, where McGuane's first ranch was. Then he came back to San Francisco to die. That, I think, is part of a migratory pattern. McGuane is permanent, he likes it where he is, and he's going to settle. His background is Michigan and Florida, as Brautigan's was Oregon.

There have been a lot of migrants. What's his name—I can't remember any names this morning—*Rock Springs* [1987, Richard Ford]. He paid no attention to the local history or geography. He had gold mines outside of Rock Springs, Wyoming, and things like that. He didn't give a damn— after all Keats said Cortez. The locals who do give a damn about history and geography and want it straight thought he was a kind of carpetbagger writing southern stories about Montana. And they're pretty bleak, Tobacco Roadish. . . .

We were talking about the diversity of that group who's moved into Montana.

Well, Ehrlich is a California girl . . .

Gretel Ehrlich.

. . . moved up to become a rancher. Well, all right, that's legitimate. She's like Tom McGuane. Of the natives, Bill Kittredge is from eastern Oregon, so he's a legitimate westerner, at least.

James Welch?

Welch, and then Ivan Doig, and I guess Dorothy Johnson—a number of people like that who were all natives. Maybe a-little-jealous natives, so that they didn't always respond to this crowd that moved in on them. Gretel Ehrlich, and to a degree McGuane, at least, are responsive to the country and try to get it straight. When McGuane writes *Missouri Breaks*, he has at least been there; he knows what they look like.

Some imports become part of the native scene, and some do not. Some who went there because of the native scene have been pretty well adopted into it. And others have not. But I think there isn't a *very large* number of native Montana writers. It's too small a population. What is the population of Montana—a half million or so? Something like that, and it's a big state. I've been astonished in going up there—everybody knows everybody in the state. All the politicians and all the local county supervisors, and everybody else. And so do the ranchers. People have the dignity of rareness, and that may be another development of westernism that I like. The space not merely between towns but between people.

I think those things force responses out of sympathetic people like Gretel Ehrlich. So that they do speak with something like the local voice. But it's certainly not going to be a populist literary movement. It's not going to be widely spread, and I don't know that it has spread, to Bozeman or anywhere. It seems to me pretty well isolated in Missoula. Nothing in Great Falls, nothing in Butte, so far as I know. Strictly a Missoula operation. No, wait a minute, it is true that there is some of it in Bozeman because [David] Quammen comes from Bozeman, or lives in Bozeman. One of those Montana Norwegians, of whom there are a lot. There were a lot of Scandahoovians coming up along the old migration route to the Northwest that my family once followed and stopped en route.

Is that same kind of combination true, say, of Santa Fe and Taos? The combination of people like Leslie Silko and N. Scott Momaday, in this case both Native Americans who grew up in that general area, and John Nichols, who comes in from the outside, and Richard Bradford, earlier on.

For that matter, Oliver LaFarge was an import . . .

Conrad Richter, too.

Conrad Richter, yes, and so was Willa Cather, when she was a Santa Fean and wrote her books on top of La Fonda. So, I guess was Witter Bynner. He was from New Jersey, or somewhere.

Well, in a new country you're bound to have a lot of immigrants. At a time when the world elsewhere gets so very crowded and people want space, they're going to go where the space is. And some of those are going to be the most sensitive people, some of those are going to be bright. The artistic impulse sometimes arises at home and moves out, and sometimes it arises outside and moves in, which is fine and healthy. I don't see anything wrong with that, except that it . . . probably in terms of opportunity, more people are going to move out than move in. Doig has already moved out to Seattle. You have to have some money or make it big enough to be able to stay; otherwise you may find yourself just pinched out, going where the opportunities are greater. McGuane has some money from his family or from the movies. He makes a pass at raising and training cutting horses, but as a horse rancher, I'm sure, he doesn't make his living.

It seems to me that the key person in that Missoula colony or circle, right now, is Bill Kittredge. He's something like H. G. Merriam was earlier.

Yes, and there always has been one central figure in such a group. Hugo was that for a while, Joseph Kinsey Howard before him, Merriam before Howard. It's nice to have an address like Upper Rattlesnake, too, where such a group can congregate. That's a good, prideful western address. There is a real advantage in having a crowd and a gathering place. Writers have to have somebody to talk to. Generally in the West, companionship comes from the local academy, whatever it is, because that is where some writers will be making their living. In the Missoulas of the world there aren't any Bohemias that will support you. I don't think that Upper Rattlesnake is Bohemian in any sense of the word. It's a kind of middle-class academic community in most ways. But that's where Kittredge lives, that's where Welch lives. Several members of the English Department live in Missoula, who, if they're not writers, are sympathetic to writers who form a kind of critical leadership.

They're short a lot of things. They're short music and theater and things like that. But they make do and make a lot of it at home. Kittredge's friend . . .

Annick Smith?

Annick Smith did the *Heartland* movie, although I guess Bill wrote the script, or part of it. But that's a real accomplishment, a landmark movie in my mind. And that sort of accomplishment doesn't depend on anything from the outside, except money, maybe. You don't have to have a theater to make a movie. You don't have to have anything except talent and a source of funds.

They were also coeditors of that marvelous anthology, The Last Best Place.

Yes, they're certainly central to that group. I don't think Jim Welch is active in quite the same way, though he is certainly one of the prominent members and one of the best writers.

I'd like to shift the focus to you. It's rumored that you're doing your autobiography. Is that true . . . ?

I'm afraid I started that rumor with you, and I'm afraid it's not true. I started summer before last, I guess. I agreed to write a 10,000-word autobiography for Gale Research, which does contemporary writers, five or six people to a volume. I was irritated at the fact that I couldn't get my precious life into 10,000 words very handily. It took me quite a while. I had two or three problems. One was that I had the feeling that I had read all of this before, in one form or another. And two, that it was hard to get my whole life into 10,000 words. Three, that I kept wanting to invent. Writing an autobiography, you shouldn't do that—I don't think. So I didn't get very far with it. While I was playing with the idea, I wrote an essay about my mother, which I had been wanting to do for a long time. It was published in a Book-of-the-Month Club Christmas volume, called *Family Relations.*

I wrote something else. Oh, for Clarus Backes, the former Book Editor of the *Denver Post,* who was doing an anthology called *Growing Up Western.*

I did him a piece essentially about Saskatchewan-Montana, that part of my life. I also did a piece for another of those anthologies they did in Montana...

On the Great Falls years ...

Yeah, on the Great Falls years. So I wrote four or five random pieces, altogether, and that's where it still sits. I've never got beyond Great Falls. And not very emphatically up to Great Falls. I was piecemealing it. I would have to take the long business apart—the Gale Research thing, the 10,000-word one—and fill it all in with things like these chapters in order to make the start of a full autobiography. And I don't know, I'm a little bit like Robinson Jeffers—I never go anywhere except to dinner. Nothing much happens in my life. I don't have any world events or any shocking revelations, or anything like that, which makes . . . a problem.

I didn't even have . . . I began to realize that I don't even have a wide literary acquaintance, having lived in the West and been too busy with teaching and occupied with other jobs. So I never sat around in cafes or went to literary cocktail parties. I've got a lot of acquaintance with younger writers because a lot of them I taught. And that would have to be a good chunk of the autobiography. But apart from that, the only writers I knew well and had a lot to do with were people around Cambridge, Boston, and Bread Loaf. That's where I first met a lot of writers, including Frost, DeVoto, Louis Untermeyer, and the whole bunch that used to . . . John Ciardi . . . it was the Bread Loaf crowd. Along with that, a lot of publishers who used to come up—Alfred Knopf and people—so that for a while I was in a kind of literary community. But when we moved out here, that was cut off as if by a guillotine. We met a few during our year in Rome in 1959–60—Bill Styron, Phil Roth, a few others.

But other people came to you here.

Yes. There were people like Malcolm Cowley, Frank O'Connor, Katherine Anne Porter, C. P. Snow, Saul Bellow, Cheever, sure, quite a lot of them. But known only briefly.

I was thinking of the McMurtrys, the Keseys, those people, who started coming here in the 60s to study with you.

And the Wendell Berrys, the Ed Abbeys, the Bob Stones. They actually started coming here in the 40s. But the class of 60, I guess, was one of the most remarkable. A lot of prominent writers came out of it.

There's a literary history to be done: the Wallace Stegner literary influence at Stanford, and on western letters.

I shouldn't write that because my influence was not good upon every-body, and the way I see it would not be the way other people would see it. In fact, there are a number of people who I'm sure got nothing whatever out of coming. There are others who got quite a lot. I shouldn't write that because often the reason for their not getting anything was some lack in me, or some blockage between me and them, some blindness on my part to what they were doing. I was certainly not infallible—I could have been blind to anybody. Particularly the ones who didn't want to work irritated me.

So several of us are going to have to gang up on you to finish those auto-biographical chapters . . .

This could still happen because I don't have anything else on my mind, and when I get clear of this latest deadline which suddenly moved back from February 1st to January 1st . . . so I have to grind one out in the next few days. After that, I don't have anything much to occupy me. I might at least write some more essays. And I suppose one place to begin would be just to write the history of the writing program, which nobody really knows but me. That would have some usefulness. It already has a good many errors in the popular view. Funny, even R. F. Jones, who was a very dear friend and head of the English Department when I first started at Stanford, had it wrong. His brother funded it in the first instance. But R. F.'s version of it differs from mine. I think mine was right, but I'm not . . . he's dead, so he can't argue with me. Al Eurich was the acting president of Stanford, when I came there, and was running the Aspen Institute when I was up there a few years ago. He told me the story of the founding of the writing program in a form that I had not heard before. It gets modified. Lots of things get modified. Also I suppose there is some usefulness to that. Writing my own boyhood is just a walk in the steps of the novels I've already written. I'm not sure that that should be a very large part. . . .

Would the years in Salt Lake be the most traumatic for you to write about?

Well, I don't know. Probably so. But not all the years. I was very content with a lot of things in Salt Lake. Some dire things happened too, but I've got around them so far by inventing. If I couldn't change them, if I couldn't make them fit in the form I wanted, I might find them more difficult to deal with.

You would invent into a novel, uh?

I have a sense that every novel is to some degree an autobiography; and probably every autobiography is to some degree a novel. I suppose Phil Roth really has the right dope in *The Facts*; have you read that book?

Nope.

It is supposed to be the autobiography of Philip Roth, as distinguished from Zuckerman, his stooge. But Zuckerman enters in, and comments, and by the end the facts and the fictions are blended like butter and sugar in a frosting.

About ten years ago, I asked you about the future of the West. Those comments of a decade ago seem both optimistic and pessimistic. But what words would you use now in describing your views about the future of the West?

I guess I would be a little more pessimistic than then. Partly because every boom-and-bust leaves the West physically a little poorer, a little worse damaged. Too many people are part of the damage. Salt Lake City, for instance, which I liked very much when its size was about 100,000, is now at least three times that big and fills the whole valley. The smog that used to be there from the smelters is gone, but the smog from automobiles is even more poisonous. Not as dirty but more poisonous. The Chamber of Commerce boosterism that used to be just a little noise in the bushes is now a very clangorous sound in Salt Lake. They're all beating the drums to get bigger and bigger. All that fiction about the goods of growth.

I don't think Denver is as good a town as it used to be, before it got populous. I guess I'm just conservative. I don't really want the West to change from the way it was when I liked it. On the other hand, I can see why people from other parts of the country want to come out there, why they want to live in Denver, even in a suburb like Englewood. Because the mountains are close, there are some real advantages. The mountains are getting so crowded, though, that it doesn't help to have them close.

I suppose what I would like to see is some kind of sustainable economy come to the West. Mining by its very definition is not sustainable; it's extractive and once the ore is dug the industry is gone. The towns are gone too. You can't make it as a cattle rancher either. You have to have it big, with big grazing privileges on the public lands. That means a kind of baronial existence—a few big families and a lot of underpaid cowhands, or a few underpaid cowhands because they don't use cowhands much any more. The whole ranch is run with one helper. Farming is not an option in most of the West, not a big one. It could support a small population, and that's probably limited in time in a lot of the hotter parts of the West too, simply by the fact of salinization. Every field ultimately becomes an alkali flat. You can't live by taking in each other's laundry either. You can do that only to a certain extent. One of the few things that you can do is provide recreation and all that lovely open space. That makes the West into a playground, which is a little offensive too. The play ethic is not as good an ethic as the work ethic. Somehow it creates a cynicism or contempt that is different from the kind of feeling you get in a working community where the people rely on other people for all things you do rely on them for in a working community.

So I guess if I'm looking a long way ahead I don't see a lot in the future for a lot of towns in the West, unless manufacturing comes in, which would make even larger changes than came in after World War II. And that would mean pollution of the air, more than at present. It is also not the greatest place to be a manufacturer either—because of the short-haul trade rates and the mere business of getting goods to market. Getting things to market is harder in the West.

So that is a kind of pessimistic look at the future, even of a town like Salt Lake which is always going to be a city and always going to have some manufacturing and does have a kind of hinterland of farming up and down along the Wasatch Front. It seems to me that the oases will get bigger, noisier, dirtier, and more crowded, and the spaces will get all torn up by mining, by overgrazing, by reckless recreationers, by off-road vehicles, and so on unless the BLM gets smart and stops them.

I think probably we have to get over our oil addiction. If the rest of the country gets over it, the West will get over it too. How that's going to be done, I can't imagine. I don't think methanol or the other alternatives are going to take care of a lot of it. And yet you have to. You cannot look forward many generations—a couple of generations at the most—in this oil-burning economy. If we don't poison ourselves by that time, we'll be out of oil. Maybe both. And the West, like everybody else, is going to have to trim its expectations. It just doesn't have the kind of rich agricultural productivity that California has or the Midwest has. The cattle industry is gone. Even at its best, it raised about 3 percent of the beef raised in the United States. It took endless amounts of range to raise those, and the range deteriorates because they all overcrowd it trying to make their extra dollars, which are hard to make. So I don't see much but deterioration and loss of population—or the conversion of the West into some kind of manufacturing economy, which doesn't look very likely, or the dedication of large parts of it to recreational use, which is better but still not good.

If you run out of oil, you have to dig coal, and then it will get dirtier than ever. I don't think we are going nuclear because there's no place to put the waste. We have the problem now even if we never make another nuclear warhead or generate another kilowatt of power. I don't think they have found the right place to put it, and I doubt that they ever will. Maybe they could bury it in Mt. St. Helens.

*I think most historians who've written about the recent West and the fu-
ture are quite pessimistic—if one uses Limerick and Worster as examples.*

Worster has focused upon water, and Limerick on the boom-and-bust
at large. But they're certainly in the same vein. Do you know anybody
who is optimistic, apart from the Chambers of Commerce, the boosters
that Benny DeVoto used to hate so because, in his view, they were raping
their own habitat?

*I was thinking of a variety of visions. For example, if I see the Ivan Doig
vision correctly, it's not basically a pessimistic vision. But if I view Joan
Didion's vision aright, it is extremely pessimistic. Not only about now
but about what is likely to happen in the future.*

I'm afraid that Ivan Doig may be a little like me. He was raised in the
West when it was a nice place to be raised in. His part of the West still is.
He grew up in the Smith River Valley and around the Sweetgrass Hills, and
when he revisits that country, it's still pretty much as it was. I guess the last
book was written about the country around Choteau.

*I mention Doig quite often because I identify with him as a sheep-
herder's kid.*

Sheepherders are still a possibility in the West, except you've got to deal
with the coyotes. A lot of the cattle ranchers that we know have turned to
a sheep-cattle mix because sheep are just a little bit more profitable than
cattle. You get your wool as well as the meat out of them. And they'll eat
anything, I guess. Won't they? They have no sense. They'll eat anything.

*Let me turn to something else. It seems to me in the ten years since we
talked you have become increasingly recognized as a major person of
American letters and perhaps the leading spokesman for the American
West. Do you feel comfortable with those two designations—one national
and one regional?*

It depends on where the emphasis is put. Obviously, if you're always
referred to as a *western* writer, that is a diminution. That means that you're
in some second-rate category. On the other hand, I don't think you can be
anything but yourself. By talking about what you know, understand, and
are, you're inevitably going to be western-oriented—or I am. Whether that's
opprobrious or not depends on whether the West gets more respectable as
a literary area. There's a lot to be overcome there because so many expect
a West full of Billy the Kids and romance, adventure, and danger. And
that isn't my West.

I suppose there is a lot more recognition in the last few years. A couple of prizes and things like that. But also, duration will do something for you. I think there is a kind of sentimental tendency in the American public not necessarily to revere but to respect writers who have got old in the trade, the way they used to respect Frost and think of him as Santa Claus, which he was not. Quite apart from his greatness as a poet, his mere age made him attractive to a lot of people. And to some extent that has happened to me. It doesn't necessarily bother me, but it's happened in some extent.

I don't know what being a "spokesman" of the West means. I suppose it means only that there aren't very many literary people who have set their minds to try to understand the country as widely and deeply as possible. There isn't a lot of competition. Often that "spokesman" label is nothing but a kind of journalistic phrase, anyway. Like the *New York Times*, which describes me as the dean of western writers, and then makes me into William Stegner. That's a good, salty deterrent to pride.

I don't know when the fact began, but I do notice . . . I was up in San Francisco talking a week or ten days ago to the Friends of the San Francisco Library at Herbst Theater, and all of sudden I realized (was told) that in this series which had included a lot of people like Updike, Louise Erdrich, and people like that, they often had empty seats, and this one of mine was sold out months in advance. People were scalping tickets out in front of the theater for a literary lecture, which is a sign, at least *locally*, of a kind of recognition I never had before. I'm part of planned duration. Stick around and become a figurehead. But talking almost anywhere, indeed even in the East—Toronto last summer and New York Public Library last fall—there were full houses. So I lucked out.

You never know, because you don't have the kind of contact with readers that you do with listeners in a lecture hall. Lecturing is a kind of public art, but writing is between you and the guy in the armchair, as Frank O'Connor used to say. You talk and you don't hear from him even if he likes you. And sometimes the people you do hear from are so literarily naive that you worry about whom you are reaching. If they like you, there must be something wrong. There are some unsophisticated readers in the world. Still, they're readers, and that's essential.

When you give these talks, are you asked to speak on a specific topic, or are you talking on environmental themes, or something else that comes from your western background?

This last one was a literary talk, actually on this relationship between autobiography and fiction that we were speaking of earlier. It came down to *Crossing to Safety*, which after all is the latest book, the one that most of the audience had been reading.

Some of these public appearances—and I don't make a lot—are just readings too. They're easier, but I don't think they are what I like the best because I never quite got over the notion that reading your own stuff is a little bit . . . pretentious.

But there is an audience, quite clearly. Mary and I were talking about it on the way home; quite clearly there is a big following in San Francisco. In Toronto last summer I seemed to be the dean of Canadian writers because *Wolf Willow* is required reading. There was a big audience there. I get a lot of letters from people, many of them people that I respect—but I don't see my name very often in the critics who summarize American literature. Most of them have never heard my name, or would think of me as William. So—it's mixed.

A review of your latest novel included this comment: "Mr. Stegner is a wise man as well as a skilled writer." How about that as a brief summary of your career?

The wisdom I'll accept, oh sure. Well, I don't know what they mean by "wise." I guess probably when I'm writing a novel I'm a lot more sympathetic with people than I am when I am living my life. I get irritated in life, but I have enough time to get over my irritation when I'm working on a novel. I don't know what wisdom amounts to, actually, except as I guess I wrote in *Angle of Repose*: accepting what you have to. I don't know that I've ever taken the line of assaulting the universe for its injustices. You'd better accept, you don't have any choice. If that's wisdom, I'll buy it.

I do think that I'm probably a reasonably skilled writer. I'll accept that. I've been working at it long enough, reading other people long enough, to realize that I can do some things that a lot of people can't. I know some things I can't do that some people can, too . . . but I don't try to do those.

Your mother would be a very good illustration of the definition you have just given of a wise person, wouldn't she?

Yeah, except that her times and her general bad luck prevented her from ever becoming what she might have become. That's sad. I don't know that she knew it really, but she had a lot of capacity and never had any chance to develop it.

Stoical quality along with that?

Oh, yeah, sure. She was almost Russian in her stoicism. You remember the old peasant woman in Chekhov who tells her daughter, who's about to be married to the local dissolute wastrel, "Marriage is a necessity my child, so we must accept it." I guess that my mother, having made that bed, she lay on it. But she would have been a lot happier if she hadn't had to. Nothing in her background, nothing in her psychology, would have permitted divorce when she had two children.

Let me build on that. You said you would never as a novelist attempt what Saul Bellow did, to create whole cloth. You create out of your experience, invent, elaborate . . .

I'm an incorrigible realist, sure. Even if that is an unpopular word, I'd better admit it. Realism hasn't been popular, God knows, for a good while. I'm sure it'll be popular again. It comes around, in cycles. But I still would rather have written *Tom Jones* than *Tristram Shandy*. I probably would have been incapable of writing *Tristram Shandy*. I've got to write what I can write. Invention . . . curiously enough, the book of Saul Bellow's that I took most pleasure in, maybe that I didn't admire the most, but I took the most pleasure in, was *Henderson the Rain King*, which is pure invention. Exuberant invention. Out of anthropology books, I suppose. I couldn't do that. Books aren't that real to me.

I was thinking that Doris Grumbach particularly liked Crossing to Safety *because you were so realistic about friendship. She didn't use these words, but I think that was what* especially *appealed to her. Friendship was so persuasively and realistically portrayed in that novel.*

That's partly because I was trying to be as honest as I could, and friendship isn't all sweetness and light. There are all kinds of things about your friends that irritate you or that you don't understand. You irritate them. It is something that wears itself into shape like the old too-tight auto engine which you had to work for 5,000 miles before you could speed it up to fifty.

Any second thoughts, any things you would do differently, as long as we're discussing your life and career? And while you're writing those autobiographical essays that all of us want?

There are a lot of things I would just as soon undo, if I could. But . . . most of the big changes in my life happened sort of by accident. Because, maybe, I was a little like my mother; I never really knew what I wanted to do. I just suddenly found myself able to do something, then started doing it, and found that I liked it. I became a schoolteacher quite by accident, and while schoolteaching, I became a writer by accident. A friend, Wilbur Schramm, got me a fill-in spot at Bread Loaf which gave me entrée into a literary community such as I had never seen before. It was like turpentining a mule; I went straight up in excitement, in emulation.

I often use a cliché with my students—I suppose it is autobiographical; probably I learned it from my immigrant father—hard work pays off.

That's been a lot of Wallace Stegner's life, too, hasn't it? A hard worker from the very beginning of your literary career.

I have no problem with work when it's work I like. The morality probably arises from the habit. You do it, and so therefore are irritated with people who don't. I sometimes find myself making a morality out of work, so that I almost judge people by what kind of workers they are. I wouldn't know what to do if I hadn't worked. I was generally doing two or three things at once. Partly out of necessity because I was poor, but partly for the same reason that some horses run at a hill. A mule has more sense but a horse will kill itself. I suppose that's the way I was.

I'm not even very discriminating about work. I like all kinds of jobs. Pencil sharpening, making a woodpile. The more brainless, idiot's delight it is, the more satisfying and peaceful it is. I think writing is always hard work; it isn't peaceful at all. It's very disturbing, but then it feels good when I quit, it feels good to have *done* it.

It would be very easy, I sometimes think, to be lazy and just sit on your can. Watch television and swim in the pool, putter around the yard. But I don't seem able to do it. I might as well go on doing what ultimately gives me the most satisfaction.

1. Biography

Etulain: I gather from what you have written in Wolf Willow *[1962] and* Big Rock Candy Mountain *[1943] that your boyhood experiences gave you a strong sense of place. That's what you mean, isn't it, when you say: "I may not know who I am, but I know where I am from"?*

Stegner: Yes, I suppose it's double. I suppose that when you grow up in the short-grass country you may be more impressed with topography even than when you grow up in mountains, because, as I think I have tried to make plain in both of those books, the plains are so dominant and simple, so geometrical a world, that you feel yourself noticeable even when you're small. You have a sense of that place more than of almost any other place you're ever going to see. I've noticed that people who did grow up on the plains nearly all feel it's a special culture. I don't know whether Pocatello will do it; you're a mountain fellow, but if you've had experience out on the flats anywhere east of Billings, probably you do feel it. There isn't anything to see except a long way off and your immediate world is very simple, very disk-and-bowl. I think the geometrical simplicity is reflected in the religious feelings of Plains Indians. All those deferences to the directions. You blow smoke in all the directions, in ways you probably wouldn't if you grew up in, let us say, Yosemite Valley.

The plains were very definitely an imprinting force on me. But also, so was the relatively primitive sociology that I grew up in, and that's another matter. It wasn't a society, as Willa Cather might say, it was the stuff out of which a society was going to be made. You don't know exactly who you

[1]

are, but you are very aware of the erratic and half-formed influences that come upon you from many directions. That's probably what I had in mind. I think it was double, not simply a matter of place but a matter of place in the process of forming a society—which, incidentally, is precisely the same theme that Page and I are dealing with in this new book [American Places, 1981]. We're concerned with the making of Americans at least as much as with the places and the topographies of America.

You mention other writers, and I think of the experiences of Wright Morris and Frederick Manfred, who also grew up in the plains areas, who also feel that same strong sense of place.

I think it's maybe the most dominant kind of topography. I don't know whether you could test this, it might not be sensible even to try, but I keep wondering, where is Swiss literature? Partly that lack is a function of being dispersed around the sides of mountains into three or four different languages so that you don't really know if Swiss literature is German, Italian, French, Romansh, or something else. But it seems to me that literature, maybe art too, is much more likely to come out of a plains environment than out of a mountain environment. I don't think of the Grand Canyon or the Rocky Mountains as having produced much in the way of literature, but I can think of a lot of prairie and plains literature, maybe because of what that environment does to the people who live in it. That's a theory I can't prove; it's not even a theory, it's random rumination.

Well, we talk about the oases kinds of civilizations in the American West, and they have not tended to be mountain villages or towns.

No, they've been more in the desert and on the Wyoming plateau and places like that, haven't they.

On one occasion you wrote: "I grew up hating my weakness and my cowardice and trying to pretend that neither existed." Were these limitations especially apparent in a frontier community like East End, Saskatchewan? Had you grown up in Salt Lake City, for example, would as much masculinity have been expected of you?

Oh no, oh no. Salt Lake City is a residual frontier town, or was when I grew up in it. Certainly it's another thing now—it's becoming an energy-conglomerate town—but it was still an environment, even in the 1920s, much more protective of the individual than the Saskatchewan frontier was. There were all kinds of social groups in which you could find shelter; you could go to the Boy Scouts, or you could go to the Mormon wardhouse and take part in Mutual, and be a member of a society, which actually was very good for me. I was grateful for it because I was a kind of lone particle, and

I was looking for something to attach to. But the demand for absolute masculinity, something like machismo but not really machismo—not that show-off really—but certainly a stoical kind of machismo, was much much much more dominant in East End than it's been in any other community I've known since. I think it is a demand made by all frontier communities, particularly in hard countries, hard climates. That was a terrible climate. I listen to the weather reports on the television every morning, and northern Montana and Saskatchewan are brutal. There is nothing between you and the North Pole but a two-wire fence; it is really a rough country to live in. And so, babies, whiners, people who suffer from one thing and another and who complain a good deal are simply tromped on. Complaining is simply not done. That is the moral code, the ethical code, I grew up in. And it's tough on a sickly child. I've had all my life, for instance, a thing called— what is it called?—Raynaud's disease. My fingers go dead—some kind of spasm in the blood vessels. My hands were always cold. Well, you shouldn't mind about your hands being cold. They could be white clear to the wrists and people would say, "Put on your God damn mittens and shut up," which I don't think was bad for me in the long run, but it was rough at the time.

You mention in Wolf Willow *that so little of your pre-high-school education was relevant to the life that surrounded you, that too much of your schooling smacked of European and classical traditions. When did you become aware of this disparity?*

Not until very late, about the time I began to write *Wolf Willow*, I suppose. That awareness, in turn, may have been a long-delayed reaction to the writing of *Big Rock Candy Mountain* and having to think about that country of my childhood and live in it imaginatively for a long period of time. I suppose reading Emerson's "Self-Reliance," "The American Scholar," whatever else, may have suggested parallels between my frontier and a much earlier frontier, between my reactions and the reactions of Americans in an early nationalistic period. In any case, somewhere in my maturity I began to be aware that the education that was given me was essentially no different from what would have been given a kid in Ontario, and not too much different from what would have been given an English child. The literature, for instance, was all European, and the system was all memorization. The system led very directly on to the study of Latin and possibly Greek, as it did for Willa Cather in Red Cloud, Nebraska. She was memorizing all those passages of the *Aeneid*, which didn't have much to do with life in Red Cloud, but which probably didn't do her any great harm either. I'm actually grateful for the memorization and the exposure to— not graded and reduced and limited kinds of verbal experience and limited vocabularies—but to poetry. What we were exposed to was largely Tennyson and people like that who weren't terribly difficult, or at least didn't seem difficult. Nevertheless, it was poetry and not Dick and Jane, so I am ambivalent about the primary education I got. It didn't have the content that it might have had that would have taught me how to deal with my own life, but it did have certain rigors that I'm grateful for. We went to school from eight to four, and we went six days a week and ten months a year, which kept us out of mischief.

Your community, then, was the school?

Oh sure. We lived in school, and we were glad to get back to it. I remember coming back from the homestead in the fall after a couple of months out there on the flats and being uplifted with anticipation of winter and school. That was a town I liked living in, and I was sorry to leave it.

Can you remember reading any local history or any writers who dealt with the Far West?

Nobody in the whole town knew anything about history, local or otherwise, except Corky Jones, whom I didn't know then. Well, I knew who he was, but I didn't know he knew such things. He kept it to himself. He probably knew—I'm sure he did—*The Company of Adventurers* by Isaac Cowie [1913], which was essentially the basic document in the history of that town. He undoubtedly knew a good deal about the quite recent Indian occupation of the White Mud River valley, because his reminiscences speak of his finding Indian burials up on racks, and he had a lot of Indian artifacts in his museum.

Is he the person you thank at the beginning of Wolf Willow?

Yes. He came over as an eighteen-year-old in the late 1880s. As a matter of fact, I had him in mind as the Englishman in "Genesis."[1] He came over to be a cowboy, but his father had been a doctor at Cowes on the Isle of Wight and had been Queen Victoria's doctor when she came to Cowes for the sailing. So Corky had had more advantages in his early life than most of the people who came in, and he wound up being historian, anthropologist, and paleontologist to the town. He made violins and learned to play them. He had a great cultural potential which got starved on the frontier but eventually made a kind of home for itself in the basement of the school where he created a museum, a paleo-anthropological museum. He collected fossils, particularly Tertiary mammals, which up in the hills were very thick; he himself discovered two or three new species of Tertiary mammals. He was the only person in town who could have told us anything.

---

[1]*Wolf Willow* (New York: Viking Press, 1963), p. 139. For complete bibliographic information on books mentioned in the text but not cited in the footnotes, see M. Lewis and L. Lewis, *Wallace Stegner* (Boise: Boise State College, 1972), and see note 3, below.

The memory of most of the people in that town went no further back than their own childhood, and they were, most of them, cut off. They were Texas cowpunchers, or Cockney immigrants, or Ontario men come west, or people we called French who were mostly métis (French-Indian), who lived by themselves by and large and had a separate culture which was Catholic and other than ours, or Scandinavians coming up the old Scandinavian route from the Dakotas and Minnesota through Montana and into Canada. All of those people were orphans of a sort. All of them had a very limited and almost completely unliterate kind of memory. More than that, the Indians before them had left no marks on that country at all, except a few tepee rings. There weren't many relics of the past, books or otherwise, and so I couldn't have learned anything about the history of that town, although I could now. People in the town have gotten interested in it, and the person who made me that ceramic boot is living in the old Z-Bar-X ranch house now; he's a retired schoolteacher. He knows a great deal of local history. There are a few like that.

You mention, I think it's in Wolf Willow *or perhaps in* The Sound of Mountain Water *[1969], that through a Canadian radio broadcast your old teacher was located.*

Yes, he's still there. I have a picture of him somewhere around. I remember my first day in that first class; I think I was five years old. He had just come across the Atlantic, this fellow. So he spent the first day telling us about seasickness, various kinds of seasickness, the degrees of seasickness. And he said, "Wouldn't you think that the big, large waves like that would make you seasick, but no, it's this kind that make you seasick"—and he drew them on the slate he had for a blackboard, the kind of North Sea waves that really do make you seasick. I think he may be still alive—the last time I heard, about a year ago, he was about ninety years old.

And he was the source of your European and classical kind of education, or did you just have him for one year?

I don't remember. No, I didn't have him very long; he actually became something else. I think he did something else in town, maybe farmed, I don't know; but when he first arrived he took over the school, which was in the loft over the local pool hall, the first school in the town. Later they built a schoolhouse, first a couple of rooms and then a couple more, making it four, and there were other teachers. I remember a Miss Bell, and I remember some woman from Kingston, Ontario, whom I loathed. I remember a lady principal, also from Ontario, who got sick with the flu in 1918 and caused a great laugh all over town because she was found in bed with a bottle between her knees. She was nasty-nice, you know, and it tickled the town to see her humanized. Also, there was a man teacher, whom I loved, who was very good. He did me the honor and probably the disfavor of jumping me from the sixth to the eighth grade. When I moved to Great Falls, Montana, he sent a letter along with me saying "Wallace is fully prepared for eighth grade work," and so I skipped the seventh grade. I was in the eighth grade at the age of what, ten or eleven, or some damn thing. I was way beyond my depth—humiliating marks on my first algebra test and things because I'd never even seen algebra. I had never heard the *word* algebra.

And I suppose it exaggerated your sense of being small and being behind other classmates in size?

Sure, and it also accentuated my desire to shine in school. By the end of the year I was the star of the class, but it was a very, very rough time in the beginning. But anyway I liked that Saskatchewan teacher, who was a good egg and put on a lot of communal musical shows that we were all in. "Cantatas" they called them. We all got up and sang and did vaudeville acts. He played with the kids and spent a lot of time in the river swimming hole; it was good to have a man teacher just once in that school.

What did you mean when you referred to your boyhood in Saskatchewan as the life of a "sensuous little savage"?[2]

Well, I suppose I was thinking not of school in that case, but of the time outside of school. For one thing, twilights are very long in Saskatchewan. The days in summer are very long—even in spring they get pretty long—and even after four o'clock there's a lot of time to horse around. We lived right on the river, with our backs to wild country. There were still beaver and muskrat swimming in the river, and weasels and mink and all the rest of it. My brother and I trapped that river every winter, and every boy in town had a gun from the time he was nine or ten years old. We also took off on expeditions into what we called the Sand Hills, which were just some little residual badlands, erosional forms on the edge of the river valley. We would go up and dig white mud out of the band of kaolin in the river bluffs and make marbles of it and bake them in the oven. All kinds of little outdoorish and generally savage activities. Sometimes I had the job of herding the town cows, which we'd drive up in the morning and drive back at night and distribute to the various houses where they were going to be milked. We lived outside, especially in summer, but even in winter there was a lot to do. The river very often froze smooth because that was essentially dry country. If it froze before it snowed we would get good skating ice. We could skate for miles up the river, up to the next rapid, wherever that was, where it was

---

[2]*Wolf Willow*, pp. 19, 25.

broken, and we could portage around that and skate some more. We would make sails of our sheepskins or mackinaws and sail down the river before the wind. We had big fires on the ice at night, because by mid-winter the river would be frozen clear to the bottom, two or three feet, four feet sometimes. All of that was great, and I remember it with pleasure. It was completely a life of the senses, though; there was nothing bookish about it. All of the spare time that I might have been spending in libraries or museums I was spending out shooting or trapping muskrats, or skating, or driving cows or something.

If Big Rock Candy Mountain *is fairly accurate family history, yours seems to have been a close-knit family despite the strong personality conflicts. Is that right?*

Oh yes, and I think that was much more often the case than not on the frontier, because in a community like that everything broke down except the most basic human institutions, and the family is the most basic of them all. They may not have had happy lives, but happy or unhappy they were tight families. There was no other body that anyone could rely on. The ultimate reliance was on the members of one's own immediate family, what I guess they refer to now as the nuclear family or the core family. It often included, again not always happily, the extended family elements, like my poor old grandmother with her senile dementia.

Your father's mother, or your mother's mother?

My father's mother. My mother's mother died when she was twelve and left her with the whole family to care for. Anyway, I don't know how it went for the fringe elements of families, but for the mother, father, and children it was very tight. And that's been corroborated for me by a number of the people with whom I grew up whom I've seen later; I run across them here and there through the world.

Bruce Mason in Recapitulation *[1979] speaks of that same tight-knitted-ness being true in Salt Lake City.*

Oh, I think you grow up that way. That's the way it goes. That's why "blood is thicker than water" in a pinch, particularly when you have no social alternatives to the family. In Salt Lake I began to feel some social alternatives and to make use of them, but even so, it was always a movement out from a family core.

Father–son relationships play an important role in several of your works, and you have written about your father on several occasions. Can you characterize your father? Was he like Bo Mason in Big Rock Candy Mountain *and in* Recapitulation?

Essentially. Not by any means precisely, because he becomes a fictional character the minute you begin to think about him in fictional terms. Fiction demands some changes in a character in order to make him fictionally persuasive and coherent. Real people are full of contradictions, as indeed so was he. He could be enormously entertaining, he could be very funny, he knew all kinds of ballads, he could be a good egg. He was also, unfortunately, cursed with a wicked temper, and as he got older I suppose he . . . I don't know, I have no way of knowing; I wasn't that close to him, particularly as I began to be an adolescent and the rift began. I never got very close to him. We walked around one another pretty warily. So I don't know whether he was disappointed in his life, frustrated in some ambition or other, I don't know. He was a boomer, and I suppose he was always hoping to strike it rich somewhere. Since he never quite did, I suppose he must have been disappointed. I imagine that a lot of the relatively surly times in his later life may have been a product of that; but that's thinking after the fact. I had no way of understanding that at the time.

Was he the kind of person who was likely to have self-revealing talks with his wife or your brother?

I'm sure he did with my mother, but I don't think he ever did with us. The further it went, the further his sons steered away from him, shied away. On the other hand, there's a strange mixture in that kind of relationship, and there were times when one could feel very proud of him; other times when one would have willingly strangled him.

It seems to me that Bruce Mason feels differently about his father at the end of Recapitulation *than he does at the end of* Big Rock Candy Mountain.

I suppose I may have had the feeling that I had judged too early and too harshly, yes. That's what I meant to imply in *Recapitulation*. The only way I could imply it without doing what you say Forrest Robinson thinks I do in *The Big Rock Candy Mountain*, talk too much from an authorial stance, was to put it in some such terms as the buying of the tombstone— which incidentally I've never done, and don't suppose I ever will.[3] I'm not that upset. I do think that the Bruce Mason that I have created and the Bo Mason that I have created would have come around, somehow, to some reasonable reconciliation. Not a real liking, but some kind of reconciliation, at least more understanding.

---

[3]Forrest G. Robinson and Margaret G. Robinson, *Wallace Stegner* (Boston: Twayne Publishers, 1977).

As I move from Big Rock Candy Mountain *to "The Blue-Winged Teal"
to* Recapitulation, *I see Bruce having, in a way, small moments of epiphany when he thinks about that relationship.*[4]

Oh sure. Because the old Oedipal conflict is not a comfortable situation
for anybody. It's absolutely routine, standard Oedipal; there isn't anything
funny about it, or odd.

When thinking about your career I have wanted to ask, can *a man come
home again? How much could you have said about Bo Mason in* Big
Rock Candy Mountain, *if he had lived on?*

I don't think I could say much more about him. He was defeated, he
was done. It wasn't a life that got crowned by anything . . . . And it gathered
no moss.

*Though you've written extensively about your father, you seem to have
been more drawn to your mother than your father. What sort of person
was your mother?*

If I were Frank O'Connor I would say my mother was a saint. She was,
sort of. Frank really meant it literally about his mother; he thought she was
in heaven. I don't suppose my mother is, but she was a gentle and affec-
tionate, yet at the same time very durable woman. She could take the kind
of life that she got handed. But it killed her too, she died at fifty, so I never
really knew her in my later life. What was I when she died, about twenty-
two, twenty-three, or something like that. But we got on very well; I could
talk with her endlessly, and did. She also had, I think, like Corky Jones, like
a lot of people with no particular training—she left school in the sixth grade
or something because she had to look after her father's family, her brothers
and sister—she had a lot of cultural hungers and a real cultural capacity.
While we were living in Canada, some uncle of hers in Iowa died and left
her a thousand dollars. It came in very handy, I'm sure, but she insisted on
saving out of it enough money to buy a piano so that my brother and I could
have piano lessons, which we took from the wife of the drunken French
doctor. It may have been two hundred out of the thousand, but she insisted
on the piano: I can remember those debates yet. She got the piano and we
all fussed around with it for a while, and then it was pretty clear, after about
six months, that neither my brother nor I was inclined to be a pianist. So she
learned to play it herself, making the most of it, by herself, just getting sheet
music and working it out. And she was a reader.

Was she a culture carrier in other ways?

---

[4]"The Blue-Winged Teal," *Harper's* 200 (April 1950): 41–49; reprinted in *The
City of the Living and Other Stories* (Boston: Houghton Mifflin, 1956).

Oh yes, she communicated a lot of echoes of her childhood, and through her childhood of remembered Norway. She did speak Norwegian before she spoke English. She had a lot of stories about the old days in Norway— which she had never seen; she was born in this country—but that she had heard about from her father and mother. And she was also a cultural carrier in the sense of that whole traditional cuisine, for instance, of Norwegian cookery, which she had to learn the hard way. Somebody wrote me a few years ago about remembering my mother in the hard times in Saskatchewan. When somebody brought in a bushel of apples, they were all distributed around the neighborhood. That wasn't fruit country. You had to get them when you could, and you couldn't always get decent apples. She made a lot of applesauce, and then she made jelly out of the peelings, which impressed some people but was perfectly natural for her. That was the way she had been brought up. That frugal, Old World business of putting up sausage and head cheese in the fall when you slaughtered a pig, the Christmas baking, other kinds of things. Sure, she was a cultural carrier, and I suppose there are echoes of her and others like her still reverberating up there. There were a lot of Scandinavians in that part of the world.

I suppose that modern readers looking back at her story might read in the word "trapped," and yet as you discuss her she doesn't seem to exhibit that kind of feeling.

I don't think so, no, I think she assumed that a wife's place is with her husband, for better or for worse. Women's Liberation came a long time after that. I'm not sure that she could have subscribed to it even if it had come in her time. No, I think she had some kind of stoical notion that even when it was tough you bent your back. She wouldn't have said with the Mormon emigrant, "The Lord shapes the back to the burden," but she somehow had that same notion.

Which I suspect would have been shared by many pioneer or frontier women.

Of course. Nevertheless, she was hungry, you know. She was hungry for women's company, she was hungry for all kinds of intellectual excitement, and she had very little way of getting it, except by reading. She was a big reader.

The separation that she might have experienced in Saskatchewan because of its isolation, then, would be expressed in a different way because of your father's occupation or because of the dominant Mormon faith in Salt Lake City?

Oh, she had a few friends in Salt Lake. They were likely to be the wives of brakemen on the Union Pacific, people like that. Very, very humble companions, and almost always either non-Mormons or renegade Mormons, people who had "busted off." That, I think, was pretty standard too. Adults couldn't make it into that Mormon society the way a child could, the way that *I* could. I went off to Mutual, played basketball, went to ward amusement halls, but there were no such entrées for her. It seems to me, thinking it over, that she had a terribly limited and lonesome life. She had to do what a lot of women in the past have had to do—get a vicarious life out of her children.

You don't mention much about your older brother Cecil except in Big Rock Candy Mountain. *I would gather that his interests were quite different from yours, particularly as you grew older.*

Yeah, he was always an athlete, he was always big and strong. He actually wound up not as tall as I am, but he was a kind of bull. He played football in high school, and he was a good pitcher. He was probably good enough to play in the big leagues if he had got any breaks. Some of the people he pitched against, and used to beat in high school, went on to become pitchers for big-league teams. It could have happened that way, particularly because that was something that my father really did encourage: he had been a ballplayer himself. He knew ballplayers, and they used to come up to the house all the time. Tony Lazzeri, Lefty O'Doul, a lot of people then playing in the Pacific Coast League, would come out for a beer, after ball games. Fritz Coumbe used to live with us. You wouldn't remember Coumbe, but he was a pitcher, had been in the National League, and then was in the Coast League. So my brother knew a lot of ballplayers, and he grew up thinking baseball. Somehow that never came about. But his activities in high school were almost all associated with athletics. He wasn't much of a scholar. On the other hand, he was a singer. He had a good tenor voice, and he used to be in all local operettas. He was a kind of activities man, whereas I was the grind. The fact that I had been boosted out of the seventh grade by Mr. McGregor in East End and then boosted again out of the tenth in Salt Lake—so I jumped two grades—meant that I graduated the same time that my brother did. That was always, I imagine, difficult for him; . . . two years make an enormous difference when you're fourteen or fifteen. I graduated from high school when I was sixteen, and he graduated when he was eighteen. And I hadn't even started to grow. I probably weighed ninety pounds about the time we stood up together on this graduation platform. That could be difficult for him, I think. I was held to be smarter than he was, but I was such a runt he couldn't help being ashamed of me. Nevertheless we got on very well, and we were good friends, partly because we were in no sense competition— he for me or I for him. We were two different objects. He never did have any ambition to go to university, I don't think. He got married early and was out playing semipro baseball and working in the mines on bull-gangs, the kind of phony job they gave ballplayers in semipro leagues. After high school I saw very little of him—here and there, Christmas holidays.

Was there ever any question about your going to college—especially since your parents' education was limited and your brother had not gone to the university?

No. I was automatically headed there, and they supported the idea without any question—approved and applauded. Actually, my brother's example was not in question, since he graduated from high school at the same time I did. He was headed for a job and semipro baseball, I was headed for college.

After your undergraduate years at Utah, did you choose the University of Iowa for graduate work because of its creative writing program? Which scholars did you study with there?

My choice of Iowa for graduate work had nothing to do with the creative writing program—which in any case did not begin until the fall I arrived there. My choice of Iowa, even my choice of graduate school, was as purely accidental as I made it for Bruce Mason's choice of law school in *Recapitulation*. I had worked my way through college as a delivery boy, truck driver, and salesman for the I&M Rug and Linoleum Company. I expected, in my dumb way, to go on working there after I graduated. Then the head of the psychology department offered me a fellowship for a year of graduate work. The head of the English department, Sherman Brown Neff, was aghast that I would consider psychology and went to work to see what he could turn up in English. He turned up a teaching assistantship at Iowa, and off I went, just like poor old Maurice, the campus moron, given a nickel to buy a root beer. When I got to Iowa, I found that Norman Foerster (who later directed my dissertation) had just established the School of Letters, which among its other conditions allowed people to take an M.A. with a creative thesis. I beat my way in, more or less against Foerster's best judgment (I was barely twenty-one, and green as grass), and wrote some short stories for a thesis. Later, when the Depression settled down ominously, it was easier to stay in graduate school than find work outside. I stayed. Because I didn't think a Ph.D. in creative writing meant anything in the marketplace, I took a degree in American literature. Of the people I worked with at Iowa, the ones who most influenced me were Foerster, whose New Humanism I quarreled with but whom I personally respected and liked, and Henning Larsen, who revived the latent Scandinavian in me.

And, I should add, my roommate for two years, Wilbur Schramm, who taught me more than most of my professors did.

Since you have always been intrigued with history, how is it that you did not decide to do your graduate work in history?

At the time, I neither knew any history nor knew I was interested in it. One of my graduate student friends, Vernon Carstensen, did just what you suggest—switched from English to history. I was, I suppose, more literary then—literary in the worst sense of the word—than I was later. I knew nothing, literally nothing. I had a million books to read to catch up with my country and my generation and my classmates. I haven't yet read all of them that I should have. But they kept me busy for a long time. I discovered history incidentally, along the way, in the cracks and between the lines. Thinking about *The Big Rock Candy Mountain*, I had to think some about the movement of which my family had obviously been a part. I read Turner, Paxson, some others. It was only much later, when I began to write *Wolf Willow*, that I began to be serious about history. Or maybe a little earlier . . . when I was at Harvard, out of sheer homesickness for the West, I wrote *Mormon Country* [1942], and that was probably the true beginning. It didn't take me very far in.

You left Iowa in 1934; where did you teach before coming to Stanford in 1945?

Apart from my two years as a teaching assistant at Iowa, my first teaching job was at Augustana College, a Swedish Lutheran institution on the bank of the Mississippi at Rock Island, Illinois. That was one semester only. I taught one course of freshman English, one course of historical literary criticism, one sophomore survey of English literature, and one course in *Beowulf*. In 1934 that was called half time. I was also commuting to Iowa City to read for my degree three days a week and courting my future wife on the side. I left Augustana when a big fight broke out between the Evangelicals who had hired me and the Fundamentalists who thought dangerous latitudinarian standards were being followed. I was, in effect, fired for being one, an atheist, two, an agnostic, three, an unbeliever in the principles of higher Christian education, and four, a nonbeliever in the Augsburg Confession. Since I didn't see how I could be an atheist and an agnostic at the same time, and had never read the Augsburg Confession, and had not had the principles of higher Christian education explained to me, I was a sitting duck. Dr. Neff at Utah rescued me with an instructorship, and Mary and I were married before we took up the job in September 1934. Then there were three years at Utah, which ended when I won a Little, Brown novelette contest with *Remembering Laughter* [1937]. We quit and spent the summer of 1937 in France and England, on bicycles. Come fall, we were broke, or near it, and I took a job at Wisconsin—still an instructorship. I was at Harvard from September 1939 to March 1944, when I took leave to do a wartime-patriotism book, *One Nation* [1945], for *Look* magazine. By that time I was a faculty-instructor, which translated as an assistant professor. I had been teaching for ten years. Remember, these were Depression times, and I was a western waif. Then at the end of the *One Nation* assignment, Stanford offered me a job with a jump to a full professorship, and I came like a nine-inch trout on a copper trolling line.

Tell me about the creative writing program you set up at Stanford. Was it modeled after programs at Iowa, Harvard, or the Bread Loaf School? What were fellows in the program asked to do?

That's a large order, and I'll have to summarize. I arrived at Stanford just as the GI students were flooding back—the best students, and the most motivated, that any professor ever had. Many of them were gifted writers; the first story I read in a Stanford class was one by Eugene Burdick which was later published in *Harper's* and won an O. Henry prize. I scurried around to find some means of encouraging all this talent, found some prize money from John Dodds and the Division of Humanities, and the next year, by a concatenation of circumstances too complicated to go through here, found permanent funding, through Dr. E. H. Jones of San Angelo, Texas, for both fellowships and prizes. That was 1946. Through the years the program developed and changed, dropped its prizes (too many hassles, too much bitter competition, since our prizes were a thousand dollars), and gradually leveled out as a program of fellowships for advanced students and a ladder of courses, of increasing difficulty and expectation, for undergraduates. The models were all of those you mentioned—Iowa, Harvard, Bread Loaf. Fellows were asked only to help pick their successors, for with several hundred applications and a small faculty the reading burden was enormous. Otherwise, they wrote. They didn't, and still don't, have to be candidates for degrees. They didn't, and still don't, have to be qualified to matriculate at Stanford. They had to be good writers, and a lot of them were.

Who were some of the students you worked with?

Over the years a great many, many greatly gifted. Bud Burdick, of *Ugly American* notoriety, was the first, but there have been many since. An article on western writers in the *New York Times* recently (in which, characteristically, they managed to call me the "Dean of Western Writers" and get my name wrong, all in the same instant) featured Tom McGuane, Ed Abbey, and Scott Momaday, all former writing fellows. Tillie Olson was a fellow, Robert Stone, Jim Houston, Larry McMurtry, Ernest Gaines,

Wendell Berry, Max Apple, Nancy Packer, Philip Levine. Ken Kesey and
my son Page, though never fellows, were students in the program. There
have been many good ones since I retired a dozen years ago—Bill Kittredge,
many others. It's a long list, and a long shelf of books—many of them first-
rate. There is also a long list of people who went through the program and
wound up not writers but editors, teachers, foreign correspondents, and
so on. Bill Decker, long an editor at McGraw-Hill, Dial, and Viking, and
now a novelist as well, was in the program; so was Don Moser, the present
editor of *Smithsonian*. Many others. They have been a talented and productive group. I sometimes had the feeling that I was reading American
literature just a few months ahead of its breaking on the world. And there
have been some prize-winners: Robin White won the Harper's Novel Prize,
Scott Momaday the Pulitzer, Bob Stone the National Book Award. I try not
to take credit for any of that. The people who won fellowships in that program were so talented that there would have been no holding them down.
A year or two at Stanford helped them get their act together.

Since you had a heavy work load at Stanford, I suppose you retired early,
in 1971, to devote full time to writing.

That was the theory, yeah. I also was pretty fed up with the disruptions
of the sixties. It was no fun teaching. That didn't apply to the writing
students, actually, because writing students were still a pleasure to teach;
I enjoyed them and learned from them. But the undergraduate teaching
that had to go on was so disrupted, and the kids were so hassled in so many
directions. The intolerable ones came with answers and not questions, and
the others came with just confusions. Between them there was no way you
could feel you were not wasting your time in the classroom. So I decided
I had other things to do, and it was getting on toward the time when I had
only a few years to do them in. I retired at sixty-two, knowing that I had
some books I wanted to write, and I didn't know how many years I might
have. I have, after all, a history of a senile grandmother and I might not
have my buttons. So I retired, and I've managed to get three or four books
into the years since.

I was going to say five or six.

It can't be that many. I finished up *Angle of Repose* [1971] in my last
teaching year, but it was written . . . . Well, I'm trying to think what I did
now. I guess I wrote—certainly I wrote *The Spectator Bird* [1976] and . . .

Two DeVoto books?[5]

---

[5]*The Uneasy Chair: A Biography of Bernard DeVoto* (Garden City, N. Y.: Doubleday, 1974), and *The Letters of Bernard DeVoto* (Garden City, N. Y.: Doubleday,
1975).

Were those after I retired? I guess they probably were. I had begun thinking about DeVoto . . . quite a lot earlier . . .

Recapitulation?

Yeah, four at least, I guess. One of those, the DeVoto letters, was just a spin-off from the other. I was really just making use of my notes, but there are at least three substantive books, plus *American Places* [1981], which I wrote with my son. And I've collected another volume of essays, *One Way to Spell Man* [1982].

So many people seem to have a love–hate attitude toward California. Do you find yourself sharing some of this feeling? In this regard, I was thinking about what you told John R. Milton about a decade ago: that you didn't feel about California "the way I feel about the short-grass plains or the Rocky Mountains."

Of course I don't, and I think imprinting is the answer. This isn't my childhood heath. Recently we went back to the Midwest, to go down the Mississippi. Mary obviously feels about that country, limestone-bluff country along the river, exactly—well, maybe not exactly, but with a similar intensity—as I feel about the plains and the mountains. She was a child there. Still, California is a country that I knew pretty early. I came to Los Angeles and registered at UCLA at the end of my freshman year, 1926. My family had moved down there and lived in Hollywood, and I went down and *started* to join them. But before I ever took up the first class, I decided that was a mistake and went back to Salt Lake, lived in a boarding house, and went back to the University of Utah—for reasons, I'm sure, simply of homesickness. But I have known both southern and northern California since away back in the twenties. It's not strange country, it's just not *my* country. Yet we have contemplated moving to different places—retiring from here to some place where we do feel completely at home—and we've decided that we feel about as much at home here as we would in Santa Fe, and the climate of the places where we feel most at home is not for retiring to. Vermont has been a kind of constant and has had a big influence on our lives, but that's a summer place. We spent one winter there, and a pretty brisk one, too, and I find I don't like cold weather that well. I had it when I was young. For summers, I'd as soon be in Vermont or New Hampshire as anywhere in the world. But for winters I like it here, and I don't suppose we'll ever move.

Little of your fiction seems deeply rooted in your postgraduate school years. Except for the closing years of your father's life, you seem to have drawn little on your personal experiences in later years. Or am I overlooking too much there?

There, you may be overlooking something. It's certainly true that my own undisguised and bald life is not exposed as much in later writings, but I'm certainly drawing on my own experiences in all of the Joe Allston books. I'm writing right off this hill. I'm looking at it out my window as I put it down, and I'm dealing with the problems that a bedroom town like this encounters on its way to becoming a community. I'm looking at the kinds of neighbors we have had, the kinds of people they are, and the kinds of lives they live, so that my own experience is very, very much present in those Joe Allston books, though I am not Joe Allston. I would deny it to my dying day. He's brighter than I am, for one thing, and a good deal more cantankerous. He's a construct, a literary figment, a voice, a persona, and I found that I could speak through his voice though I am not he. Neither am I the Lyman Ward character in *Angle of Repose*. And a lot of the book, of course, is laid in northern California. So when you come right down to it, four out of my last six books have been laid wholly or partly in this part of the world, and so was *A Shooting Star* [1961]. I think I've used California, and the experience of living in it. It just doesn't appear in quite the autobiographical guise. I suppose I should also repeat the warning that what looks like pure autobiography in *The Big Rock Candy Mountain* or *Recapitulation* may be no more autobiography than what appears in the Allston books, or even *A Shooting Star*, or *Angle of Repose*, where the leading character is a woman. You project yourself in various ventriloquisms and various guises.

Do you have the feeling sometimes that you ought to have a little statement as Mark Twain did in Huckleberry Finn—*for prospective readers —since they want to read too much of Wallace Stegner into Joe Allston, Lyman Ward, or Bruce Mason?*

I'm constantly warning them against that. I've given up warning them against reading too much of it into *The Big Rock Candy Mountain* because everybody reads that as straight autobiography, which it isn't. But I'm resigned to it. By writing too close to the bone, I asked for it.

I noticed that several of your early works are dedicated to your wife, Mary, a later work to your son, Page, and that you've collaborated with your wife and your son on book-length projects. Does this suggest that the three of you have had stronger mutual interests than those of the family in which you were raised?

Oh, absolutely. Sure, we're all literary people. Mary was studying English and working as a librarian when we met, and was just about to go take a job in a rare-book store in Los Angeles when I saved her from that fate. Page, after a lot of circling around like a dog trying to lie down, not really wanting to walk in my tracks, and wanting to be his own person (which we respected), finally did lie down in that same place. He took a Ph.D. in American literature, and he teaches and he writes. He grew up seeing quite a lot of literary people come in and out of the house, and I suppose that's a strong bending force. But also he's got a gift, and it's natural for him to find that he wants to exercise it. Sure, we have a lot of mutual interests and they're most of them literary.

Nearly every commentator on your literary career has mentioned your idea of a "middle ground." A combination of fiction and history is one example of middle ground, but it seems equally apt for your combination of imagination and autobiography, fictional and personal history.

I suppose I'm open to criticism for not making clear lines, but, obviously, I do it on purpose, so I must be unrepentant. I don't see any reason why not. I can't imagine anything you can imagine *with* except the facts of real life, but you don't have to be restricted by them. By nature I'm a realist, but I'm not going to be a flat-footed realist. The real world exists, as far as I am concerned, and I find it very exciting to look at; but when I'm writing about it, I don't want to be pedestrian. I would rather pick up my feet a little more nimbly. The middle ground, I don't know. Forrest Robinson says I used that phrase. I don't remember it, and I never quite recognized the middle ground as he defined it, but it's probably there. I certainly have played the game of blurring the boundaries between history and fiction, as in *Wolf Willow*, as in several historical works where I have attempted to enliven history by what seem to me expressions of the kind of fictional truth we're after, and sometimes have even enlivened fiction by the literal historical truth that gives it solidity, bones. I wrote a couple of essays, which you probably know, on that general theme.[6] I don't see any reason when one is frankly writing a novel why the imaginative and the real cannot be mixed—or fused. Truman Capote certainly didn't invent the nonfiction novel. After all, there is *An American Tragedy*, whose whole second half deals, in documentary terms, with the trial of Chester Gillette. Some of the D.A.'s speeches at the trial, as well as other things, are reproduced verbatim in the novel. I don't see anything wrong with that. That's simply making plastic use of all the materials that a novelist has.

Moby Dick—*the middle section of* Moby Dick?

All right, sure. You break experience up into pieces, and you put them together in different combinations, new combinations, and some are real

---

[6]"On the Writing of History," *The American West* 2, no. 4 (Fall 1965); "History, Myth, and the Western Writer," *The American West* 4, no. 2 (May 1967).

and some are not, some are documentary and some are imagined. But since the whole thing is an imaginative construct, I don't see anything wrong with the mixture. It takes a pedestrian and literal mind to be worried about which is true and which is not true. It's all of it not true, and it's all of it true. It's true in fictional terms, and it makes no pretense of being true in historical terms, even though it may make use of literal history. I seem to be defending a point somewhat heatedly, but it is one that I have pondered for a long time. Any material that comes under my eye is legitimate for use in an imaginative re-creation.

> *You've served recently on several committees where you've read many contemporary novels and had to judge which ones would win prizes. You've done this as a teacher of writing. Does it seem to you that as you look at your career and compare your novels with those you've read recently that you've used your own life more than many contemporary American novelists?*

I don't think so. I wrote one book, essentially, out of my own life, or more out of my own life than out of imagination. Then wrote a trailer to it, but it's still essentially one book. You said something recently about the fact that Bruce's post–high-school career seems to get foreshortened in *The Big Rock Candy Mountain*. Well, all *Recapitulation* is, is that stuff that was foreshortened out of *The Big Rock Candy Mountain* and put into other terms. The business of growing up, the view of that experience from an adolescent's point of view, instead of from the point of view of the whole family, or somebody within it. I don't know. Is there anything else I should say about that? . . . I don't think I've been an autobiographical writer in the Tom Wolfe way. Most of my novels and histories haven't anything to do with me, though anybody is bound to put a good deal of himself in somewhat disguised terms into any book. But the Joe Allston books, *Angle of Repose*, *Shooting Star*, the DeVoto biography, *Mormon Country*, *The Gathering of Zion* [1964]—those are not autobiography, any of them. *Wolf Willow* is to some extent autobiography, but in that case the autobiography is used as an adjunct of history. The process is reversed. Instead of history's being used for fictional purposes, this is fiction and autobiography being used for historical purposes. I intended to write a historical work in *Wolf Willow*, and not a fictional one.

2. The Early Works

Etulain: You have mentioned several times in interviews and in your autobiographical writings that your parents had a limited education, but were they interested in books; did you have easy access to public libraries in your early years?

Stegner: My mother was interested in books and used to buy books, but she bought books from the places where she *could* buy books, which was generally from the T. Eaton or Sears Roebuck catalogue. There was no library in East End, Saskatchewan, and nobody really had any books. I suppose we had as many as anybody in town. People used to borrow them from us, God help them now. But she did buy books, and I can remember my brother and me, on our muskrat-pelt money, buying books for ourselves for Christmas. I remember buying Owen Wister's *Red Men and White*. Here's the beginning of the western myth. We had no notion what it was about, but it looked pretty interesting in the catalogue: *Red Men and White*. I remember another one, *On the Trail of Tipoo-Tib*, something about ivory hunters and slavers in Africa. We bought those with our own money. My mother bought most of the books in our house, mostly novels of the popular kind, the Graustark novels and things like that. There was no library there at all. There was a library in Great Falls which I began to use a little, but it wasn't until I got to Salt Lake that I began to be a real addict. I would go down to the library two or three times a week and bring away three or four books each time, without any direction whatever. A lot of them turned out to be things like G. A. Henty, historical novels for boys, and a fellow named

Tomlinson, who used to write historical novels about American history, the dark and bloody ground of Kentucky, Indian fights, and so on. More western myth. I remember Tomlinson and Henty; I don't remember much else from that period. But I remember just devouring books, one a day, sometimes more.

We were always moving, and once in a while we would rent a house in which there was a residual library of some kind. I can remember when I was about, I guess, a junior in high school, setting myself the job one summer of reading through the Harvard Classics on the theory that that was good for my mind. I didn't understand one damn word of Locke, Berkeley, Hume, and the rest! I remember reading almost all of Conrad, though, in some rented house. Somebody there had been a Conrad fan. That didn't hurt me any. I can remember reading in another house a certain amount of exploration, Captain Cook's reports of his explorations in Australia, the discovery of New South Wales, things like that. Again the selection was absolutely random and accidental. I don't suppose anybody began to direct my reading until I got into college. Then it was a direction primarily by temporary fad, the fad of the times. It began with James Branch Cabell and Hemingway and went on to Joyce and the rest of them. I was simply following people whose judgment in books was better than mine, more original than mine, and ahead of mine. If I found them interesting I would go read them.

You mention, I think it's in Big Rock Candy Mountain, *Bo Mason's buying a very expensive set of Shakespeare, isn't it?*

That's a detail out of our actual life. Yeah. We had that set of Shakespeare, but I don't know when he bought it. He got hooked by some traveling salesman. It always impressed me because it was bound in red calf. It looked very gorgeous. I don't recall reading any of that Shakespeare; God knows, I couldn't have. It was too remote from my dialect and anything that I understood. I don't think I ever read any Shakespeare until high school.

You mention Ridpath's histories.

Ridpath's histories I did read because they had pictures in them, the rape of the Sabine women, and the Gracchi with their swords outthrust. I did read in those histories on rainy days, days when I didn't really want to go out—partly, I suppose, because my hands were always cold and white and numb. I stayed in the house more than my family thought I ought to. I was always being urged to go on outside and play, with the result that I stayed inside and, in order not to have my mother on my neck, would pick up a book. As long as I was reading, she wouldn't bother me.

Would you have come in contact in either Saskatchewan or in Great Falls, or maybe in Salt Lake City, with the works of Owen Wister, B. M. Bower, or Mulford?

Oh, sure, I read all the Bar-20 books of Clarence B. Mulford and some of B. M. Bower. Most of those I read, as I recall, and the Tarzan books as well, toward the tail end of our East End years and during the two years in Great Falls, when I was nine, ten, eleven.

I suspect B. M. Bower was living in Montana about the time . . .

She may well have been. I wouldn't have known. But I remember *Bar-20 Days, Hopalong Cassidy,* and all that. I wonder where one picks up the word that those are things to read? I was simply reflecting, I suppose, the reading tastes of that pretty uninformed town on the upper headwaters of the Missouri. On the other hand, I remember kids who had got the latest Tarzan book and brought it to school, and were envied, and the book coveted. As soon as they were through with it, it'd get loaned around. It would go around through ten or twelve people and be devoured in a day or so, the way kids I suppose swap around records now . . . or comic books in your youth. But these were at least real books; they were in words.

You cannot remember, then, a book person, before you went to college, who suggested specific titles or authors for you to read?

No. I remember meeting people like that in college, though, who impressed me without being in any way directive or pedagogical. They impressed me as being so much more sophisticated and knowing than I was that I felt small and envious and leaped off to try to bring myself up to their level. There were two or three people like that in my college life, some of them students. One was a bookman in Salt Lake, ran a bookstore, Bill Winder, who was always indulgent about releasing *Funny Hill* from underneath the counter, but who also steered us to a lot of books that we would never have read otherwise. I remember reading Joris Karl Huysmans, for instance, and people like that when I was about a sophomore. That was entirely Bill Winder's doing. The thing that impresses me now about all of that is how random it was, but also I suppose, in the sum, how much I actually did read. Most of it was junk, but I read a lot.

You have mentioned the disparities between your boyhood experiences and the content of the books you were reading in the statement: "Books didn't enlarge me; they dispersed me."[1] In other words, did your early reading whet your interests in people and ideas beyond East End?

---

[1]*Wolf Willow,* p. 26.

I think I have to correct that statement. I may have given a wrong impression. It's not so much the books that I was reading outside the school that I was talking about. I was talking about schoolbooks and the education in books that came with school. I was thinking of school rather than reading as dispersing me. School did divert me to various kinds of things a long way off from life in Saskatchewan. I suppose I was thinking when I wrote that sentence that it might have been advantageous to have been better focused, to have started learning from the ground up, instead of learning at large, at random, in a void, and then trying to focus all that down upon the immediate life that I was trying to live. I don't know. At this moment I'm not prepared to say whether it's better to go one way or the other. I suppose it didn't hurt me to be without history for the first thirty-five years of my life. I found it, finally, and so far as Saskatchewan was concerned there wasn't an awful lot there to find. So, fortunately I didn't have much to catch up on. If I had had history early, God knows what. I might have wound up some county historian, a local history buff called on to determine whose buffalo skull that was so-and-so plowed up last week. There seems to me to be a certain limitation about being THAT interested in the local . . . .

I thought you were just going to say in being a historian . . .

No. And I'm grateful to county historians too, and to people who do dig in the local lore, because without them a more general historian wouldn't have any of the details to play with that he does. At the same time I would rather hate to be limited to the local digs.

Had you decided to become an author before you went to college? Was that in your mind?

No, no. I hadn't the slightest idea about becoming a writer. I didn't know you *could* be a writer. Writers were something far off and a long way back in time. I'd never seen one. There was none in Salt Lake. The only one that I ever saw in Salt Lake, and I didn't think of him as a writer then, was Vardis Fisher. He was writing a novel, and we all knew it; but somehow it was an unreal occupation. He was *really* an English instructor.

No. I just started going to college. That was exciting enough. I think at first I was an economics major. Then I fell into Fisher's freshman English class, and Fisher felt that I could write. He gave me good grades and patted me on the head and boosted me out of freshman English at the end of the first quarter and into an advanced writing course with him. I got the impression pretty early that writing was something that I could do, but I still didn't have any notion of a major. I suspect that I changed majors sometime midway of my sophomore year and became an English major because all of the people that I liked most on the faculty, and the classes I liked the most, were in English: Syd Angleman and people like that. Pretty early, I guess, maybe in my sophomore year, I took a writing course from an old fellow named L. A. Quivey, who was sort of odd, but excited about writing and able to communicate his excitement. You could hang around his office and learn things. He liked it when you did well. I feel he took a fatherly interest in me. Before I was through, I read papers for Quivey, and I read for Syd, and for several of those people. I suppose I was an English Department addict by the end of my sophomore year, but I had a real sophomore slump, too. I went to the University scared to death. People had assured me that college was very much more difficult than high school. I had no background, no perspective on anything, and I ran scared from the opening bell, with the result that I started out straight A in my freshman year. In the sophomore year I discovered beer, and cigarettes, and girls, and all kinds of things, and I went down to straight B's. But about the time I was discovering all of those things, I was also discovering and getting excited about books, and I suppose that's when I became an English major for sure. I don't really remember the precise day, but sometime in 1926.

You mentioned that Fisher was your teacher in English composition. What do you remember about him as a teacher? What kinds of things did he do, encourage you to do in class . . .

He was one of those teachers who liked to take can openers to unopened minds. He had the notion we were all Mormon provincials, that we'd never seen anything, and that a real idea would shock the pants off us. It was thrilling, in a way, to be treated almost like an adult. He formed a thing called the Radical Club, of which I was a member during the tailend of my freshman and through my sophomore year. We'd have meetings and discuss the historicity of Jesus Christ, methods of birth control, and such matters. Once or twice we had a chance to bring in speakers who were talking in Salt Lake. Vardis got them, and they would meet around with us over a beer. Scott Nearing, I remember, was one of them. He had been thrown out of the University of Pennsylvania for his radical leanings, and after his lecture in the Tabernacle he came to Fisher's house and opened our eyes. Don Lewis, a teacher of speech and a close friend of Fisher's, was in the group. Another member was Margaret Trusler, who later married Fisher. . . . At sixteen or seventeen years old I didn't really belong in that company, which thought itself the most emancipated company at the University. Nevertheless, I liked it.

Were you writing for campus publications?

I didn't write. I was working a forty-hour week at a rug and linoleum house after my first quarter at the University. I didn't have any time to write for anybody or to go out for much. I did go out for tennis because my best friend, whose father owned the store that I worked in, was also on the tennis team. He was a lot better tennis player than I was, and his father could hardly let him go out without letting me go too. So those afternoons of practice, we just cut out of our working hours during tennis season—and, once in a while, a meet that we would get off for. Then we'd have to cut class to make time up at the store. It was always learning that suffered.

Your master's thesis was a collection of stories. Did some of those stories become some of your first publications?

Yeah, one of those, let's see . . .

Was that the "Pete and Emil" story?

No, "Pete and Emil" I think I probably wrote at Iowa. But one called "Bloodstain" was the first story I ever did write.[2] I harked back to the old river bottom of the White Mud River and wrote a story about a kid who accidentally shot his friend's father, mistaking him for a rabbit, down in the willow brush. Some fool reprinted that just a year or so ago. I wouldn't let him print it under my name. I read it—it's terrible. But that was the first one I wrote. One thing it did was cement my acquaintance with Bill Winder and make Professor Quivey begin to think I was his star pupil.

That was written at Salt Lake, then?

It was first written in Salt Lake. Later I rewrote it, many, many times and finally included it in the thesis. I guess I wrote "Pete and Emil" in Iowa City. I've forgotten. What else is in that thesis? There were only three stories, I think. What would the other one have been? . . . Sometime, I think when I was about a junior, about 1928 or so, Quivey arranged with one of the Salt Lake papers to hold a college short story contest, with a prize of twenty-five dollars. I won that—but the story that I won it with I had the wit to bury quietly among the dead leaves. That was not in the thesis.

So then when your dissertation on Clarence Dutton was published, that was your first book, is that right?

Yes, but it really isn't a book. It's about a fifty-page pamphlet, a sort of abstract of the thesis. The University of Utah Press made itself available for publications by local faculty. I dug it out; it was after all on a local subject.

Did you feel pressure as a young faculty member to publish or perish?

Well, you bet. Those were the years when there was no promotion whatever in any college. We were all worked to death, and skimping our work,

---

[2]"Pete and Emil," *Salt Lake Tribune*, December 9, 1934, p. 3; "Bloodstain," *American Prefaces* 2 (Summer 1937) : 150–53.

teaching four classes of freshman English with thirty-five people in a class. You couldn't properly read a hundred and forty themes a week. I'd go through a set of themes in an hour—zip, zip! But you had a feeling that if you were going to get out of that rut at all, you had to do it through something exceptional. Utah was always a place in the old days, and I suspect it may even still be, where publication is not pressed the way it is in a lot of institutions. There were some very good teachers, but they weren't pressured to publish, and in consequence few did any publishing at all. On occasion, maybe a textbook. The people with whom I was in direct competition for a promotion at Utah, though, didn't think of it in those terms then; none, I think, had published anything. I had published, I guess, a story in *Frontier and Midland*, and then that Dutton thing. Then I published, or at least sold to the *Virginia Quarterly*, a story which is a piece of *The Big Rock Candy Mountain*. "Bugle Song," something that came on like a poem. I wrote it in one afternoon.

Is "Bugle Song" the one about the boy, the rats, the snake, the feeding of the weasel?

Gophers to the weasel, which is again pure autobiography. So I had published three little things, and I thought that was pretty good. It was more than anybody else around me had done. When I won the Little, Brown contest with a novella, I was kind of a blockbuster.

That was really a break in your career, wasn't it?

I felt that entitled me to promotion. I'd been there, what, three years. I was at the end of my third year, and I thought it was time I got promoted. I couldn't persuade . . .

Did you start as instructor or assistant professor?

Oh, instructor. You worked for ten years to get to be an assistant professor in those days. I *wanted* to be an assistant professor, but I couldn't persuade the head of the department, though he was a friend of mine, I'm sure, and would have done it if he could. I couldn't persuade the president either, so I quit, in my brashness, thinking, "Okay, I'll make it some other place or some other way." That's how we left Salt Lake in 1937.

How did you come to write the novella Remembering Laughter?

I just saw the notice of a contest. I didn't have a class till ten o'clock, so I'd sit down at eight every morning and write until I had to whip up the hill—we lived on Twelfth East, and it was only about two blocks to class. I could be up there in seven minutes, half-trotting. So I could write for two hours every morning, and it went reasonably fast. A story really that

Mary had told me out of her background. Remote family relations or friends of the family, something, and this turned out to be *Remembering Laughter*.

You've mentioned that the work load was such that it dulled you for a couple of years after you got to Utah, yet the novelette came on quickly, didn't it?

It wasn't really the work load that dulled me—no. I was never one to work too hard for my wages. What dulled me was really the business of grinding through a Ph.D. That kind of study was not my native habitat at all, and though I did it as faithfully as I knew how, I don't suppose I was ever very good at it. None of it stuck. I'd have to fight to hold it in my head, to try to memorize the *Cambridge History of English Literature*— and then try to read all the books second. I should have done it the other way around. But, in any case, I was a fairly unwilling graduate student, and I had enough to do with teaching four classes. Also, I was back in Salt Lake, and we were a young married couple. There was a lot of partying going on, and lots of hikes, and picnics, and so on, up in the mountains. Salt Lake is an easy town to get out into the country from, and I had grown up doing that. So what I remember about those years in Salt Lake is how many times we were up picking dog-tooth violets in the mouth of Hughes Canyon, instead of being down on the campus interviewing students. Oh, I met my classes and I read their papers. But I did them both with the greatest speed possible. I don't think it was the teaching that kept me from writing any-thing, because when it got the time when I sort of bubbled over and had something to write, I did sit down and write that "Bugle Song" story in an afternoon. From there on, it all began to run.

Was it through the publication of Remembering Laughter *that you came to know Bernard DeVoto?*

Benny was one of the judges who gave it that Little, Brown Prize. I wrote him a letter of thanks—the kind of asking-for-advice letter that young writers are always writing older writers—and got back a very decent and very intelligent response. So the next year, Christmas time, when the Modern Language Association was meeting in Chicago, I went in from Madison and met him. The following summer, the summer of 1938, I met him under much more intimate circumstances at Bread Loaf—two weeks of the closest kind of association. He lived in Cambridge, and we were just moving to Cambridge the next year, so that as soon as we moved to Cam-bridge, the first place we went to dinner was at Benny's. He and Frost were both living there—Frost in Boston at that point, but later in Cambridge.

You were still in your late twenties. Was there a sense of exhilaration that you had arrived already?

I was too busy to be exhilarated about anything. I think of it now as a very exhilarating time because for the first time in my life I was moving among people who really rattled my brains. Benny was always happy to act as a guru. When I told him I had to write some stuff for money, because we were just too poor to make it otherwise, he took me over one afternoon and said, "My boy, here are my files." He showed me all the files of his *Collier's* stories, how you did it, and laid me out formulas. I could never write to a formula, but I thought that was decent of him. Once in a while during those years I'd write something for *Atlantic* or someone and make enough money so that I could feel relaxed for awhile.

In the novella Remembering Laughter *you use a long flashback to tell most of the story. Was this your first experiment in finding the best way of connecting the past and the present?*

I suppose it was, though it was certainly—like so much of what I'd done —totally unconscious. I guess some sense of form, some rudimentary groping notion that you don't just splatter it out chronologically, must have been in my head while I was dealing with that rueful little legend left over from an earlier time. I suppose I thought it was easier to take a stance which permitted the backward look, which is what I finally gave myself. I didn't have any point of view. I just did it as a flashback. I was there as author. I probably wouldn't do it that way now, but I did set it up in the present and then slipped back into the past and then came back to the present at the end. It involved, as you say, a long flashback, a kind of envelope or pair of parentheses around a story.

Often literary commentators like to see resonances of one writer in another. Several people have commented that they see parallels between your novel, Edith Wharton's Ethan Frome, *or the writings of Fisher, Nathaniel Hawthorne, or Henry James. Were those people the kinds of writers you were reading at the time, whose ideas you might have picked up?*

No. Somebody said that about *Ethan Frome*, some reviewer, when the book first came out. That daunted me because I'd never read *Ethan Frome*, but I whipped out and read it right away. It's very easy to see why they thought I had done some borrowing, particularly since both are novellas, both in that middle length. I don't know where the form came from. It certainly didn't come from Edith Wharton, for though I admire Edith Wharton now, I don't think I'd read any of her then. Fisher could have had an influence upon me that I didn't understand, but, actually, I never had the highest respect for Vardis's novelistic skill. He told some good stories, some very moving stories, but I tried once reading him aloud and it didn't work. This goes back to DeVoto again. Benny DeVoto had written a piece in *Atlantic* or someplace, damning all the Mormon novels. There wasn't a one worth reading, nobody in Utah could sign his name, and so on. Then came out *The Children of God*, which had won the Harper Prize. Benny had to concur, it was a good book; and so he ate crow publicly and wrote another piece in which he, I think, overpraised *The Children of God*. So while I was writing *The Big Rock Candy Mountain*, finishing it up in Vermont that winter, I tried reading *The Children of God* aloud to Mary. It didn't read aloud. It wasn't good prose. It hurt my ears, it seemed so blunt. It was made with an axe. I think I must have felt that about Vardis pretty early. He was a very forceful character, but not the subtlest that you ever dealt with. He did many, many things for me, and I liked him, but I— just on the basis of literary admiration—I'm quite sure I never modeled my writing on his. Who else was on your list?

Hawthorne and James.

Hawthorne and James, huh? Neither one of them would have been a favorite of mine. I would have thought myself much more likely to be influenced by . . .

Conrad?

I wouldn't have thought of that, but I did read Conrad earlier than almost any major writer, and that business of backtracking, of coiling back, advancing a story to a certain point and picking it up again, I could have got from Conrad, though it never occurred to me until this minute. No, I would have thought that somebody like Mark Twain was much more likely to have influenced me because I admired him so much more. I never did admire James. I came to a kind of reluctant admiration, or a reluctant respect, pretty late. Hawthorne always seemed to me a little chilly, and also he didn't write the American Language. He wrote schooled English.

You had been reading Twain though?

Oh, yeah, well from forever, I suppose.

The Potter's House *[1938], the story of a deaf-mute, is quite different from your other early works. Was it written before* Remembering Laughter? *Wasn't this novelette the expansion of an earlier short story?*

No, to both questions. I wrote *The Potter's House* in Madison, I think the second year we were there, and I had already by that point—wait a minute, let me get this absolutely clear. I think I wrote it in Madison, but so help me, I'm not absolutely sure. I know I sent it to my friend Wilbur Schramm, who was then editing *American Prefaces*, and that's where it was published.

It was published there the first time?

American Prefaces became the organ of the writing program at Iowa for a while, and Wilbur edited it, and he did publish that rather long story. I'm sure I wrote it in Madison. If that's true, then I had already published *Remembering Laughter,* and I might even have already begun *The Big Rock Candy Mountain,* and I might already have written *On a Darkling Plain* [1940]. *The Potter's House* was a little experiment. I was trying to write a story with no auditory images in it at all, just playing games. I don't think it's much of a story. I haven't gone back to reread it for a long, long time. It got picked up by the Prairie Press in Muscatine and published on gray paper with blunt type, with red rubrics and all that. The only laid paper job I ever had.

Someone suggested that you emphasize in this novel two of your favorite themes: the dangers of people isolating themselves from society and the importance of close family relationships.

This is in *The Potter's House?* Well, maybe, although those weren't very heavily on my mind at the time. I had in mind a pottery place that Mary and I had seen in Laguna Beach when we went down for Christmas to get out of the Salt Lake cold—one of those places that make garden pots and the kind of pottery that, in those days, all young couples had to serve coffee or iced tea out of, mugs with iron or brass or bronze handles. The image of that lot, of the place where all these things were made, in the sunshine of Laguna during the time when we were escaping the December snows in Utah, I suppose was something bright and vivid in my head. But I don't think I would have gone so far as to think about the danger of people isolating themselves from society as part of the meaning of that story. He didn't isolate himself from society. He was isolated from it by a handicap. But I guess maybe there's something to the close family relationship. The deafness would be isolating to a degree, and that may already have been in my consciousness as something important.

Isn't On a Darkling Plain *the first of your novels to draw on specific personal experiences? I'm thinking of the flu epidemic. Were you committed by this time to the idea that autobiographical fiction was your medium, your métier?*

No. I wouldn't call *On a Darkling Plain* autobiographical, either, in any but the most rudimentary sense. Though it deals with country I knew—a homestead out there in Palliser's Triangle—and with the town I knew, none of the experiences are mine except, as you say, the flu epidemic. I *had* been shut up in the schoolhouse with the whole town, with about ten people on their feet and the rest all sick or dying. But nothing autobiographical.

The trouble with that book, and there's plenty of trouble with it, is that it's entirely *made*. It's an imagined novel, and war heroes I knew not one damn thing about. I knew nothing about war. I wasn't even grown up when I wrote the book. So, the experiences of this character Vickers are purely hypothetical, disastrously so, I would say.

He appears in The Big Rock Candy Mountain *briefly, doesn't he?*

Yes. I had already invented him, so I put him in *The Big Rock Candy Mountain* where Chet is left at home alone with the bootlegged booze. That, of course, is all invented, too—that business of people trying to hijack the stock.

That's the "Chip off the Old Block" story?

That's right. It was made into a TV movie by the Canadian Broadcasting Corporation.

It was?

I saw it in Toronto [1973], that's the only time I ever have seen it. Quite faithfully done.

It seems to me that more than anything, On a Darkling Plain *deals with an idea that has always intrigued you—relationships between individuals and the community.*

That was pretty much on my mind, because when this was being written —I guess it was written about 1938, published in 1939, everybody was saying: "Are we going Fascist or are we going Communist? Which way do we go, left or right?" As if there were no middle alternative. There in Madison I had my first experience with the intense political consciousness, and for a while I went around to meetings of the Young Communist League to see what was going on and listened to speakers back home from the Spanish Civil War. I got two very strong impressions out of that experience. One of them was that this was not my bag at all, that I didn't have any such political feelings. The other was that in any choice between left and right, communists and fascists, I was going to have to go down the middle, because neither one of them seemed to me an absolutely imperative alternative. I had the same feeling, even stronger, when I later joined the Harvard Teachers' Union in Cambridge. F. O. Matthiessen was the president of it. We spent all our time getting Earl Browder out of jail, sending me home frothing at the mouth: "God damn, that's not what it's *about*." Anyway, in Madison I was made conscious of the outside world in ways that I had never been before. That was my first experience with people who were committedly, frantically, tensely political. Out of it came these questions of what one owes the society, and where does the individual fit in? *On a*

Darkling Plain isn't a political novel, but it does get on to that problem, as you say. I suspect that problems in the novel came to some extent out of my own rather asocial life. I had grown up, more or less, withdrawn from organized society, and I'd been in the habit of living sort of withdrawn from it. But as a teacher in a university, I couldn't be that withdrawn from it, and so I was being made to think about it some. I dramatized it cheaply and not very intelligently in that book.

One of the ideas that strikes me as I read this novel is the difference implied between the West Coast and the Prairie Provinces. Is the province of British Columbia treated in this novel as if it were the California of the Canadian West? As something essentially different from the real West?

I think so, and I wouldn't be at all surprised if that's a reasonable perception, that British Columbia *is* unlike the rest of the Canadian West. Something happens about the crest of the Rockies, and from there on it— I don't know—Victoria and Vancouver are very different from Winnipeg and Calgary.

It seems to me you were implying something in this novel that you say did not come to you until Wolf Willow, *but it's already here, I think, in this novel—unconsciously perhaps.*

Well, I think I must have been aware even then that a lot of people had left Saskatchewan, moving on, driven out, turned out, and that the direction of their flight was very commonly either to California or to British Columbia —further west, and to warmer places.

To a milder kind of West?

I think I was aware of that even before we left Canada because some of my friends had gone the same way. Well, I don't know, maybe I was already leaning toward that perception. It wouldn't be remarkable. I should have known that with my mother's milk, but I probably didn't know it more than tentatively.

I notice that in your biography of Bernard DeVoto you give extended coverage to DeVoto's discontent with Marxist ideas and writers of the 1930s. Your fourth novel, Fire and Ice *[1941], suggests that you may have shared some of his attitudes toward Marxists.*

Well *Fire and Ice*, of course, is the culmination of my feelings in Madison that this plus-or-minus, left-or-right business was an artificial and rather hysterical dichotomy. That feeling in me may have been partly innocence, coming as I did from a totally nonpolitical environment. But, it may also have been regional, my protected sense of being deep in the continent. The

closer I got to the East Coast, the more I ran into these people who were
hysterically running around being Trotskyites or Stalinists. They seemed
to me to be hysterical, and I got that feeling corroborated in spades by
DeVoto and Frost, both of whom had a deep contem
would have put it, un-American kind of politics. The
dichotomy wasn't native politics at all. It made no allow
middlists and for the strength of the democratic traditi
turned out Frost and DeVoto were right about it. We
either communist or fascist. We're always in desperate da
way or the other, but we always seem to totter in toward t
where. It's a very uncertain kind of life, but I'm not yet pro
that the other was a reasonable statement of the case. I put som
ing into *Fire and Ice*. Many of the people I saw in the Young
League were Jews from the East who at that time used Wisconsin
of substitute for the Ivy that they couldn't get into. Unbelievable as
now. There were real quotas on Jews in Harvard, Yale, and many p
and so a lot of bright boys from the Bronx, Brooklyn, and New York cam
to the Big Ten. The school that they chose to come to was more often than
not Wisconsin, because it had a progressive political tradition which looked
liberated. I saw quite a few of those people, both as students in my classes
and as people with whom I had something to do. The Young Communist
League, particularly, of which I attended three or four meetings—that puts
me on the Dean's list, doesn't it?—struck me as being quite insane.

In Fire and Ice *you seem interested in the central idea of Hemingway's*
For Whom the Bell Tolls *and Steinbeck's* The Grapes of Wrath—*the
individual and the group—and, as you pointed out, this evidently was a
theme that appealed especially to writers in the late thirties. Were you
influenced by those books or had they . . .*

I wrote *Fire and Ice* before I read either of those books. *The Grapes of
Wrath* came out, I think, while *Fire and Ice* was in press, and I read *For
Whom the Bell Tolls* several years later—after we had moved to Cambridge.
No, I wasn't influenced by those, but I was certainly influenced by the
climate of opinion. It was a legitimate question in the Depression. You had
somehow to make up your mind where you were on questions of social
justice, on the one hand, for all kinds of people, and the liberty and independence that had been traditional in America on the other. It's a theme
that Hemingway did earlier in *To Have and Have Not* and that was done
over and over and over again in a lot of strike novels—*Union Square* by
Albert Halper, Steinbeck's *In Dubious Battle*, things like that. The problem
certainly wasn't anything that I invented, but it was something that we all
talked about.

One thing that I ran into in Madison was a whole group of very intelligent young instructors, all of them about my age, all of them better educated by far, and many with experiences very different from mine. Claude Simpson was one; Stuart Brown, who wound up at the University of Hawaii, was another; Curtis Bradford, who later did a couple of books on Yeats, was another. Brown came from Princeton, Claude from Texas, via Harvard, and Bradford from Yale—one of Tucker Brook's boys. There was also Phil Gray, who was another Yalie, whose father had bankrolled Henry Ford when he turned the bicycle shop into an automobile factory. Phil was the rich boy of our group and one of my closest friends all his life. (He died last year.) We were all interested in the same things, and the quality of the conversation at parties and so on, as between Salt Lake City and Madison, was—whew!—up like that. It was like the first year in graduate school. You had a feeling you were learning at four times the normal pace. It went on, of course, at Harvard, the same way. But Madison was definitely a step up, intellectually; and a lot of ideas came into my head that had simply never lodged there before. This is one of them. I suppose the history of my father was in my mind—I was already working on *The Big Rock Candy Mountain*—the recalcitrant individual, the outlaw individual, essentially, as against the society, and whose rights are whose, was also at work here.

He's a bit like Morgan in To Have and Have Not, *isn't he?*

Oh yes. So that both personal and social reasons pushed me toward consideration of how the demands of the individual and the demands of society could be reconciled.

Big Rock Candy Mountain *is much different from the first novels. Were there "lessons" you had learned in the writing of these first works that you wanted to avoid or to repeat in your first "big" novel? Still, you were writing them at the same time, weren't you?*

I was writing some of them at the same time. I started writing *On a Darkling Plain* during Christmas vacation of 1938, when I had about three weeks free. I wrote a big chunk of it in three weeks. I wrote it fast, too fast; and I finished it, more or less, before the end of that school year. *Fire and Ice*—I'm not quite sure when I did write that, whether I may not have finished it in Cambridge. But I wrote both of them after having started *The Big Rock Candy Mountain*, and I wrote them partly because I was having difficulty with all of that selective process—the business of knowing what to put into and what to leave out of *The Big Rock Candy Mountain*. How to make some kind of coherent narrative out of a great mass of material.

I was thinking of general lessons, like: How do you tell a story? How do you flash back and forth? What's the role of the narrator? Those questions that seem central to an understanding of your career.

I didn't know anything about flashing back and forth particularly, though in *Remembering Laughter* I had done it unconsciously, perhaps learning from Conrad, or somebody. I certainly had no literary theory, no notion of what a proper novel should be. The form itself had to be worked out on the typewriter, with the material itself dictating it. The business of narrators didn't come into *The Big Rock Candy Mountain* because I was never in anybody's mind first-person singular; I was over several people's shoulders; I suppose that was then the only point of view I knew or understood. I never wrote anything in the first-person singular for a long, long time. Once I started doing it, it seemed to me to offer devices, possibilities, that other points of view didn't, so that I wrote all the Joe Allston stories, and *Angle of Repose*, by deliberately creating a narrative voice and then taking advantage of it—both as a unifying device and as a device for syncopating time. You can syncopate time in a phrase, if you're talking through somebody's mouth, but you can't do it nearly so readily if you're writing in third person or over somebody's shoulder. I was learning as I went; I had no conscious thought except trying to get the thing done. *The Big Rock Candy Mountain* came to me in big lumpish nineteenth-century terms, and I just did it chronologically, from beginning to end. When I finally cut out the hundred and fifty thousand or so words I had to cut out for the armed services edition, my first act was to cut off the whole front porch. The armed services edition starts in North Dakota and not in Iowa, and what happens between Elsa and her father and her new stepmother is all suggested in flashback or in a letter or two—much more economically than my original strategy of working it clear out. I would have done much more of that, I suppose, if I had known enough to. It would have been a way of reducing some of the size without losing anything substantial.

How do you react now when you reread your first fiction, the novels and the stories? Some writers get itchy fingers and want to rewrite their earliest stories. Do you react that way?

I wish they weren't there sometimes, certain things. *On a Darkling Plain* embarrasses me. *Fire and Ice* rather embarrasses me, too, because it's politically naïve in the same way that *On a Darkling Plain* is psychologically naïve.

You feel pretty good about Remembering Laughter?

Remembering Laughter, somehow, yeah—I would certainly change the phrasing and be a little less hush-hush and tiptoe, but—but no; it seems to me at least well-made. I found the parentheses that would hold it together, and I don't think that the landscape, the background, the place, is badly done. We're dealing there with figures who are not real figures from life. They stand a little taller and a little more distant; they're like stage figures, in shrouds and cloaks. They don't really have—these are just people who got into a mess and couldn't get out of it except by keeping their peace, by silence, and that gives them a stagey look rather than a real look. But I'm never tempted to rewrite them now. I guess I always lean ahead, not backward. I haven't always liked to see some of the things that are frequently reprinted—reprinted that often—because they don't seem to be the best stuff that could be picked. But I have long since had to shrug off the fact that I got my education in public, by and large, and some of it shows.

I notice that your first five volumes—the study of Dutton and the first four novels—were put out by five different publishers. Did you work directly with these publishers, or were you working through an agent who was searching for an ideal publisher?

I can tell you the whole dismal story. The study of Dutton doesn't really figure; that was just a little thing, to get something on my dossier. But the first four novels—here is the history: *Remembering Laughter* won a prize and was published by Little, Brown; then I wrote *Potter's House*, which wasn't a book. It was too short for a book; it really was a magazine piece, so that really doesn't figure here. I was happy enough to have it published for nothing by the Muscatine Press, just to make a pleasant, handleable book out of it. The next one, *On a Darkling Plain*, I submitted to Little, Brown, which had an option. Raymond Everitt didn't like it and rejected it, assuming, I think, that I was such a naïf that I would accept his rejection and throw the book in the can and give them the next one. But when they didn't pick up the option, I sent it to Harcourt Brace. Sam Sloan at Harcourt Brace liked it and published it right away. Then Raymond Everitt was very upset because he hadn't expected to lose one off his list. He just thought, well, have the kid put this one away. I told him he'd bought me on margin and hadn't covered, and so I assumed that finding another publisher was the thing to do. It *was* the thing to do, too; otherwise I would have got screwed by Little, Brown. Then when *Fire and Ice* came on, Sam Sloan, Cap Pearce, and Charlie Duell, all of whom had been junior editors at Harcourt, were faced with a bad situation. Frank Morley, Christopher Morley's brother who had been with Methuen in London, came back to the United States and took over the head editorship at Harcourt. All of a sudden the slot at the top that all of them had been hoping to fill was filled up. Frank Morley was then young—they were looking ten or fifteen years ahead before they had any chance—so they broke off and founded Duell, Sloan, and Pearce. Because I liked Sam, and he liked me and my books, I just naturally went with Sam Sloan to Duell, Sloan, and Pearce. That's three publishers on three books. Duell, Sloan, and Pearce then published *The Big Rock Candy Mountain* . . .

Up to this point, you had not had an agent . . .

Yes, I got an agent right after *Remembering Laughter*. Raymond Everitt signed me up with Bernice Baumgarten. She worked primarily on magazine stuff, but I also consulted with her on this. I guess she sent the books in, I don't remember; but we agreed that the thing to do was to sell them—if they were worth publishing at all—and not to take Little, Brown's rejection as final. She agreed that it was useful to follow the publisher that liked you and that you liked and liked to work with. I went with Duell, Sloan, and Pearce with those two books, and then they also published *Mormon Country*. So they published three. After that it was wartime. I was teaching ASTP[3] at Harvard and had already agreed to do *One Nation* for *Look*, who sold it to Houghton Mifflin. They got a couple of prizes, which I probably wouldn't have got without the aid of the elbow-twisting that *Look* could exert.

When I changed to Houghton Mifflin, I changed because of that *Look* magazine deal. At Houghton Mifflin I found that I liked those people very well indeed. About the same time, they proposed—we had moved to the West Coast for the *One Nation* job and were now moving to Stanford— they proposed that we act as West Coast editors. So Mary and I acted as Houghton Mifflin's West Coast editors for a long time. We got them some good books, like *Mister Roberts*, which came in because Tom Heggen was my cousin. Some other good ones came in because we were here, and on the spot. We did that for quite a long time, eight years or so. When I finally shifted from Houghton Mifflin to Viking, I did so because I had a feeling that for two or three years I had been falling through the grating, that they looked upon me as an employee and not as an author. I thought they ought to take a little more pains. I left Viking after what? three books?—because, to tell you frankly, I found Viking a penny-pinching outfit. They make good books, good-looking books, and they had some of the best editors in the business, but the policies of the company were very tight-fisted. When the time came to see what I could do about retiring from teaching and living on advances for a long time, I just had to look for somebody else. We looked around several places and the best offer by far was Doubleday's. I've been perfectly content with Doubleday, primarily because of Ken McCormick and Sam Vaughan. So that's the history of my publishing career. It's not desirable to have that many publishers. It's hard to keep your books in print

---

[3]Army Special Training Program.

because publishers whom you've left have very little impulse to put you back in or keep you in print. So I've been dispersed in that way, too.

One survey of the first decade of your writing asserts that two questions dominate your early work: "who is man and what can he affirm when he lives at dead center?" I suppose the writer means between isolation and a kind of other-directedness. Do you find this a useful comment as you look at your early fiction?

I don't know quite what it means. Who made that remark?

Chester Eisinger[4]

Eisinger? Well, I guess I don't necessarily believe Eisinger. I read some article of his a long time ago in which he upbraided me for not taking sides, for leaving issues ambiguous—as if there weren't a clear decision to be made between this choice and that choice. I think his analysis, if not his judgment, is profoundly true. There often *isn't* a clear decision to be made between this choice and that choice. In some book I had left it that way, and he wanted it pushed over the edge. I don't know what "dead center" means. Since it comes from that source, I'm not sure I think it means much. I think he misreads me. I think probably I have emphasized the difficulty of choice because choices are often made by forces outside the will, that they're made by circumstance. Elsa Mason goes somewhere because she must. She doesn't deliberately make a choice to do this or that. Life forces her to do that. When I'm writing about people like the Masons, who were poor and down in the scale, I don't give them the kind of free will that Henry James's characters have. He invented them rich so that he could give them free will, but God didn't do that for everybody. You bend where you're pushed hardest. So I don't understand what living at dead center means. I don't think anybody lives at dead center. That sounds like complete inertia, silence, rotation around your own navel, and that isn't what I mean any of my characters to be doing.

I am intrigued with this period of your career. Your first big novel had just come out, The Big Rock Candy Mountain, *and you were making the decision to come west. Did you see this as a kind of turning point in your career—'forty-three, 'forty-four, and 'forty-five?*

Yes, it was a very, very upset time, of course —in the history of the world, too. The war was on, and I wouldn't have been able to take the *Look* job, I suppose, if it hadn't been that just by the grace of everything, I had practically the highest draft number in the world. I was going to be the last guy

---

[4]Chester E. Eisinger, "Twenty Years of Wallace Stegner," *College English* 20 (December 1958): 110–16.

in the United States drafted in my age level, so that I could take a choice whether I wanted to go to OWI [Office of War Information], as Wilbur Schramm was urging me to do, or whether I wanted to do something else. I thought at that time that going to do this job for *Look* was the best possible way to reach a mass audience with a message about equality and fraternity. Wartime patriotism took strange forms, but *One Nation* did seem to me to be a thing worth doing. As it turned out, *Look* didn't run all those articles in the magazine, and so it didn't turn out to be what I thought it was going to be, but the book had some impact and maybe did some good. I remember having a conversation with Rudolf Serkin at a party at Harvard. He couldn't imagine why I would resign or take a leave from Harvard to go to work for *Look* magazine. The way he put it, it did seem kind of strange. But I wasn't by then so sure that the OWI was doing anything very substantial for the war effort, and a lot of people had come back from Washington pretty disgusted with the bureaucratic entanglements and the red tape. At least on this job I would be essentially my own boss, and I could be doing something that I thought was important. Also, it offered me the possibility of a major book. So, for two reasons, I did take the leave from Harvard. I suppose that was a real edge of some kind, a divide. For a year and a half, then, I was a journalist, not a college professor. I did a lot more traveling all over the country, and in more intimate ways than I had in the past. We'd go down to Elizabeth City, North Carolina, and shoot Jim Crow, or we'd go out to Dubuque, Iowa, and shoot a lot of monasteries and Catholic institutions in the Middle West. Traveling all through the West doing Mexican barrios, Filipino pickers in Stockton, Indian reservations, I got to see some of the country, and I think that was useful to me too. I don't regret that choice at all. All it did was take me away from Harvard at a time when I probably couldn't have been teaching anything important or doing myself any good toward promotion anyway, because we were all teaching the dregs and leavings. Harvard essentially wasn't functioning. It was just marking time. I don't think that even if I had been there and caught a few opportunities and done brilliantly at them it would have made any difference in the matter of promotion beyond the assistant professorship I then held. When I became a journalist and we came out and were living in Santa Barbara, I had already made a break with Harvard. I wasn't at all sure I was ever going to go back. When the offer came from Stanford giving me a double jump from assistant professor to acting full professor, it was very clear that I had made the appropriate break—that the *One Nation* book and the year and a half of journalism were not really wasted time. It hadn't actually interrupted anything much.

3. *The Big Rock Candy Mountain*

Etulain: A good friend tells me that when she read The Big Rock Candy Mountain, *she felt as if she were prying into your private life. She thought the writing of the novel must have been a painful experience, especially since you revealed so much about your family in your early years. Is she correct in assuming that it was a painful experience and yet a cathartic one?*

Stegner: Oh, sure it was, although she may be wrong in assuming that everything in it is autobiographical. You know, the imagination does work; though there was a good strong basis of autobiography in the book, it isn't by any means all autobiographical. Some parts of it were painful—I wrote some of it through tears—but other parts were like anything else. You put things together, and they come out either satisfactory or unsatisfactory, depending upon how well you put them together. The whole experience of writing that novel was, in a sense, cathartic, because I had to recreate a lot of my past, and it was a long way past. Times do change and you get into other areas and you forget about the past. When I was a graduate student at the University of Iowa, Steve Benét came through, and I told him I wanted to write a three-volume peasant novel. I'd been reading a lot of Scandinavian novels because I had a couple of Scandinavian professors, and my background was Scandinavian, and somehow or other I was reading a lot of those. I thought if an American could write a *Growth of the Soil*, I could. I had discovered just about then, as a graduate student in Iowa, when I was twenty, or barely twenty-one, that my experience was different from that of almost anybody that I talked to. It seemed interesting to them, and that's a temptation to any writer, even a budding writer. You know, if what you talk about seems interesting to people, you instantly talk about that and nothing else. So that's the impulse I started out with a long time ago, the impulse to write a peasant novel about Saskatchewan homesteaders. It was about nineteen thirty, 'thirty-one, something like that, a long time back.

Had you thought of writing this book before you actually started in . . . ?

I never did until Iowa. I began to think about it then because I got the impression that somehow my life, which had seemed to me very dull and unimpressive, was different enough so that other people took an interest in it. I of course never wrote any part of it for a long, long time after that, but that was where it first came on.

You once told two interviewers, "I don't believe you can write about anything . . . without drawing deeply on your own experience."[1] The Big Rock Candy Mountain *seems the best illustration of this credo among your early works.*

Well, possibly. Because I did recreate all the places where we had lived in a wandering life around the West, and I recreated some people, fairly realistically, in the book. I was drawing on my own experience a lot, but also let me repeat what I've said here, that the book isn't by any means all personal experience. And even when you do draw on your experience you don't have to write autobiography. Somewhere or other, I think in *Recapitulation*, that most recent novel, I remark that the memory can be an artist as well as a historian. You draw on it, but you don't draw on it literally. You draw on it all the time. I don't suppose you can do anything else *but* draw on your own experience, in the same way that you can imagine only what you have seen. You can't imagine creatures you haven't seen. The only thing you can do is put together some monster made up of pieces of the creatures you *have* seen. When I said that you can't write out of anything but experience, I certainly didn't mean literal experience. *The Big Rock Candy Mountain* is by no means literal experience. Some of the father–son stuff is of course pretty literal: I was exorcising my father. But a lot of the rest of it is invention, and I would have to insist on that.

Then I suppose you'd give the same answer to the next question. In some ways, isn't The Big Rock Candy Mountain *an attempt to reach your own "angle of repose"?*

---

[1]Robin White and Ed McClanahan, "An Interview with Wallace Stegner," *Per/Se* 3 (Fall 1968): 30.

Only with regard to my father. That obviously is a kind of experience that is central to a child. The dominant figure in your life probably is your father, if you have one, and if he happens himself to be mixed-up, irritable, and frustrated, and to feel himself many times a failure—those things do bounce off the child's head and leave knots. Surely, I was exorcising my father, and in a sense making some kind of recompense to my mother, who led a very rough life with him. Whether that's reaching my angle of repose or not, I don't know. The effect, I'm sure, of such a dominating and hair-trigger kind of father on many kids is to breed a kind of insecurity which may never be healed. I was probably looking for security.

I was thinking that, not only, say, with your father, but in the sense of your whole past. In the same way that Bruce wrestles with it in Reca-pitulation.

Yeah, an American life is a very strange thing, because you do go so many places and, particularly if you start pretty much at the bottom at some Neanderthal homestead in Saskatchewan, you have to try to come up the whole way in one lifetime, to something like the peak of your civilization, whatever that may be. It's demoralizing. I can remember talking to an association of Greek writers in Athens about 1963. George Seferis had just won the Nobel Prize, and there were others there, eminent people. The best writers in Greece. And here I came on a Fulbright, carrying culture back to Athens from the Saskatchewan prairie. The whole thing struck me as so ironical that I had to speak about it, and they thought it was marvelous to hear a man without history. They're oppressed with too much history. Most Greeks feel the weight of the Bronze Age weighing on them. How do you become a man of the present with all that past weighing you down? Well, I was trying to become a man of the past without any past, with all that present. My speech was reprinted all over Athens and was a great success—the only spontaneous speech I ever made in my life that was. It sprang out of my sense that growing up without history is a deprivation. I have no sense, or hadn't until then at least, and still really don't, of the obverse of that—how it might be to grow up with too much history. As a matter of fact, the Greeks reprinted *Wolf Willow* in modern Greek—the only book of mine, apart from a book of lectures, that *is* translated into Greek. That one somehow struck them because of that ironic juxtaposition of postures.

> *Someone has written that you began* The Big Rock Candy Mountain *in 1937. Since the book was not published until 'forty-three, were you at work on the novel throughout this time, or did the events that transpired in your life during this time prolong its preparation? I'm thinking especially of the death of your father in 1940.*

No, as a matter of fact, that sort of told me where the book ended. I don't think that was what delayed the book. What delayed the book was the fact that I was teaching full time and jumping around besides, jumping, specifically, from Madison, Wisconsin, to Harvard. I began it just after Christmas in 1937—during Christmas vacation. I remember I got a new portable typewriter for Christmas, and I instantly sat down and started to write this novel. I worked on it the following summer at Yaddo, and I worked on it during the next four, five, six years. It was not an easy book to write. For one thing, I had too much material. I had to find ways of shortening it. Somewhere in the midst of it—I'm not quite sure where; I think during our first year in Cambridge—I threw away two to three hundred pages of North Dakota. That was all invention, not personal experience, incidentally. I left North Dakota when I was about two and a half years old. But because it was important in the lives I was writing about, I had to try to recreate North Dakota—and I recreated too damn much of it. Eventually I threw a lot away, and I also threw other parts away in the course of writing the book. But the principal reason I was slow is that I was teaching all the time and moving from Wisconsin to Harvard.

> *And you wrote other books during that time?*

When I'd get stuck, I'd write another book. I really did have quite a lot of energy, I see now. I didn't think so then. I thought I was a sickly soul, but I must have had a good deal of energy because I wrote a lot—not only books, but quite a lot of stories and articles. For thirty dollars I would write anybody an article. We were poor and motivated, hungry. I remember the first year in Harvard. We were living in Newtonville, and I wrote fast and well because I was working then on the Saskatchewan part of the story, childhood stuff which just bubbled up like hot springs. I wrote several stories that fall: "Goin' to Town," "Two Rivers," "The Chink," "Chip off the Old Block" –at least those four stories which were later incorporated into *The Big Rock Candy Mountain*.[2] Most of them I sold to the *Atlantic*. Ted Weeks was notoriously slow in responding to manuscripts and kept losing them in his desk. But I knew his secretary, who was the wife of a friend of mine. Jeanette Cloud would get these things into Weeks's hands, and sometimes I could get *Atlantic*'s response to a story in a week—something that nobody else in history ever succeeded in doing. Those stories came relatively easily, piecemeal. The book is, as you are quite aware, episodic anyway, and those things that came more or less naturally were the coalesced cherty nodules that had got deposited in memory. I could write them fast, and I did write them fast because I was hungry.

Those were mainly Saskatchewan stories.

All the Saskatchewan ones, yeah. Later I wrote some other stories which were incorporated, or which were intended to be incorporated into the book. Some of them got in, some didn't. There was one called "In the Twilight," about a pig-sticking, and one about my grandmother, "The Double Corner," I guess, which I wrote here many years later.[3] Neither ever became part of the book. Back then, when I had used up the easy stories and got stuck, I'd divert myself to other jobs. Sam Sloan was my publisher at that time, and Duell, Sloan, and Pearce wanted a book on the Mormon country in a series that Erskine Caldwell was editing. When Sam spoke to me about that I said, "Yay, sure, fine," because I was homesick for red ledges. So I wrote *Mormon Country* in about a year, interrupting the book. I never did entirely quit on *The Big Rock Candy Mountain*, but I would take months off it and work on these other things. That's another reason why I took so

[2]"Goin' to Town," *Atlantic* 165 (June 1940): 770–76; "Two Rivers," *Atlantic* 169 (June 1942): 745–52; "The Chink," *Atlantic* 166 (September 1940): 349–56; "Chip off the Old Block," *Virginia Quarterly Review* 18 (October 1942): 573-90.

[3]"In the Twilight," *Mademoiselle* (November 1941); "The Double Corner," *Cosmopolitan* (July 1948). Both reprinted in *The Women on the Wall* (Boston: Houghton Mifflin, 1950).

long. But one reason why I was content to take time off and work on something else was the difficulty I had finding a shape for that large, amorphous mass of remembered and invented material. I never did find much shape for it.

The novel seemed so different from your previous novels, much longer and more ambitious and more autobiographical. Was this book a conscious effort to break away from the novella, to write a big work?

Nothing I do is very conscious. No, I don't think it was a conscious effort at all. It may have been an unconscious one. I wrote the little ones first because those were the ones that came to me, they seemed there to be written. The big one did take a long time and was many times interrupted because it was a big and a hard one. But I wasn't making a conscious effort to do anything. I wasn't looking to produce a magnum opus or take a giant step forward. I was just writing what came naturally. It turned out, obviously, that it was a change, and the experience of writing it was good for me because everything in my writing past had been pretty much hand-to-mouth. You get into the habit of writing short stories because that's the way you begin in college classes, and that's what you have time to do. You can finish one in a week or two, at the most. Those other things which take such big blocks of time and constant submergence I never had the time to do. I would have been better off, I suppose, if I had put even more time on *Big Rock Candy Mountain*. That's a piecemeal book.

You mentioned, a couple of times, getting stuck. Were there any specific kinds of things that . . . I was thinking of the famous story about Huck Finn *where Mark Twain got stuck on the raft incident. Didn't know what he was going to do and put it on the shelf. Then came back, apparently with what he felt was the answer. Were there specific places in the novel that you . . .*

Well, I didn't have a raft going the wrong way towards freedom. I didn't have to reconcile my plot with the fact that my raft was escaping deeper into slave territory.

But you did have a young boy growing up.

Oh, not really. In the beginning I was writing a story from my parents' time, and as it got along toward the time when I understood it better, I obviously switched the point of view. The point of view begins with the mother and then switches to the two boys alternately, and occasionally to Bo, and winds up with Bruce since he's the only survivor. But . . . no, I wasn't thinking of writing a book about myself, at all. It just happened that when I got into that part of the story the point of view was inevitably my own because that's the way I remembered it, almost unchanged and unmodified by art. The Saskatchewan episodes are much the closest to autobiography. Those are memories of my childhood, most of them. But to return to your question, I wouldn't think that there was much that was conscious about that book. The intention shifted and changed on me. If I were rewriting it at this moment, I would write it very differently, I suppose, because I would be a lot more conscious.

Is Bo Mason's story that of Colonel Sellers in Mark Twain's The Gilded Age *or that of the hero in Sinclair Lewis's* Babbitt? *Is Bo the archetypal, dreaming, boosting American?*

Well, he's certainly that. I don't think he is as funny as Colonel Sellers, unfortunately, or even as George Babbitt. Also, he's closer to, well maybe not closer to the frontier than Sellers, but conceived in a less genial mood. When Sellers lights the artificial fire in the stove and warms his hands by it, it's both pathetic and funny. I never conceived Bo Mason as being either pathetic or funny. He is a strong, dominant kind of man, and in a way a dangerous one . . . but still deluded, socially deluded, the product of frontiers which now all of a sudden have closed. He was made to be a frontiersman, he's a frontiersman *manqué*. He would have done very well as a mountain man. Been just as careless, just as reckless, just as wild, just as greedy. Whatever else, the American way was made for him.

I was rereading your comment in the revised edition of Sound of Mountain Water *[1980]. You comment about the . . . what the western American has been taught or thought about his background and what he has lived through. The disparity between the two reminded me a great deal of Bo Mason.*

Obviously he's a manifestation of something that I have been learning all my life. Learning sometimes the hard way and pretty slowly. I see plenty of people like him. Some of them are developing subdivisions around here now, and I hope they all go broke.

Elsa Mason seems to represent the female figure one encounters in much western fiction, the woman who desires stability, society, roots. Did the life of Mary Hallock Foote, the woman on whom you based much of Angle of Repose, *appeal to you because it reminded you of the life of Elsa Mason?*

Not consciously. It never occurred to me that there was any relation between *Angle of Repose* and *Big Rock Candy Mountain* till after I had finished writing it. Then I saw that there were all kinds of connections.

There was the wandering husband and the nesting woman, and the whole business reproduced in many ways in somewhat more cultivated terms and in different places what *The Big Rock Candy Mountain* was about. It's perfectly clear that if every writer is born to write one story, that's my story. I wrote it at least two ways, but I certainly wasn't aware of repeating it. I was working from the Foote papers, and I set out thinking of Molly Foote as a kind of heroine. Then as I worked on her I began to see her as a heroine with a foot of clay. She was a snob, unfortunately, and she wasn't made for the life she got into. I wound up thinking of her husband rather than of her as the hero of the piece. But it didn't occur to me at the time that the story was anything like *The Big Rock Candy Mountain*. I was a good deal more aware of the fact that somehow these wanderings tie together elements of the national life, that the East and the West are both in it. The Midwest, unfortunately, isn't much in it, but the East and the West and Mexico and lots of places are, and different classes of society, so that in many ways *Angle of Repose* is a book with a lot more range than *The Big Rock Candy Mountain*. I think it may be historically more significant for that reason.

I remember your commenting on the significance of women in western fiction as symbols of the desire for roots. I think it was probably in "History, Myth, and the Western Writer."[4]

I came up on that, again, belatedly. I should have known it all my life, but I was writing an introduction to a collection of western stories edited by J. Golden Taylor, and reading through those stories, I came across that woman many times.[5] Then I realized that I'd come across her before, many, many times, not only in western, but in midwestern stories—in settlement stories of one kind or other—anything that involved the frontier and all the hardships thereof; a life in which the woman was very secondary, almost like an appurtenance to be carried along. She's in the *Grapes of Wrath*. She's in all kinds of novels.

The Virginian, *the Molly figure.*

Yeah, oh sure. *That's* a man's world; the frontier everywhere was. Women were trying to make it theirs, but they didn't succeed for a while.

Well, let's back up. From one perspective, Big Rock Candy Mountain *is the story of the closing frontier in Canada and the United States. Isn't*

---

[4]"History, Myth, and the Western Writer" appeared first in *American West* 4 (May 1967): 61–62; 76–79; then as an introduction to J. Golden Taylor, ed., *Great Western Short Stories* (Palo Alto, Calif.: American West Publishing Company, 1967); and then finally in *The Sound of Mountain Water* (Garden City, N. Y.: Doubleday, 1969).

[5]See note 4, above.

Bo Mason's problem that of a frontier pioneer in a changing and changed world—a world calling for more organization and settlement and stability than he's capable of?

It's perfectly clear that he doesn't have the qualities for the changed world. He's made for a world that's just passed, just barely passed, and so he goes looking for a place where that world is still possible. It's undoubtedly the drive that moves people like that. There are still people hunting it, too. They head up to Humboldt County, or the San Juan Islands, or Alaska, wherever it is said to be open and wild—McCall, Idaho, wherever—and they wind up growing pot in somebody's backyard and getting busted every now and again, as Bo Mason was for bootlegging. It's by no means a history that's over, though the opportunities are pretty well over in physical terms. One of the things that marks people like that, it seems to me, is an unwillingness to accept or understand change and also an unwillingness to understand or accept the responsibilities that go with the change. One of the nicest things about American independence, which was born of free land, as far as I can determine—was born of free land from the very first settlement—is that you can tell the world to kiss your behind and go off. That is freedom; it is also irresponsibility, social irresponsibility. When the world tightens in around you, you can't do that anymore, and it probably means a lot more unhappiness for people of that stamp.

I was thinking of the problem a writer has in recalling something after a change. In Recapitulation, *Bruce Mason walks down the street hoping that change does not wipe out memory, that even though changes must come they won't destroy all his memories.*

Oh, well, that's probably pure self-indulgent nostalgia. I don't . . . I hope change doesn't wipe out the memory of the time when we were all free on wheels, when we could wheel around the West, any place we wanted to. That's not going to go on forever, you know. I had a feeling last fall going through southern Utah that it was probably the last trip of that kind that I was going to make. It becomes irresponsible after awhile to waste that much gas just to look at Bryce Canyon or Capitol Reef. So we'll all have to go by public transportation, find another way. As you know, I'm hooked on history, I am committed to the notion that we can change as the history changes. People like Bo Mason can't. They grow up without history, and they live without history, without any sense of history. They're trapped in the present.

Is that the problem of the young people in Angle of Repose?

Well, I don't know. It is, certainly, during that phase of their lives. You don't know what their lives are going to become. I don't know. This girl in *Angle of Repose* isn't stupid. She's just part of her times, and her times are anti-historical–ahistorical. I already see signs that that attitude begins to go away, but it'll take a long time, I suppose. When it came on, it was merely another, perhaps desperate, flurry—like the last flurry of a fish before you bring him in—of American independence, and the notion that you can tell the world to kiss yours and go on off where you want to and live your life. The whole notion of a life style is curious and totally ahistorical. It's as if society were some kind of experimental business, completely pragmatic.

A. B. Guthrie uses the same idea in Boone Caudill, who tells everybody where to get off, goes to the mountains, and then he realizes when he talks to Dick Summers at the end of The Big Sky *that he's spoiled the mountains.*

Yeah, sure, spoiled the mountains, killed a lot of his friends. I think our ancestral Western Civilization myths operate through there. You know: myself am hell.

We can still—our politicians, say, our western politicians—can still play on this idea of individualism . . . the idea of the Sagebrush Rebellion, too.

It's our absolute sure-fire business in certain parts of the West. It seems to me that the Intermountain West now is the most politically reactionary part of the world because it's closest to the frontier, maybe barring Alaska. It's all Sagebrush Rebellion. The thing that catches people's imagination and stirs them up to fight somebody, or elect somebody, or throw somebody out, is a kind of assurance that some of that old freedom still lasts, that it's still there. I don't think it is.

Why does Bruce Mason become a bookish man, a man of ideas, rather than like his father or his brother Chet?

I suppose because the sickly son of that kind of father is going to revolt against him, be dominated by him but revolt against him and try to become what his father is not. And since his father is uneducated, ahistorical, whatever else, I suppose you revolt upwards, don't you? Lots of middle-class kids revolt downwards, but a guy like that has to revolt upwards, towards culture and away from his violent, independent frontier syndrome. I think that's certainly what happened to me. I found the kinds of consolation in books that I didn't find in my family, and so all of a sudden I was living another life, and that other life just sucked me away over a long period of time. But also in me—not in Bruce Mason because I didn't write this into him—but in me, I know it happened through other kinds of insecurity. See, we moved from Saskatchewan, where I was really very happy—it was a beautiful place for a kid—and left all my friends behind. I was about eleven years old, something like that. I went down to Montana for a couple of years and then to Salt Lake, with the result that just about the time when I think kids are most groupy, and feel in junior high school a sort of addiction to friends and companions, all of that security was cracked open. So I found the public library. I didn't really find it until we got to Salt Lake, but I lived in it in Salt Lake. Books are a habit, and once you've created a book-habit I suppose it lasts.

The picture you give of the older brother is that he comes closest to his father's ideals by becoming the star athlete. I wonder if he isn't something of a new pioneer of the 1920s in his competing with and defeating others in athletics.

Well, sure. Bo Mason likes him much better than he likes the younger son, which is again part of the difficulty between the younger son and father. But there's no great affection between Chet and his father either, because the dominance, the hair-trigger temper, the rest of it is just what you don't love a father for. On the other hand, if it came to a pinch, a certain grudging admiration is present in each case. I turned my brother—I did have a brother who died young—I turned him into something more of an athlete than he was. I suppose, in order to make a contrast between the two boys, and . . .

Is Bruce Mason less of an athlete than you were?

I wasn't much of an athlete, but I wanted to be. I was a real jock in spirit.

You played tennis, you played basketball, but Bruce is not involved in these activities.

No, no, no, I guess I wanted Bruce to be the sickly, scholarly one, and Chet to be the athlete, and to demonstrate that the paternal dominance destroyed them both, or might have. It's not a very supportive element, anyway.

Now, the frustrations . . .

That's one of the ways in which the memory is an artist as well as a historian. It makes a better story if the two boys are different than if they are alike. Actually, we got on very well. Once, we got to beating each other's brains out, you know, at the age of eleven or twelve, but from there on we were very good friends. Excuse me, I interrupted a question of yours.

I was thinking that the frustrations of the older brother aren't quite as apparent in the novel as the younger brother's.

Well, there's all of that macho business and the early marriage and the annulment and so on. The frustrations are there, but I may not have written them as vividly because they weren't mine.

Perhaps his point of view too doesn't come through as much since Bruce is going to be a spokesman for more of the novel than Chet is.

Toward the end Bruce takes it over, yeah. I don't suppose Chet is a spokesman in more than a couple of chapters. One in the orphan asylum in Seattle and one, I guess, while he's falling in love with his babe, whatever her name is, in Salt Lake. There may be others, but those are the ones I remember.

Was that one of the places where you got stuck, his point of view?

Perhaps. I don't remember. I wouldn't do it now, shifting the point of view in quite that fashion, and yet I could see no other way of doing it at the time. I thought I gained something by it—in the way of variety and a sort of shifting of gears. I'm not sure I did . . . . I might not be able to write that book now. I like to think I could write it better now than I could then, but I might not be able to write it at all. I reread it pretty carefully not too long ago when the Franklin Library issued it as part of a series of signed editions or so in full leather. I hate to see errors, pure old stupid typos, in a beautiful, gilt-edge, full-leather edition. So I insisted that I read the proof on it; so I had to read the whole book over again for the first time in many years. It was troubling here and there. It felt clumsy to me, a little too obvious, a little too direct, a little too straightforward, too nineteenth-century. All of the technical options of the modern novel are ignored. I don't make any use of them. I have made use of them since. I make a lot of use of them in the *Angle of Repose*, which is, technically, many, many cuts above *Big Rock Candy Mountain*.

You're playing with more periods of time.

Yeah, and I'm doing a lot more fancy footwork. That was a hard book technically to write, but I think it came off technically. *The Big Rock Candy Mountain* was not hard technically to write. It was just that I wasn't a very skilled writer. I was not even sure of what to leave out and what to put in, and I put in many things that I later had to throw out.

If Bo and his oldest son Chet represent figures who learn little from the past, Bruce seems, in the last few pages of the novel, to see and accept the ambiguous impact his father has had on his life. He seems to conclude that there are redeeming qualities in Bo's life.

I suppose any son is going to feel that way about his father, if his father has dominated him that much. No one wants to think that he has wasted all his submission—or all his irritation and rebellion. Bo was a strong man but still a failure, so what does Bruce do about that? He regrets it, he wishes his father had done something better with his life, he thinks maybe there was good raw material there. . . . I am now going to say something that flies in the face of contemporary education, which doesn't think much of mere memory. I think it's a great gift. Bo had a sticky memory for ballads, for poetry; he didn't read much, but whatever he heard, he remembered. That's a gift, you know, it's a talent. If you assume that talent with training and guidance could have come to something, then of course Bo could have come to something. His gifts are literary, essentially, though he is not in the slightest a literary person, whereas somebody like Elsa Mason has no literary gifts at all, though she's much more of a person than he is, a much better person. You would never find her name in the papers, but you might find his. As I thought him over, I felt he had the possibility of being somebody who could have made a mark on something.

The kind of person who would have appealed to Carl Sandburg, for example, because he had a grass-roots, folkloric sort of Xerox mind.

Yeah, and of course it's the kind of mind I have myself, so I have to respect it. The business of words sticking in the head, ballads, poetry, or whatever. Either he taught it to me or he endowed me with it. I'm very grateful, actually, for the kind of education I got in that scrubby town of East End, Saskatchewan, because it was all memorization. We were never made to think in the John Dewey way. We were never given Montessori toys to play with, to improve our imaginations. We were simply given poetry to read, and we read it aloud and it stuck in my head. My head is still full of stuff that I learned in the second grade, and it wasn't all junk either. The textbooks that we were given way deep in the primary grades when we were barely able to read contained some things which were worth remembering. They gave you some sense of the beauty of words and the way in which words can be plastically used. Having them in your head is like having foreign songs in your head, the way they can teach you something about the language itself, so that you refer back to the song to find out how a tense is used or how an idiom comes out. I was reading the "Man in the Holocene" the other day in *The New Yorker* and was struck by one of his little notes: "Without memory is no thought." Right. I'm now indulging my affinity for history again, I suppose, but I do think without memory you can have problem-solving maybe, but not thought.

Bruce seems to think, too, that not only has he been provided these raw materials but that because he's experienced a difficult kind of life as the son of Bo Mason these arduous experiences have toughened and strengthened him.

I think so. It's not unrelated to that notion of Hemingway's that some people are stronger at broken places. The bones heal with a lot of callus around them. Certainly he has been broken in several ways but . . . but— I suppose that the only way a boy like that can resist his father is by hating him to the death. Hatred is a kind of strength, and in a kid without any particular strength to begin with, it may be the only one. Somewhere Elsa Mason says in the book that Chet was too soft, that he wasn't as hard as his old man. Whereas Bruce, in spite of the sickliness, is just as mean and ornery as his old man is.

I'm wondering if Bruce doesn't discover that like most historians the past that he remembers (or constructs) may not be the past that others recollect (construct). This difference seems clear when Bruce and Elsa, toward the end of the novel, come to different conclusions about the same people and events.

Well, you remember the story "Two Rivers," in which the whole family is forced by this little business of finding a stream up in the Bear Paws to do some remembering. The boy remembers a stream in the Cascades somewhere out of Seattle, and he remembers that day in particular ways. His family remembers it in very different ways with very different details, and his mother says in effect, rather wonderingly, "It's funny, the history is the same, but the memory is very different." I'm sure it's bound to be. There's some of that in *Recapitulation*, too, where Bruce Mason remembering is not quite sure whether his memory is a historian or an artist and whether it may also not be a psychological healer, twisting things in order to make them more attractive or palatable. He can't even remember—and here is *one* thing I got myself into and had to paint my way out of—he can't even remember how it was he finally broke with his father, and the reason he can't remember that is that he hears a different version, so I had to have him waver between the two memories, one of which may have been the product of wishful thinking or a dream—a kind of reverie in which he conceived it all without its ever becoming real. That's one of the troubles you get into when you write a trailer to another book. I wrote *Recapitulation* in the first place not as a trailer to *The Big Rock Candy Mountain* but as a quite separate book, and then because it was about Salt Lake and because it seemed convenient to cannibalize three different Salt Lake stories, two of which, "The Volunteer," and "The Blue-Winged Teal" were spin-offs of

The Big Rock Candy Mountain. The other one, "Maiden in a Tower," was not.[6]

That's the opening scene, is it not?

Yes. But putting those stories in there meant that I had to change the names in all of them, and to some extent the characters. It also meant that I was stuck with all of the history that was in *The Big Rock Candy Mountain* and the background of all of those people had to be made to conform, which wasn't easy, took a little doing. I had to juggle the book in order to make it come out. *Recapitulation* as it came out finally is quite different from the first draft.

I read an interview with you recently where you said you had written it in first person, the first draft.

I think I wrote it in the third person first, and it didn't seem to go right, didn't have the kind of immediacy I wanted. Then I switched it to first person, thinking "Well, all right. Let the man remember it personally." The minute I got it into the first person, I began to see that it was really trying to be a trailer to *The Big Rock Candy Mountain* and a kind of personal recollection, or one that was tinged with personality. So then I rewrote it again in third person, but changed that third person into Bruce Mason. Somehow or other, doing that took the curse off. Maybe also getting some resonance from all of the emotional entanglements of *The Big Rocky Candy Mountain* made it feel more right to me.

I was thinking that in history we use the term historiography to mean the multiple interpretations of a single event—what caused the Civil War, what the Puritans were like. You wrestled with something like that in the writing of The Big Rock Candy Mountain: *here's Elsa looking at an event that involves Bo, here's Bruce looking at the same event, they come to different interpretations about the meaning of that event.*

I'm a spoiled historian.

What were the conscious breaks between history and imagination in the novel? For example, how did you decide not to mention your grandmother who was living with you in Canada? Why did Bruce go off to law school rather than to graduate school in English, and why was Bruce's life after high school telescoped so much?

I think the answer to that question is essentially one word, economy— for the same reasons I threw away those several hundred pages; bringing

---

[6]"The Volunteer," *Mademoiselle* 43 (October 1956): 124–25, 146–56; "Maiden in a Tower," *Harper's* 204 (January 1954): 78–84.

new characters into what was really a tight, internal, intramural war in the family would have maybe spread it so wide that I was afraid to. I did use the grandmother, actually, in a story, "The Double Corner," which I wrote many years later and placed in California. Why did Bruce go off to law school rather than to graduate school in English?—just the meekest of rudimentary disguises, I suppose. Maybe a sense that the *New Yorker* is right—that writers should not write about writers or about writing, and that nothing is worse as a character in your book than a sensitive young man who's going to become a writer. Maybe also some feeling that the rebellion of a youth like that is likely to take the course most opposite to his father. Since his father is essentially a born lawbreaker, he might take up law. There is, I think, a certain logic to that pattern. Why is his life after high school telescoped? Because the whole book gets telescoped toward the end. It narrows down into a chute and suddenly, like bath water, it's all going out one hole. The alternative to that would be to carry it on beyond any bearing. No reader would want to follow it because I think all of the problems are stated, the personalities are developed, the conflicts are there. To carry it on beyond a certain point would simply have been pleonastic. I did the same thing very, very drastically, as a matter of fact, in *Angle of Repose*; there, as you know, those two people lived together for forty-five years after I left them. I couldn't possibly have reported those years.

The Grass Valley years are left out in a way.

They're there only as Lyman Ward remembers growing up in his grandmother's house. None of the presumably successful years of their lives are there. The lives up to what I invented as a break between them are there in great detail, but it would have been, I think, dramatically bad to let it go on, so I telescoped that story at the end in exactly the same way.

How far along were you in the writing of Big Rock Candy Mountain *when your father died in 1940? Like many novelists, you say beginnings and endings have always been difficult for you. Had you thought about other endings previous to his death?*

No, I was . . . sort of waltzing ahead on the assumption that something would turn up. I remember thinking rather bitterly, "Oh, that's the way it ends." How far along was I—that was 1940 . . . well, I had written a whole first volume including all of that North Dakota stuff that I later threw away, and had sent it to a publishing friend of mine who didn't like it. Thought it was too long and tedious, and he was quite right. So, then I threw it away, and during the fall of 1939 in Cambridge and in the spring of 1940 I was writing a lot of the Saskatchewan stuff, all of those stories. I was probably halfway through the Saskatchewan part, in the middle of the book, maybe further along than that, though I finished it finally by going up to Vermont, taking a semester off, and writing hard on it all summer and all fall, and on up to about Christmas of 1941, I guess it would have been, or maybe 1940 . . . it was Christmas 1940. Yeah, that was it, that same year. I came back from his funeral and went straight up to Vermont and all through that summer and fall, up to about Christmas, I wrote on it. I must have written three or four hundred pages of it during that time. Then my wife went to the hospital, and I spent the next two months running back and forth to the hospital and trying to revise this vast thing in odd hours. I can remember sitting up late at night, night after night. Then we went back to Cambridge about the first of March. So . . . I started the book at Christmas 1937; I finished a draft about Christmas 1940. It really is only three years, isn't it? I thought it was longer than that.

So about two-thirds of the way through you had come to the conclusion that this was going to be one volume, but a long book?

Oh, yes. It *was* a long book, too. The manuscript was about twelve hundred pages. I can remember Louis Untermeyer during the war when he was given the job of cutting it down for the armed services editions. You know, those little paperbacks which had to be brought to a certain weight because they had to be shipped so many to the box for overseas use. *The Big Rock Candy Mountain* had to be cut down to a quarter of a million words from about three hundred and seventy thousand. Louis gave it to me saying, "Well, you cut it." I took out about thirty thousand words and then it began to hurt, and I said, "No more. I can't do this. You've got to do it." So Louis tried it, and he got an extra forty to fifty thousand words out, and it began to hurt *him*. Finally turned it over to Philip Van Doren Stern, who finished it. I have never looked at it. It must be a terrible book, as cut.

A commentator or two faults the final sections of the novel as containing too much authorial commentary. Would you revise the final chapters if you were writing the novel now?

I'm not sure I'd revise it in those terms, though my wife tells me I'm always a little inclined to underline the significance of scenes, and I might find that I would want to cut some of that out. On the other hand, some of the meaning of the book for me lay in the growth of understanding, and the growth of understanding can't be fictionalized unless you have somebody grow *into* understanding, which amounts to authorial comment. It isn't really authorial comment, it's Bruce Mason's comment, and I don't think I would take it out. I don't know who the commentator was you're thinking of, but I would argue with him.

One was Forrest.

Oh, Forrest, oh, really?

He doesn't use the words "authorial comment." He suggests that some of the ideas Bruce thinks about do not seem to come directly from what he has experienced.

Well, that may be. I'm perfectly willing to admit that I could be guilty of that.

If I remember correctly, he says something to the effect that the long journal entries might not be necessary, that Bruce is learning without having to include those questions raised in the journal.

Yeah. Well, I guess those do come pretty close toward the end, at least within the telescoped section.

I'm interested in the words reviewers used in trying to describe the novel. Is it a western novel, regional fiction, fictional autobiography, a story of initiation?

I don't know. I guess to me it doesn't make any difference. Simply *non importa.* The label that's put on it is maybe useful to a reviewer trying to explain it to readers, but it makes no difference whatever to the person who wrote it. I didn't care what it was. It obviously is a western novel because it takes place exclusively in the West. It obviously is a regional novel for the same reason. It's obviously autobiographical fiction, at least to a degree. And it obviously is one of those—it becomes in the end, as Bruce Mason begins to take it over—if not quite a spiritual autobiography, at least a story of initiation and education. So it's all of them, but I wouldn't think that any of those terms necessarily describes the book. They label it without describing it. What you hope a book is, is some kind of longitudinal section of life which is valid in its own terms, and I would hope it's valid in its own terms even when it's clumsy. I think it is, as a matter of fact. If you're going to make a judgment on a novel, ultimately, it's the truth of what it says within the terms set by its characters that makes it worthy. That's about what Leavis had in mind when he began to define the great tradition.[7] He limits it rather more than I would.

You used the word "clumsy." I suppose that if I were given the novel to review, I would agree with Howard Mumford Jones when he described it as a "vast, living, untidy book."[8] But it seems to me that the episodic, sprawling plot allows for the treatment of so many moods and details, like Huck Finn or H. L. Davis's Honey in the Horn *in that respect. Did*

[7]F. R. Leavis, *The Great Tradition* (London: Stewart, 1948).

[8]"World Out of Nowhere," *Saturday Review of Literature* 26 (October 2, 1943): 11.

you have trouble finding an appropriate structure for the story that you wished to tell?

Oh yes, and I don't think it is a structure essentially. It's a nonstructure. It is pretty episodic. There are gaps such as the transition from North Dakota to Washington. That's the place where the whole of North Dakota fell out. I decided the quick cut was the only way to get across that and jumped to the tent in the woods of Washington where Elsa is remembering. What really happens is that you make a big jump and then you flash back in some kind of Conradian fashion. That seemed to me to work reasonably well. I was pleased when I worked it out, because that was one of the places where I was stuck. I was just plodding through it, and I decided finally not to plod at all. If I were going to get from the door to the window, I would just suddenly appear in the window, rather than counting every step across the room. But generally the difficulties were primarily of exclusion and selection of stuff that, whether remembered or imported into the memory from elsewhere and thus made almost a part of memory, was profuse. I had God's plenty of material for that book. I think I liked Howard's word "overflowing," because it did overflow on me. He didn't mind that, and neither did I. I winced a little bit at the word "untidy," because though I thought it was sometimes clumsy, I didn't think it was untidy. I thought I had cleaned up the messes at the edges. I like that word "vast" too; that doesn't bother me. It is a big book and ought to give a sense of a great profusion of life. I don't think it's fair to judge, let's say, *War and Peace*, by the same standards you would use for judging *The Great Gatsby*. The one is one kind of novel, and the other is another kind. This is clearly over on the *War and Peace* side rather than *The Great Gatsby* side, whereas *Recapitulation* or *The Spectator Bird* are both on *The Great Gatsby* side. They are tight. Their architecture is a lot more precise.

A parallel experience comes to mind: Thomas Wolfe writing during this time, his stack of ledgers, and the calling in of Maxwell Perkins to decide what would be done with the organization of these materials. You served as your own Maxwell Perkins.

I think one should. It doesn't seem to me a writer should ask anybody else to do his artistic work for him. You can ask an editor to spell for you, if you can't spell, but beyond that I wouldn't think it was fair. The trouble with Wolfe was that he really didn't have any sense of structure. He was no engineer at all. And he had total recall, so that he had my problem of profusion of material without even my limited capacity to deal with it except to pour it out. That's precisely what's the matter with his books, which are sometimes for pages at a time marvelous but as books leave a great deal to be desired, even after somebody has hacked and sawed and stapled and done all the other things to them.

> *The Big Rock Candy Mountain is similar to one kind of book or novel that's been written about the West. Think of, say,* Roughing It, *or H. L. Davis's* Honey in the Horn. *Large episodic novels in which people move often and experience many, many things.*

That's in the nature of things, isn't it, because you know, if you get into tight structure, you'll be dealing in the unities of time, place, and action, and the West almost precludes unity of place, just by the nature of things. It also, therefore, may preclude unity of action, though it doesn't necessarily. Unity of time, something else. A shoot-'em-up like *Shane*, for instance, is tight. Unities of time, place, and action. But it doesn't make any pretense of being a sociological report on a whole civilization. And I suppose I feel the West in something like epic terms so that it has epic rather than dramatic impulses in it. There are a few things, like Conrad Richter's *Sea of Grass*, which are small and tight but still have some of the sweep. I don't think of very many.

> *I think of you as writing both the tight-knit and the panoramic kinds of novels. Clark did the same in* The Ox-Bow Incident *and in the* City of Trembling Leaves; *he did both kinds.*

We waver, I suppose, and that's to some extent the luck of the subject. Sometimes you have the luck of the subject, and the subject dictates its own form, or at least you find out it does by the time you have worked with it long enough. I fully believe in form as discovery. You find out while you're writing a thing what shape it is, what shape it has to be.

> *It seems to me that* Big Rock Candy Mountain *participates in one of the major themes of American fiction—the journey motif, for example, in* Huck Finn, Grapes of Wrath, On the Road, *to mention three novels. It participates in this larger theme that's been at the center of a lot of American fiction.*

Of course, the journey is one of the absolutely basic ways of imposing form upon fictional experience, not only in America but anywhere. You can think of any number of short stories, for instance, which are based upon the theme of a journey, because a journey has a beginning and at least an implied end. Chekhov's "The Steppe," is just the journey of a boy across the steppe in a drought year. Maupassant's "Boule de Suif" is an interrupted journey, a kind of bead on the string of a journey. Journeys do recommend themselves, just the way days and seasons recommend themselves as having automatic and almost symbolic stopping and starting places. When you get into a society as mobile as that of western America, it's almost inevitable that somehow or other you're going to do something like *Grapes of Wrath.* You're going to start somewhere and end somewhere, and in the meantime you will have seen a civilization. *Huckleberry Finn* is pretty much a standard.

You like Paul Horgan's little story "To the Mountains," which is about those two boys going to the mountains. I was thinking of the difference between that story and the kind in which there is another type of journey. For example, Steinbeck's "The Leader of the People," where the journey is perhaps toward understanding and realization, but not a physical journey.

One of the big problems in any piece of fiction, as you're undoubtedly perfectly aware, is to find the place to begin and the place to end and the way to impose on an experience some sense of completeness. Hemingway was absolutely right, the ending—the only ending—of stories is death. But you can't have a death in every story; you have to fake these appearances of completeness. The journey is one very plausible way. I wouldn't have said that *Big Rock Candy Mountain* was quite so much a journey as all that, though it involves some journeying. Seems to me it has elements of the journey—several phases of it—but it also has elements of the novel of settlement. It may also have some element of that reflection of American independence which produces the outlaw story. In other words, it is much, much, much richer than you say.

Recently, historians have commented on the differences between the Canadian and the American Wests. In this novel, you seem to minimize such differences. Had you changed your mind by the time you wrote those sections in Wolf Willow *where you do compare the Canadian and American Wests?*

I wouldn't say I changed my mind. I simply didn't know anything about—I hadn't thought about—the Canadian West, or even very much about the American West, though I obviously had Turner in my mind when I was writing *The Big Rock Candy Mountain,* and the ending of the frontier and what it does psychologically to whole bodies of people. But it hadn't occurred to me that there was a difference between the American West and the Canadian, and I knew very little. I don't know when it was I began to get interested in the Canadian West and to get the feeling that I had grown up without any history and that I wanted some, but it wasn't, I think, until in the fifties sometime. Then when I began to write *Wolf Willow,* trying to be the Herodotus of the Cypress Hills, I discovered that, like Herodotus, I had very few sources. I found one book on the fur post that started that town and a certain amount on the Cypress Hills massacre, and a certain amount of the early years of the mounted police, and a certain amount on Fort Whoop-Up and the country a little bit west where the whiskey traders were coming in to subvert the Blackfeet, but very little, very meager. And so the more I got interested the harder I had to hunt for sources. I went back to the town and went through the whole file of town papers carefully, photographing a lot of them, bringing them home for further study. There was a paper that ran consecutively from, I guess, about 1914 to . . . I don't know, whenever I was up there in the fifties. Forty years, nearly, of the papers of a single town. That told me something about the Canadian West too, because our town started as a single-tax town, which is very different from Tombstone, Arizona. A single-tax town implies all kinds of things about the people who founded it. It doesn't make much room for entrepreneurs and real estate promoters and those kinds.

So I learned about the Canadian West just by that original act of curiosity in an attempt to say something about my own past, to find out about it, and to do it in this case not strictly in fictional terms but in terms that would pass for history. I wouldn't say my mind changed about the Canadian West; I just learned something about it, and the more I learned about it, the more I decided that it is a very different kind of West. In fact, I wouldn't be at all surprised if one of the reasons why historians are commenting on the differences between the Canadian and American Wests now is that I told them to. I don't ordinarily say things about myself that way. But going up to that conference in Banff shocked me almost . . . how much *Wolf Willow* was the beginning of a tradition.[9] I hadn't really thought I was the Herodotus of those hills, but I obviously was. My only claim to originality, I think, is a few things like that. It may well have been very apparent to anybody who was trained in history before I found it out, but I discovered it with glad surprise.

> *I have used* Wolf Willow *in courses in western historiography, especially when dealing with comparative western history. I also want to use it for its approach to history in a fashion different from that of the straight-forward monograph.*

Since it uses both autobiography and reminiscence, as well as fiction, it's a librarian's nightmare. How do you catalogue it? Incidentally, it has been reprinted again. Bison Books has just brought it out. That's another thing that conference of Dick Harrison's up in Banff did for me. I was so damn mad about paperback books that would come into print and be shipped out to a few airports and then be shipped back generally unopened,

---

[9]The "Crossing Frontiers" conference, organized by Professor Dick Harrison of the University of Alberta, was held during the spring of 1978 in Banff, Alberta, Canada.

and go out of print in six months so nobody could buy copies, that as they fell out of copyright, I demanded the rights back and in most cases got them —in one case couldn't— but in most cases got them and then sold the whole batch of them to the editor from Nebraska.

David Gilbert.

And Gilbert promises to keep them in print indefinitely, for life, which is exactly what I wanted. There isn't as much money in it as there is in some other kind of thing, but it's very much more desirable because most of these have some limited textbook use.

I was thinking of the way you treat history in The Big Rock Candy Mountain. *There you move more straightforwardly than when, for example, you deal with history in* Recapitulation. *In the later novel you shift back and forth, but there are times when the past and present are joined in* Recapitulation. *Some images are joined; others seem to just meld together. This joining of past and present is something you evidently began to do after* Big Rock Candy Mountain. *That novel seems to be one where you're moving chronologically with time, but later your use of time is much more complicated.*

Oh, sure. That's what I meant when I said that some of the devices that were made available to novelists in the modern period I didn't even know about when I wrote *The Big Rock Candy Mountain.* But you can't teach writing to a bunch of gifted people over a long period without becoming much more aware of the technical availabilities. If you don't discover them for yourself, your kids will, and teach them to you. And one of the things that you discover is that time is infinitely flexible. You don't have to follow chronology, you don't have to plod one step after another. You can play back and forth, and the impressionist novel, from Conrad on, has made great use of that kind of fusion. It's possible also, as Nabokov did, to fuse reality and hallucination in exactly the same sort of seamless web.

The dream at the end of Angle of Repose, *for example?*

Which started out to be a realistic scene, and I found I didn't like it as a realistic scene because it introduced at the end of the book a character who had never been in the book at all except as a name or as a kind of avoided menace. So since it was perfectly apparent that somebody was going to come for Lyman Ward sooner or later anyway, I thought it might as well be his nightmare, rather than a straightforward scene when they did come for him, and that the dream could stand for the reality perfectly well. I don't know whether it does or not. I wrote that scene all in one night and then couldn't think of any way to change it afterward.

I raised that question because someplace either McMurtry or Kesey said, in an offhand comment: "I see after wrestling with this"—and it seems to me it was either Kesey talking about Sometimes a Great Notion *or McMurtry about one of his novels—"I see now what Stegner was saying when he said how important point of view is and how one uses the narrator's voice."*

I probably did say something like that because awareness grew on me, too. I wasn't aware in the first place that I did think it was so important, but the more I study the art of fiction, the more I think it is important. For a while, I was even stuck in that Henry Jamesian notion of a very strictly limited point of view, which I think works for certain kinds of things, but which I have now decided can be frustrating in certain ways. There are subtleties to it that Henry himself didn't know about, I think. You don't have to be as rigid as he, and yet point of view is just as important, maybe even more important than he thought it was. So I undoubtedly did say such things in class, though I said very little in class, actually. I willfully refrained from making generalizations that would get in people's road and make them think they were doing something wrong. The teaching of writing is a very Socratic kind of teaching, and you should stay out of the people's way rather than get in it. But I probably couldn't have avoided saying that.

4. The Later Works

Etulain: You spoke earlier of Big Rock Candy Mountain *as something of a turning point in your career. Your next book was* One Nation *[1945]. What were the circumstances that led to the writing of that volume?*

Stegner: The circumstances were primarily an acquaintance with Harry Shaw, who had been the director of the New York Writers' Project, doing the *New York Guide*, and was teaching at New York University or Columbia when a friend of his was suddenly made editor of *Look*. Harry was brought in as executive editor or something of the kind. One of his functions was to develop some *Look* books, like the contemporary *Time-Life* books or *Sunset* books, adjuncts of the magazine. We talked a good while about the possibilities. Harry was interested in doing something on prejudice and discrimination. It was wartime and inequalities were acutely evident. Roosevelt had just issued an Executive Order making blacks equal in the armed services. Up to that point they had only been stewards and Seabees. Things like that were happening, and Harry said, "You know, this is a chance to follow a major book with a major book. You'll have all the resources of *Look* behind you. You can call on a photographer whenever you want. You can set up your studies, and we will publish the findings. We will publish them in the magazine first, serially, so that you're going to reach an audience of two or three million with something that may do some social good."

So I taught through the year, went to Mexico for a couple of weeks, just to take a break, and then came back and went to work on the book.

[65]

It appeared serially then in ...

No, this is where the whole thing was disappointing. *Look* got scared. They got afraid that people—the public that reads *Look*—just wouldn't take it. In fact, in Mexico City I ran into the editor of *Ladies' Home Journal*, whom I knew a little, and at a cocktail party I told him what I was going to do. He smiled in his beard and said, "What is *Look* going to do when, after your first article comes out, they lose 50,000 subscriptions?" I said, "I don't know, but they're boldly going ahead." But he was right. When they began to get intimations of what the effect would be, they boiled the whole thing down into one quite long, but thoroughly innocuous— and I would think, ineffective—article. A kind of abstract of the whole book, not a single piece, which would have had a good deal more impact. Houghton Mifflin published the book and did very well with it, and gave it a Life-in-America award. And it was very much used in schools as outside reading. I was told by the director of the Boston Public Library that for a couple of years it was the most-used book in the Boston Public. Boston, after all, needs some of that; they're always busting heads in that place. So, it sold reasonably well and had some effect as a book, but I was disappointed by the fact that it never got into *Look* in the way it had been planned for.

Two years later you published Second Growth *[1947], which was one of your nonwestern books. I suppose the background for this novel came from your living in New England while teaching at Harvard?*

Before teaching at Harvard. We bought an old farm when I was at Wisconsin and went in and fixed it up and spent every summer there for about, oh, five or six summers, until the war stopped us. We couldn't get gas to go up. So I knew Vermont reasonably well, and I knew the country around.

Some commentators list Second Growth *as one of your least successful books. Are they being too critical?*

Oh, I don't know. It's a minor book, surely. I wrote it pretty fast, and I wrote it primarily for the color. I wanted to say how rainstorms come in off Mount Mansfield, and things like that. I had more things like that to say than I had a story. The story was sort of inept. I still like the book descriptively, but I don't think it's very important in other ways. I don't know what commentators you're talking about, but ...

I was thinking of it as being more like books that you did earlier. It is shorter. Perhaps you did it quickly as a relief from the long haul you'd had with The Big Rock Candy Mountain.

Oh, and *One Nation*, too, because *One Nation* was really about two years' solid work and a lot of traveling, at times when traveling was difficult. During the war . . . there weren't any planes you could get on at all. You had to travel by train, and the trains were jammed full, and you often couldn't get on those, or you got bumped because soldiers were being sent somewhere. Also I got a heart infection in the middle of it, in Santa Barbara, and lost about twenty pounds. It was the kind of thing you either get over or you don't, and I got over it, but it sort of made everything hectic. By the time we came out here to Stanford, in June 1945, . . . my tongue was hanging out. I started *Second Growth*, I remember, the first year we were here and finished it in Vermont during the summer. It wasn't a very long book; it took six or eight months at the most.

Three years later you published The Preacher and the Slave *[1950], which has now been retitled* Joe Hill. *Wasn't this your first novel based, to a large extent, on historical research?*

Yes, I think it was. There was quite a *lot* of historical research in it, too. I got interested in it way back in Cambridge. You remember that ballad by Alfred Hayes, "I Dreamed I Saw Joe Hill Last Night"? In Cambridge we were playing things like that, and "Six Songs for Democracy" from the Spanish War, and I got interested in the songs that people died to. I had

had a certain remote connection with Joe Hill because I'd lived in Salt Lake, where he was jailed and executed. I used to take out the daughter of the warden of the State Pen when I was about a freshman in college or maybe a senior in high school, so that I knew the old State Pen on Twenty-first South pretty well. We used to go around through the back end of it, through the pig farm that they maintained there, and hook rides on the D&RG going up Parley's Canyon, to go up camping. So the place of Joe Hill's end was all familiar territory, and the more I read about Joe Hill, the more it seemed that I had some kind of natural interest in him. Then it turned out that my roommate in graduate school at Berkeley and later at Iowa, Milton Cowan, had been involved.[1] His father had operated the meat market which was the other side of the store in which Joe Hill was supposed to have killed the grocer and his son. So that gave me another little connection. Then about 1942 I went back to Salt Lake and looked around trying to find people, and surprisingly, I found quite a few. I found the sheriff who executed Joe Hill, commanded the firing squad. I talked with the warden of the State Pen, the new warden, who turned out to be a rather sad anti-capital-punishment man who seized upon me as an opportunity to make a point. I got him to blindfold me and walk me through a mock execution—from Joe Hill's old cell down the iron stairs and across the cindered courtyard and up the alley, and stopping in front of a door with a canvas screen across it. All the execution gear was thrown back in an old shed, just an old broken armchair to which they strapped the hands, and a backstop with a steel plate behind it, all dented in with the bullets of previous executions. I got a criminal's-eye view of what it might feel to be led out to your death.

I did take quite a lot of pains with that book, not only going around to see the country, but reading everything I could find on the Wobblies and getting in touch with anybody I could find who had ever known Joe Hill. I found, finally, seven who pretty surely had. A lot said they had, but they obviously hadn't because they had all their dates and facts wrong. They were in touch with a legend but not with a man. And I corresponded with Ralph Chaplin and Harry McClintock and a lot of people like that. Chaplin, once the editor of *Solidarity* and a cartoonist and a songwriter himself, had conducted Joe Hill's funeral in Chicago. He worshipped Joe Hill, but had never met him and thought of him as a wronged rebel. I think he was wrong, but he had nothing but the most honorable feelings.

_____

[1]Stegner began his graduate work at the University of Iowa in 1930 and obtained his master's degree in June 1932. To be near his ailing mother, he enrolled in the University of California, Berkeley, in the fall of 1932; at the beginning of the spring semester of 1934, he re-enrolled at the University of Iowa.

*You've not written book-length fiction about such western heroic types
as the cowboy and the mountain man. But in writing about a labor radical like Joe Hill, weren't you taking on another kind of western Hero?*

I can remember from almost my earliest years, when I was three years
old or so, up in Seattle, a good deal of talk about the IWW. I heard my
parents talking about them, and there was a lot of trouble in the woods and
the shingle mills where the Wobblies were powerful. They caused quite a
lot of unrest in the hearts of stable citizens. They were really the shock troops
of labor. So I had a sense of the IWW as a western phenomenon, in this
case a northwestern phenomenon, from early on. It wasn't completely true
that they were limited to the West, because there were the Lowell strike and
several others in the East; but the typical IWW is the guy catching a freight
car across Dakota, working in the grains and then in the woods, and then
coming down into California, working in the fruits. That circuit was where
the bulk of the IWW strength lay. But if he's a hero, he's more now than
he was during the time when the IWW was potent. A lot of people then
were upset about the IWW, in the way the Reagan administration is about
communist infiltration, for the same general kind of hysterical reason.

*Many people want to end the West—the old frontier West—in the
1890s, but some of the same writers who romanticize the outlaw heroes
of the 1870s and '80s go on to make heroes of people like Joe Hill.*

Oh yes. A fellow named Foner wrote that kind of book about Joe Hill,
but then Foner was or is a left-winger, a party-liner. He wrote several other
things of the same kind. No, the whole building of Joe Hill as a myth, as a
hero, was, in the first instance, a product of the labor press—the IWW press
specifically, but the labor press at large. It created the legend of Joe Hill.
From 1915 to 1930 or so, you didn't hear much about Joe Hill at all. After
the passage of the Criminal Syndicalism Act of—what, 1922?—the IWW
was suppressed. It cropped up only in events like the bombing of the governor of Idaho, what's his name . . . ?

Steunenberg . . .

Big Bill Haywood was involved in that. Well, Haywood was organizing
the Western Federation of Miners in Bingham [Utah] about the time that
Joe Hill was there, and one of the reasons why Joe Hill was, as they say,
framed—he was not treated gently, but I doubt that he was framed—was
that everybody was scared to death of Haywood and his organizers. They
had stirred up the waters which Joe walked into. Anyway, that all died
down through the twenties. Then the whole Joe Hill legend from down
underground began to emerge again. Dos Passos put a little vignette biography of Hill into *USA*, and then a WPA poet, Alfred Hayes, wrote a poem

and . . . a WPA musician [Earl Robinson] set it to music. "I Dreamed I Saw Joe Hill Last Night" was a piece of thirties left-wingism, an IWW legend with a Stalinist tinge. It was a product of a deliberate program—"Let's sit down and write a folksong." So they sat down and wrote one about a labor hero and martyr, Joe Hill. That revived the whole thing. It was 1940, maybe, when I got the recording. I suppose, in a way, I was taken in. My father had been a kind of busker himself and had a great memory for ballads. We had always had things running through the house like "The Big Rock Candy Mountain" and "The Bum Song."

Later, while I was working on the novel, I discovered Mac McClintock, who wrote "The Bum Song," "Hallelujah, I'm a Bum," and others. He said he wrote "The Big Rock Candy Mountain," too, and Victor at least paid him royalties as author. Actually, I think "The Big Rock Candy Mountain" was written by T-Bone Slim, or some other nearly nameless balladeer, a long time before Harry McClintock came along. He may have added two or three verses. In any case, he recorded all those for the first time; and McClintock had an even closer connection to the Joe Hill legend. He sang Joe Hill's "Pie in the Sky" song on Burnside Street in Portland, reading it off an envelope or laundry tag Joe Hill had handed him. That was the first time "Pie in the Sky" was sung on the street. At other times McClintock sang some other ones of Joe Hill, including "The Wobbly Casey Jones." I tried to imagine the scenes, too. Stewart Holbrook took me down to the old Wobbly Hall on Burnside Street and we spent a day just knocking around— got kind of pie-eyed, and he threatened to get me tattooed. Tattooed; that was interesting research—might have left a lasting mark on me.

During the 1950s, your only two collections of short stories were published. Were you drawn to the short story as a compatible form of fiction early in your career?

I think almost everyone who comes through a college is, because a short story is a thing you can write for class. It's short enough so you can get through it in a few weeks at the most, sometimes almost get through it overnight, if you happen to be lucky. I have written some stories that took only four or five hours. I've written some others that took a month; but at least the short story is a manageable form for a class exercise; and so all the things that I cut my teeth on were short stories. You always think, when you're nineteen or twenty, that you'll start a novel. You start it, and it gets about as far as a short story, and then it dies. You don't have the stamina for the long race; you don't have enough to write about. You always think you're more prepared than you are. In my case there were a lot of aborted beginnings on longer things, but nothing long got finished until *Remembering Laughter*, which again is only an extended short story. It's about a hundred pages of manuscript, something like that, hardly a novel. That was the longest thing that I had ever written up to that point. Until I finally finished *The Big Rock Candy Mountain*, as a matter of fact, all my novels, as you've pointed out, were short and almost tentative. *Mormon Country* was a full-length book, but it was another kind of thing. It wasn't fiction.

Why so little short fiction after the 1950s? Absence of good markets, or were you just more interested in longer works?

I think short stories are a young man's racket, most of the time—the way lyric poetry is. There aren't very many people like Thomas Hardy who turn poet in their old age. Generally speaking, short story writers have a tendency to write longer and longer. It happened even to Chekhov, who was as natural a short story writer as you could possibly be; the later stories are much longer than the earlier ones. It happened to Hemingway, so that he comes on with things like *The Snows of Kilimanjaro* and *The Old Man and the Sea*, instead of the telegraphic one-page cablese things he began with in *In Our Time*. I think that's natural enough. You get longer and windier as you get older, maybe because you have more to say, but maybe also because you have more time to say it in. You have, inevitably, the feeling that in writing a short story you are living on your principal: you're using up all your beginnings and endings. You'd better save a few for the longer pieces which ultimately are going to make your career. It's very hard to make a career on short stories alone. Some people have done it, but most people can't, particularly in a time like the present, when magazine markets are pretty well closed up by comparison with what they used to be fifty years ago. It does seem that all of the forces of our time push writers toward novels, not toward short stories. The students at Stanford were all short-story writers when I first opened that program in 1946. By now you hardly find any short-story writers at all, though once in a while someone will write one just because it happens to get in his road. Most of the stuff that's read aloud in that class these days is chapters from novels.

I notice that more than a decade elapsed between Shooting Star *[1961] and your previous novel,* Joe Hill. *How did that happen?*

It happened because . . . I gave up writing novels after *Joe Hill*. That book got a feeble press and no notice and didn't sell anything, and nobody understood it. I was irritated too that reviewers thought I was writing a proletarian novel, which I wasn't. They thought of the book as a belated trailer from the thirties. It's a long way from a proletarian novel, actually. If I had written a proletarian novel, I would have had the backing at least of labor and the leftist groups. But I didn't have anybody's backing, and I thought, "Oh, Christ, I'm throwing pearls before swine and sounding off

in the wilderness where there are no receivers tuned in. This is hopeless."
And so I just quit writing fiction.

A discouraging period, then?

In terms of fiction, yes. I wrote a few stories in there, but—see, there
were two books published in 1950, the *Joe Hill* one and a volume of short
stories. *The Women on the Wall.* And in 1950, I guess, I won the O. Henry
Prize with a short story. The short stories were not too difficult to get some
kind of notice on, but I hadn't had much luck with novels. *Second Growth*
wasn't very big after *The Big Rock Candy Mountain* anyway, and it looked
as if I was on the wrong track. I frankly thought I was a kind of anachronism. I thought I was a nineteenth-century prairie child trying to write for
the twentieth century—and it wouldn't work. I've forgotten what I wrote
between 1950 and 1960. The Powell book, for one thing, and that was a
long, hard, and difficult job on which, off and on, I was involved for about
twelve years. So most of my effort after 1950 . . .

Your second volume of short stories, The City of the Living, *came out in
the 1950s also.*

Yeah, 'fifty-six, I think something like that, but those were, most of them,
already written. We went around the world for the Rockefeller Foundation
in 1950–51—and out of that tour I did get a good many articles for *The
Reporter* and other magazines on Egypt and India and places we were visit-
ing. I also got a couple of stories. One called "The City of the Living" came
out of an episode in which our son Page got typhoid in Egypt. And we ran
into some people on the French Riviera who gave me another story called
"Impasse." So that trip produced a little writing, but no novels. On the
tour we'd been making a lot of contacts with writers in India, Japan, the
Philippines, Thailand, and elsewhere. It seemed useful to keep those chan-
nels open, because the whole purpose of this Rockefeller trip was to see what
literary activity was going on after the war, and nobody much knew. There
was then no literary contact—much more literary contact between England
and India, for instance, and the Far East, than between America and the
Far East. Japan had a beautiful, subtle, sophisticated fictional literature
which practically nobody in this country knew anything about. I told the
Rockefellers that if they would pay for a secretary and a little office material,
I would go on for a year, writing letters and trying to get some Japanese
short-story writers translated by the Japan PEN, which agreed to do this,
and I would try to place them in American magazines, which I did.

So a lot of my time when I wasn't teaching and directing the writing
program was spent on that for the next year. That takes us up to the end
of 'fifty-two. In 'fifty-three–'fifty-four, I was still working on Powell. That

biography, *Beyond the Hundredth Meridian*, was published in 1954, when we were living in Denmark. While in Denmark I was working on some of the stuff that later became *Wolf Willow*. I had some kind of half-assed notion that I wanted to do a study in village democracy, focusing on three very different places. One was Saskatchewan, where I had spent my boyhood. Another was Vermont, which had been a village democracy for two hundred years at least. There's one from scratch and one two hundred years old, and so I went back to Denmark to find one that was ten thousand years old. But I never made a book of it. What it finally came down to was concentrated on the Saskatchewan—the one from scratch—because that was obviously the one that interested me most.

In 1955, when we had come back here and I was a fellow at the Center for Advanced Studies in the Behavioral Sciences, I wrote most of *Wolf Willow*, including the three pieces of fiction that were originally intended for it, of which only two finally got published in it. One, called "Genesis," was a novella, and one called "Carrion Spring," a story. I wrote another story called "The Wolfer," which I finally pulled out. So you see, I was writing a little fiction in the fifties, in spite of my disillusionment; but I put "Genesis" away for a year, maybe a year and a half, because I couldn't figure out how to finish it. Finally, when I picked it up again, I realized why. It was finished; it didn't want to go on. It wanted to stop right there. The story didn't have to go through the whole winter, it just had to go through one blizzard. During that year at the Center I also wrote most of the history of ARAMCO. We flew out to Saudi Arabia, spent about a month and interviewed a lot of people. It was a very productive year, but not for fiction. And *Wolf Willow* never got published until . . . when was it? . . . 1962, I guess, after *A Shooting Star*.

So, it looks like you were a little bit discouraged with fiction, but so many other projects were taking . . .

Well, I wasn't unbusy. In 1959, the summer of 1959, Page got married in Ohio. We went back to his wedding and on to London and spent the summer in London. Bought a car and drove down through the Low Countries and France and down through the Alps into Italy, and spent four months in Florence. Then in January we went down to the American Academy in Rome, where I had been appointed a resident. I wrote most of *A Shooting Star* during that year, 'fifty-nine–sixty. I finished it, as a matter of fact, as we were driving north again from Rome through Provence and the Dordogne, sitting out in the courtyards of old country inns, with weeds up to my knees, on a card table, and typing the final manuscript of the thing. *A Shooting Star* wasn't a novel that I had my full heart in, but I was interested in doing it—to see what I could do with such a theme.

And it did do pretty well. As a matter of fact, it's been translated into more languages and had more success abroad than any of my other novels, though I don't think that much of it. It was close enough to popular trash so that it obviously went better—it was a Literary Guild selection, and in terms of sales and money, obviously a profitable thing to do. I suppose that's what put me back on the fiction bandwagon.

That's what you mean then when you say that there's a soap-opera problem in Shooting Star?

Well, yeah, the problem of a woman like that is inevitably soap-operish. She's tearing a passion to tatters. She's self-destroying herself with her emotions. At the same time, what's happening to her is serious. I was trying to get at something which it seemed to me I had seen fifteen different times: attractive, intelligent, advantaged women who were educated beyond anything that they were allowed to do in the world. Being decorative housewives simply wasn't enough, particularly if they had professional husbands whose lives were wrapped up in their careers. I made my woman the wife of a doctor. Now it would be another matter—quite another matter—but in the 1950s a woman had nothing to rebel with but her body. She often became either a drunk or a nymphomaniac or both, and that's what she did in this book. But that's close to soap opera material. I was walking a tightwire all the way, knowing the dangers but hoping I could get by them. I think sometimes I did, but not all the time. Maybe it can be done, I don't know.

I find your next novel, All the Little Live Things *[1967], more grim than much of your fiction. Have other readers reacted that way?*

Curiously, I get a lot of very heartfelt, intimate letters even yet on that book, from people who have come up against the problem of someone close to them dying of cancer, and the problems that it makes in the lives of the living, particularly when the person dying is young, and particularly when children are involved. Sure, it's grim; you bet it's grim. I was feeling grim, as a matter of fact, because in one year four of our friends died of cancer, one after another, all relatively young women in their forties. I was feeling peculiarly bleak during that period. I knew from the beginning that it was too glum a subject, simply a downer, unless I could do something with the surface of it to make it look lighter than it was. That's when I invented Joe Allston. A wisecracking narrator can make a story seem a little less grim than it is, though it still got grim even in his hands, I think.

Some commentators have argued that All the Little Live Things *is a grumpy criticism of the hippie generation. That seems to me a rather narrow view of the novel.*

The hippie just wandered into it by accident and became a rather half-witted Principle of Evil. The book is about "little live things" and the relations one has to life. It's not unrelated, as a matter of fact, to that story I mentioned earlier, the one called "The City of the Living," where in a life-and-death situation, you suddenly realize what the word "antibiotic" means. You maintain your own life by the destruction of other kinds of life, and your place in it is artificially kept open for you. I had a feeling—I'd been reading Teilhard de Chardin and people like that, and I was interested in his particular version of immortality, which is just an exchange of protein. That's the ecological point of view too—that you give your pound and a half of minerals, or whatever they are, back to the earth, and you've paid your debt to Nature. But it's a little hard on the individual, particularly when the individual wants to live, as this woman did, and has every reason to live. So, I accentuated that by making her pregnant, so that the course of the book is a race between life and death. No, the hippie is only a kind of dumb bystander. That was my feeling about hippies in general at that point. I've changed to some extent since, but the ones that I knew then were dumb bystanders who didn't have any notion of what went on but thought they did. So I made him a dumb bystander just standing out there with his mouth open, helpless, at the same time when he was the cause of some of the worst part of the last scene.

That harrowing scene I stole from Page. We had a neighbor named Jack Ewing, a Stanford professor who had loaned his horse to some friend from Australia, presumably a horseman. This fool tried to jump it across the cattle guard, and it got caught and broke its legs right off—not merely broke its legs, but broke them *off*. Page was going by and saw it and came up here to get a shotgun to shoot the horse. So, for my final grim scene, I borrowed the horse business from him. Later I found out that he'd been saving it for himself. Took it out of his mouth. I'll have to pay him back somehow. But it makes a properly excruciating ending to a grim book. The thing starts out light and gets ominous, and then eventually bleak, which was the way I was feeling, I guess. I disagree that *All the Little Live Things* is a putting down of hippies, because the hippie is the least important thing in that book, to me.

Joe Allston plays a major role in several of your works, as in All the Little Live Things. *Wasn't his first appearance really in* "Field Guide to the Western Birds"?[2]

---

[2]"Field Guide to the Western Birds," *New Short Novels* 2 (New York: Ballantine Books, 1955); later reprinted in *The City of the Living*.

Yeah . . . which I wrote as a short story, or a novella, really, for Mary Lou Aswell, who was doing an anthology for an original paperback. I was slow to get it in, so it wasn't in the first collection. She did another one and used "Field Guide" in it, along with a piece of Norman Mailer's and one by John Philips—who was actually John Marquand's son—and some girl I don't know. In making Joe I also made use of the immediate scene around here. We were a long time finishing the house and getting the yard halfway out of the mud and getting to know the neighbors. I borrowed for Joe's portrait the character of my agent, who was always threatening to write up what he had done for ten percent. He made a properly acerb commentator on the suburban scene. Later I wrote another Joe Allston story called "Indoor-Outdoor Living" and published it in the pilot edition of a magazine called *Pacifica*, which was being started in San Francisco and which never got off the ground. I never tried to publish that anywhere else; I used some of the same situations and little pieces or hints from it in *All the Little Live Things*. I wrote a story for *Mademoiselle*, also called "All the Little Live Things," which covered essentially the returning from the funeral after Marian had died, the cherry tree with the roots eaten off, and the forces of evil working around in the earth. The novel simply absorbed and digested these two stories.

In All the Little Live Things, *and in* The Spectator Bird *[1976], Allston seems to play the same role, in some ways, as Lyman Ward does in* Angle of Repose—*a kind of observer, commentator.*

Well, sure, narrator, observer, commentator. He's a very different type, though. He's more emotional than Lyman Ward, less over-controlled. He's under-controlled, rather than over-controlled. Lyman Ward is pretty uptight all the time. Joe Allston is likely to get drunk and disorderly and to wisecrack in the wrong places. He's another kind of character, but he has some of the same functions as a literary device, and he's the first time really that I experimented with the first-person singular, which until then I had never much liked. It always seemed to me a way of sprawl; you're windier in the first person, or I thought you were. And also, it seemed to me you couldn't deal with really strong emotions in the first person because it's simply an awkwardness for an individual to talk about his own emotions. I had a theory that strong emotions should be approached obliquely, and not talked about. So I had never played with the first-person singular until I got onto this Joe Allston business, where I was just looking for a tone of voice which had to be light and flippant. As it developed, it began to develop undercurrents of seriousness, but the tone stayed light. In *Angle of Repose* I was doing something a good deal more complicated than that. I was having Lyman Ward recreate the life of his grandparents, as one would do a research project, a work of history, from the evidence, the letters, the documents, the memorabilia—memory, and at the same time, while he's doing that, leak his own story inadvertently between the lines. That makes for a much more complicated mesh.

Isn't Joe Allston doing some of the same things in The Spectator Bird—*talking to himself, recreating out of his diary, and trying to find himself?*

Maybe. But he's frank with you from the beginning. There are some things in that diary he doesn't want to read to his wife, and he says so. Lyman Ward wouldn't have said so. You'd have to learn it some other way. They're two different people, though the methods are certainly related. I rather liked those first-person novels, once I got into them, because I found that I could do some things I could hardly do by other means. I could syncopate time, for instance, like mad. A sentence or a paragraph, I'm gone and nobody's noticed. It's much smoother than if I had to summarize in the third-person mode.

It seems to me there's some of Wallace Stegner in Joe Allston.

Oh yes, but as I think I warned you the other day, don't read him intact. He goes further than I would. Anybody is likely to make characters to some extent in his own image, but if he's at all self-protective, he'll make them also *out* of his own image, just to throw people off the scent.

Although The Spectator Bird *won the National Book Award, it didn't appear in paperback for some time and was not reviewed widely. If I remember correctly, you said something about its not getting reviewed in the* New York Times . . . *it never did?*

No, nor in the *Los Angeles Times.*

How do you account for this silence on one of your best novels?

I think the *Los Angeles Times* is explicable because Bob Kirsch, who was the book editor, and who did like the *Angle of Repose* and was respectful of my work, was abroad that year. The whole office was in a little bit more confusion than when Kirsch was at home. For the *New York Times,* I have no explanation. They didn't review *Angle of Repose* either. So they missed both the Pulitzer Prize and the National Book Award novels. And I think that must be, somehow, attributable to some prejudice. John Leonard was the editor at that point. I don't know him, but evidently my stuff infuriates him, bores him to death, or something. I know he got a lot of angry letters from people, denouncing him for not reviewing it, because many sent me copies. A national book review journal has the obligation of reporting books to the whole reading public. You can't be idiosyncratically selective; you can't leave out books you happen to have a personal antipathy to. It's notable that Leonard didn't last as editor. So I suspect we got our revenge.

Your last three novels, Angle of Repose, The Spectator Bird, *and* Recapitulation, *make extensive use of the interplay between past and present, memory and contemporary events. This technique really allows you to play with time, doesn't it?*

Well, yes. And as I was saying, first-person narrative encourages you to syncopate time, to bridge from a past to a present. It also allows you to drop back and forth, almost at will, freely. When Joe Allston or Lyman Ward is working with the past, his head is working in the present. He may be talking to somebody in the present about somebody in the past so that the relations between past and present are intricate, a cat's cradle. That's one of the things I like the most about the first-person novel. It didn't work so well in *Recapitulation.* I wrote that book first in the third person and then changed it to first. It didn't seem to me to be right, and eventually I concluded that third person was the way to do it. But it meant that I had to fade in and fade out. When Mason is having dinner at the Hotel Utah, he looks through the sunset over Saltair and thinks of when he was fourteen and selling hot dogs out there, and then we fade back in again to dinner. This is quite a different trick when you're doing it third person from what it is in first. So I had to learn how to do it there, too. But I certainly do take advantage of any way of interpenetrating past and present—whatever way I can find. I guess I have made myself public on that. I think that's what western novels too frequently don't do, and some modern novels that aren't western don't do. Hemingway, for instance, has no past in him at all. I can't think of a single bit of past in him except the suicide of Robert Jordan's father in *For Whom the Bell Tolls*; and you don't find any children in Hemingway either. Ordinarily we live a three-generational life. Hemingway is absolute present— present tense, people between twenty and thirty-five, no parents, no children.

So different from Faulkner.

Oh, absolutely different from Faulkner. Faulkner is *rich* with associations from the past. All those hoofs that are thundering through his Sartoris stories. Everybody in the South, I suppose, is likely to have a stronger sense of tradition and history, partly because of the abiding memory of the Civil War, the good days now gone, and all of that, but also because of the guilt of black slavery. Faulkner's South is a real region, essentially rural, and essentially built upon two or three crops, cotton, corn, peanuts. So that there's . . . anybody from Frenchman's Bend is recognizable by any other Southerner. Until World War II, when the South began to migrate, it was a thing which had been there for a good many generations, since the 1830s and '40s, more or less in the same form. Even though slavery had gone the land remained the same, the crops remained the same, people remained the same. I would agree: Faulkner is rich in it and Hemingway is poor in it. Somebody like Scott Fitzgerald in *The Great Gatsby* elected to write strictly in the present, but he did go back, and he picked up all of the Jay Gatsby past in order to make some resonances in his present plot, and that is thoroughly legitimate. It seems to me that's a modern way to write a novel. Hemingway was not only modern, he was limited. All he was after was the immediate sensation of the moment, how it was.

> *I was thinking that when the American historian C. Vann Woodward collected some of his early essays on the South, he used the title* The Burden of Southern History. *We use the words "usable past," but you have used the phrase: the West has an "amputated Present."[3] The West seems not to sense its past like the South; the West's past is no burden.*

No. There are lots of reasons. It isn't anywhere nearly as homogeneous in ethnic, or geographical, or climatic, or resource, or any other terms. Likewise the West was settled, most of it, after the development of modern means of communication. Telegraph, for instance, was in very shortly after the settlement of Salt Lake and California, which means that the business of provincial ripening—growing up in isolation, getting a sense of local identity and integrity before you begin to be diluted by anybody else—never happened in most parts of the West. Westerners were always, for one thing, on the move; it's a very migrant society in every part of the West I know except Utah, and maybe even there. The West exports manpower all the time. And being migrant it doesn't have the sense of roots; it doesn't have the attics and cellars and the storage of old memories, or hasn't had until very recently. And its plain life is so short that it wouldn't have an awful lot to store even if it were in the mood to store it. A lot of towns in the West that you have lived in probably have been towns only since about 1870, at the very earliest. They're about a hundred years old, some of them less.

> *In* Recapitulation *Bruce Mason remembers a good deal about his early years in Salt Lake City, but he seems afraid to make direct contact with a boyhood friend. Is that because he knows the past will be changed from the way he recalls it, or am I reading too much into something? Maybe it's just a novelistic device that you . .*

Well, it's both. I do think that when you go back to some place that you haven't been in for many years—where the associations are dense but the connections have been broken—you may hesitate to make contact with

---

[3]*The Sound of Mountain Water*, p. 193.

somebody who after forty-five years is by no means the person that you knew. All of the emotional attachments would have been changed, not only by distance but by the growth of the different individuals in different directions over all that time. You do grow away from your adolescence, and early friends grow away from you. You grow apart because the bond that held you together as adolescents isn't an enduring one. You turn out to have different interests in the long run. I do think that anybody would be inclined to shy away from reunion after long separation, except some fun-thinking kind of extrovert who wouldn't have sense enough to know that it might be touchy, might be sort of damaging to him, or to the other person, or to a feeling.

That's one thing. The other is the novelistic reason that this character has been, from his very early youth, browbeaten and dominated by a harsh father. He has lacked all his life, as I see him, a certain self-confidence. This despite a certain worldly success. I put him in the diplomatic service and made him an ambassador—which, by most standards would be a very successful, even distinguished, life. But the very basic lack of confidence remains; the whole recollection of this book is a recollection of humiliation, in places where his confidence was stepped on and where he was not really allowed to come out. He is the continuation of the boy in *The Big Rock Candy Mountain*—though that was an afterthought, not originally part of the book. I decided that this character was close enough to Bruce Mason so I might as well make him a trailer. But in the beginning I had written him in other terms and under another name. The recollections that he relives are all humiliating, up to and including the fact that his girl dumps him and that, in the end, the catastrophes of his family and the catastrophe of his love life are associated with the town, to which he comes back, half reluctantly. He doesn't really want to remember as much as he does. Given those feelings he would, I think, be particularly subject to uncertainty and feel in the long run that the best thing to do is just to turn away. In a way, that is a kind of defeat; it's an assertion of the fact that having been bent, that twig was going to stay inclined—and that though he makes his reconciliation with his father and buys him a tombstone, he really isn't free from him yet. The kind of thing that his father has done to him is still a part of him. That's what I meant. That may be a little more complicated than you thought.

Have reviewers tried to make as much of autobiographical parallels in Recapitulation *as they did in* Big Rock Candy Mountain?

Oh, no, I don't think so. No, a lot of people who grew up in Salt Lake have written me about the book. Some of them I grew up with, some I never knew. What strikes them most is the place. Salt Lake has never, I suppose, been written about in fiction. My agent thought I was mad. Why the hell put a book in Salt Lake, why? But I didn't see any reason why not. These actions and people *belonged* in Salt Lake City, not in New York City or Boston, or anywhere else. A lot of the mail I get on the book has to do with recognition of the town which people seem to feel, but nobody made any autobiographical allusions that I remember. There's a certain amount of autobiography in it, obviously, because it is a continuation of *The Big Rock Candy Mountain*. But it's all modulated and changed and altered and shifted and given new emphases and taken further. I suppose I have a certain resentment against my father for dominating me for so long, but I'm not put down quite as far as this guy was. As with Joe Allston, I just project something in myself a little further out to get an image of what *can* happen.

Generally, commentators on your fiction have tried to identify you with the narrators of your recent books, to emphasize autobiographical elements, and perhaps to downplay your created characters. How do you react to this tendency among critics?

I never reacted to it because it never struck me as being that universal a tendency. Do you think it is? You've been reading these things. I don't read them that carefully. Whom have you found reading me as autobiography?

I was thinking more of newspaper reviewers than of established literary critics; of people who are commenting extensively on your life, wanting to tell readers that they know that Wallace Stegner was in Salt Lake City and that he did many of the things that Bruce Mason did. They want to tell what they know of your life, and they make the next step in suggesting that much of this novel is personal history rather than "imagined" fiction.

That's just a vulgar error. It happens all the time with people who can't read, so they read what they want to see, rather than what's there. Or, they make these big jumps of inference for which they don't have any basis except guesswork. . . . I take it as a compliment in a way . . . it's easy to assume that a narrator who speaks plausibly is speaking for his author. I go to a good deal of pain to make him speak plausibly, but I don't necessarily want to go to all those pains to make him speak for *me*. So, I guess if I were made aware of that kind of tendency among reviewers, I would try to correct them. I would say, "Don't mistake the object for the subject." Even if there is a strong autobiographical element in a character, he's somebody else by the time he's made and put on a page, and the autobiographical element is irrelevant. What's on the page is what matters. That's the way books should be read, not with any kind of autobiographical detective-impulse, not with any listening for echoes. We all do it, but we shouldn't. It's one of the things that literary study has brought on us because we surround the study of literature with the study of biography and history, social history, literary contexts.

It's a thing that we should have learned a long time ago with that famous essay, "The Intentional Fallacy," but I guess we still go on doing it.

I don't mind looking for the essential mind or spirit of a writer in his books. I read for that. But I don't give a damn about his biography. It doesn't bother me that Conrad had a habit of flipping bread pellets around the table while he was talking, or that Milton abused his children. What is in the *book*, what comes of this distilled personality and character and intelligence on the *page* is what we ought to read for, and it is clearly a reflection of a personality. But it's not so biographical. Are you thinking of a work by C. S. Lewis called *The Personal Heresy*?

No, the Wimsatt and Beardsley essay—"The Intentional Fallacy."[4]

Plenty of people have objected to that, and I think with cause. A lot of writers, Faulkner, for instance, deliberately mess up their biography in order to confuse and put off the scent those people who are so eagerly hunting them down. Faulkner told more lies about his personal life than anybody except maybe Sherwood Anderson, and probably for the same reason. He may have learned it from Anderson. I haven't told any lies about myself, but I don't think that it makes much sense to make me at one time Joe Allston, and the next time Lyman Ward, and the next time Bruce Mason. They're very different people. I think perhaps the fact that the last one isn't in first person . . . has led to less of that autobiographical interpretation. Anything in the first person a lot of people take as eye-witness stuff and swallow whole. After *Angle of Repose*, all kinds of people wrote me speaking about my grandmother, as if I had written a family history. I had no such grandmother. I wish I had.

---

[4]W. K. Wimsatt, Jr., and M. C. Beardsley, "The Intentional Fallacy," *The Verbal Icon* (Lexington: University of Kentucky Press, 1954).

5. *Angle of Repose*

Etulain: What was the genesis of Angle of Repose? *How did you come to write the novel?*

Stegner: the genesis is clearly the Mary Hallock Foote papers. I was without book, and about that time a graduate student of mine, George McMurray, decided that he definitely was not going to make a dissertation out of the reminiscences and the letters, which he had hoped to do, perhaps with an anthology of some of her stories. He hoped to restore her, because he really admired her stuff. But he turned out not to be able to do it because he just got too old and discouraged. He would have had to learn German and a lot of other things in order to get a Ph.D., and he was a re-treaded GI student, already sixty-three years old. When these things fell back upon me, I looked into them thinking there might be a book there. I read the letters, which didn't happen instantaneously. There are enormous numbers of them, a stack that high of typed letters; it's about a year's work to read through the blooming things. I took them to Vermont one summer and read around wondering whether there might be a biography in them or whether they might be a novel. Eventually I decided that if it was anything it was a novel, but it was a year or two before I finally determined that there was really a book there. It grew during the time of reading, perhaps because that story reinforced my own notion of what a story is. It was like the *Big Rock Candy Mountain* without my realizing it. It was the boomer husband and the nesting wife, although with variations in it and on a much higher social level. Anyway, it appealed to me finally as a story, and I determined that it was a

[83]

novel. Up to that point it had come entirely out of the papers. Then I began to realize that I didn't want to write just another nineteenth-century triangle in cowpuncher's or in prospector's boots. I really didn't want to write a historical novel; I wanted to write a contemporary novel, but it occurred to me that maybe past and present could be linked together in the way that I had obviously been working toward for a long time.

So I fiddled around for a good long while, and I finally wrote the opening chapter more or less as it is, utilizing a narrator with a broken marriage and a broken body. The physical misfortunes I borrowed from the plight of my old professor, Norman Foerster. The marital problem I took from the experience of a friend of mine, whose wife—with whom he was madly, crazily in love, and by whom he had six or seven children—left him suddenly, simply ran off with some doctor, who almost immediately got himself killed in an automobile accident up at Lake Tahoe. So she was left, having abandoned her husband and having lost her lover. She tried to come back to him—she tried to crawl back to him—and he wouldn't have her; he kicked her out—implacable. Which is the origin of the Lyman Ward story, essentially. I added the crippling and the other business partly because it was there before me in Foerster and partly because it seemed to accentuate the tearing apart of people who have been very close for a long time. And that's where that came from. I don't think my friend ever did have anything to do with his wife again, and I don't know what ever happened to her; she just vanished. But it did seem to me in the circumstances that I had imagined—using Grass Valley as the place for this—taking him back during this time of crisis and healing—that in that place sooner or later they were going to come for him. If he had children, they were going to come and try to take care of him, or put him away, file him away. He was in a box, as it seemed to me, speaking from a box rather hollowly, desperately reconstructing the life of his grandmother and desperately avoiding his own. It seemed to me that the present and the past could be brought together in that way. If I could do it, I could tell one story the way a historical researcher might have reproduced it, and I could leak the other almost inadvertently. That double story created technical difficulties.

As a matter of fact it was extremely difficult for me to find a way. I threw away the opening chapter two or three times, thinking, "I can't do it. I can't find any way of getting from here to there, any way of getting back" . . . . Every time I tried it, it seemed awkward and clumsy. But eventually I found a way that I thought wasn't quite so clumsy, and when I had worked it out, I restored the original chapter. I had been smart enough in the beginning to say, "No, I won't throw it clear away, I won't put it in the wastebasket, I'll put it in the drawer." It was about a year, a year and a half, I suppose,

before I found what I thought was a legitimate way of getting from past to the present and back again and working that technical problem out.

You actually had known about Mary Hallock Foote for quite a while, hadn't you?

I'll tell you where I found out about Mary Hallock Foote. When I came up from Santa Barbara after finishing *One Nation* and taking the Stanford job, I was working on a chapter called "Western Record and Romance" for the *Literary History of the United States.* I was reading all kinds of local-color people and western explorers and so on, and I read her among others. I thought she was one of the best, actually; she was good and hadn't been noticed. I suppose she appealed to me because she was western and not southern or midwestern. So I knew about her and put something of hers on the reading list for an American literature class—The Rise of Realism, as I remember.

"When the Pump Stopped"?

No, it wasn't that. I got that story from Janet Micoleau, later. Her grandmother had sewed it together and made a little edition out of it for a Christmas present once. "How the Pump Stopped at the Morning Watch." I put it into an anthology when I finally put my class notes together as a book, but it wasn't that that I was assigning. . . . I think maybe the *Led-Horse Claim,* or something like that—some short novel. George McMurray was in the class, and he said, "I know about Mary Hallock Foote because I used to go up to New Almaden. Did you know she had done pictures and articles about New Almaden?" Frankly, I didn't. So he educated me on Mary Hallock Foote. He also said, "Her granddaughter lives in Grass Valley, and I'm going up and see her and see if we can't get her papers for Stanford." And he did. Later, through Alf Heller, who married my secretary at Stanford, we got to know the Micoleaus. Alf was living in Grass Valley and editing the local paper. We visited them several times and became friends. It was a long time between the time when George first brought those papers down and when I started to work. He was a GI student. Must have been 'forty-six or 'forty-seven, something like that. He may have got the papers down here by 1950. I certainly didn't begin to work on them before the middle sixties, fifteen years later.

What are your reactions to Professor Mary Ellen Williams-Walsh in her essay on Mary Hallock Foote and Angle of Repose?[1]

Irritable. Her case depends on a precise equation between Susan Burling Ward and Mary Hallock Foote. The reason I didn't use real names and the reason I didn't make an acknowledgment in the front of the book saying "I have based this on the papers of Mary Hallock Foote," which I normally would have done, is that Janet Micoleau didn't think we ought to use the real name, since what I was writing was a novel. So the acknowledgment I made was thanks to J. M. and her sister for the loan of their ancestors. If I had written a biography of Mary Hallock Foote I would have put her in the book by name and made acknowledgment to her papers. But it is a novel, not a biography. It has nothing to do with the actual life of Mary Hallock Foote except that I borrowed a lot of her experiences. So I don't, I guess, feel very guilty about that. It is a method that I've used, as you've said, to mix history and fiction. And whenever fact will serve fiction—and I am writing fiction—I am perfectly willing to use it that way. When fiction will serve fact, as when I did a thing like "Genesis" in the middle of *Wolf Willow,* it seems to work the other way.

No, I'm a little irritated at that particular holier-than-thou attack. And I don't feel that I did Mary Hallock Foote any damage at all because, left alone, the papers would have been simply the raw material out of which a novel might be made. Molly Foote is raw material for Susan Ward. The

---

[1] A much-revised version of this essay appears as Mary Ellen Williams-Walsh, "*Angle of Repose* and the Writings of Mary Hallock Foote: A Source Study," in Anthony Arthur, ed., *Critical Essays on Wallace Stegner* (Boston: G. K. Hall, 1982), pp. 184–209.

fact that certain people weren't able to see it in a novelistic way makes the difficulty. And she [Professor Walsh] also makes one of those leaps when she assumes that even the Lyman Ward story is borrowed from Mary Hallock Foote.

You hadn't even read the Foote story she cites?

I hadn't even read the story. I haven't read it yet. So I don't know how much she thought she saw there. As far as I am concerned the Mary Hallock Foote stuff had the same function as raw material, broken rocks out of which I could make any kind of wall I wanted to—as poor Norman Foerster's ailments, which I borrowed for that wheelchair point of view.

Or the Joe Hill stuff in The Preacher and the Slave?

Yes, the Joe Hill stuff . . . there was far less documentary background there, because there isn't a great deal available on Joe Hill. But I knew as much about Joe Hill as I could find out. If I had been writing his biography I couldn't have gone any deeper. I couldn't have found out any more.

Or the warning that you suggested really ought to be at the beginning of Big Rock Candy Mountain—*for those who want to read it as straight autobiography.*

Well, it sure isn't straight autobiography. I don't know, maybe I am perverse, but I see nothing wrong with letting reminiscence or fiction serve the purpose of history, and vice versa. I don't see any reason why real life, real people—Henry Adams, Clarence King, whoever else—Molly Foote—can't serve the purposes of a novel. The problem, I think, the real problem—which I got into inadvertently, and which I wish I hadn't gotten into—was that in order to try to honor Janet's notion that no names should be used—that we shouldn't recognize the source of this as her grandmother—I disguised the acknowledgment, and I also left the quotation marks so that they could be read as Lyman Ward's quotation marks instead of mine. That's something that Mary Ellen Walsh makes a point of. She doesn't think that's enough.

You had asked Mrs. Micoleau to look over the manuscript and to okay it, is that right?

Right. I offered to send it to her, and she said, "Oh, no; I trust you. I know you are making a novel, and I'm very busy—and go ahead." Perhaps we should both have consulted with her sister, Marian Conway, at that point. I'm sorry she was upset.

You mention the problem of trying to find the perspective that would bring past and present together. Were there other major problems you wrestled with in writing the novel?

Well, yes, because there is in that novel, too, in the forward part of it, some of the kind of thing that I was playing with in *All the Little Live Things* —the generation gap, and especially the antihistorical pose of the young, at least the young of the 1960s. They didn't give a damn what happened up to two minutes ago and would have been totally unable to understand a Victorian lady. I could conceive students of mine confronting Mary Hallock Foote and thinking, "My God, fantastic, inhuman," because they themselves were so imprisoned in the present that they had no notion of how various humanity and human customs can be. That's a secondary theme, like a subplot, in there.

I guess I was thinking of a technical problem more than a thematic one.

Everything is subsumed in a voice when you tell a story in this way. All of Grandmother's story comes in as a voice—Lyman's talking to himself, to his tape recorder, to Shelly, or to somebody. His own story comes as the occasional mutterings or half-heard mutterings of an interior voice. They are very different stories, the mood is very different; that calls upon me to make subtle variations in the voice. I go all the way from the documentary, journalistic, research-student business of reassembling Grandma's data and putting them together as you might write a thesis—all the way from that to the hallucinations of the final nightmare. Those differentiations of the voice are the real problem. Somebody, who was it, wrote an article on the narrative voice in the novel . . .

Audrey Peterson.

Yes, which seemed to me sensible. I thought she was reading the book intelligently. She understood at least some of the difficulties. Bob Canzoneri did something on that too.[2]

Yes, he did.

It was a very difficult book to write, and I constantly painted myself into corners and had to back out and start painting again. I would fall into some kind of authorial omniscience that the book couldn't tolerate. Or I would get the wrong time in the wrong place, or not have Lyman sufficiently reticent about his own problems. I had to have him absolutely reticent and his story barely leaked, accessible only in occasional clues and hints. I took out a lot of clues and hints; I found I had a tendency to overexplain.

---

[2]Audrey C. Peterson, "Narrative Voice in Stegner's *Angle of Repose*," *Western American Literature* 10 (Summer 1975) : 125–33; Robert Canzoneri, "Wallace Stegner: Trial by Existence," *Southern Review* 9 (Autumn 1973) : 796–827.

I suppose that you had the additional problem of two levels of time, past and present, and how often to have the passageways between the two time periods.

The passageways back and forth *are* different. Sometimes they're easy—present to past or vice versa, in clean blocks. But sometimes there's hardly any difference between past and present. Lyman sits there at his typewriter, he remembers his grandmother, he turns around in his chair, he looks at his grandmother's picture on the wall, and she is in a way present in the room. So there's present time as well as past time going on . . . . At this point I am not able to say exactly how it was done except that it took a long time to work it out. You know when you are there, when you've done it, when it satisfies you and when it doesn't; but the process is all chips and shavings, and you sweep them out when you're done.

Since you have utilized several kinds of narrators in your previous fiction, how did you select the narrative position that Lyman Ward occupies in this book? You mentioned that Joe Allston might have been a model for this kind of narrator.

The Joe Allston stories were the first, first-person narrative practically that I ever wrote. I may have written one—"The Chink" is a first-person story, the only one I can remember, and that is very little different from what I would have written if I had written it in third. There isn't any effective *voice* there. A child's voice coerces you. You limit the understanding and sharpen the perceptions, and that is what a child's voice comes to—a sharp perception without full understanding. Whatever Maisie knew she knew that way. A lot of the poignancy of child-oriented stories is precisely the discrepancy between perception and understanding; the reader understands more than the speaker does. I didn't want the reader, in this case, to understand *much* more than the speaker does, but I did want him to understand that Lyman Ward was holding off on his own story, that he could be trustworthy about his grandmother but not about himself. That again is a little bit difficult. I think probably I had learned something about how to do it from having written at least one Joe Allston novel and one novella.

I recall that either Larry McMurtry or Ken Kesey, former students of yours, mentioned the importance that you place on narrative voice in the classes you taught at Stanford. What points had you—or have you—usually stressed in talking about narrative roles in fiction?

I don't know. I find it hard to remember what I might have said to those classes a long time ago, twenty years ago, when Kesey and McMurtry were members of the class. (Fortunately, nobody kept notes in those classes, so you're not going to get any documents.) We were always working ad hoc on manuscript and not on any abstract formulation of literary theory. A lot of students then were turning toward first-person singular; the world has turned that way in literary practice, toward the confession, the examination of inner darkness. I don't know whether it came from Gide, Camus, or some other French writer, or whether we learned it from Henry James and *Huckleberry Finn*, but somebody seems to have adapted the French *récit* to American practice.

I am sure that in talking about first-person singular narrative I would have placed a lot of emphasis upon the central problem of making the narrator absolutely persuasive or, if he is an unreliable narrator, like Humbert Humbert in *Lolita*, giving us those subtle clues that will let us mistrust him at just the right places and to the right amount. I would also, I suppose, have said a good deal in the Henry James way about not being in two minds simultaneously and not being outside and inside simultaneously—about being consistent in the point of view. I probably used a good many times in class the image of a garden hose running with a nozzle and without a nozzle. You get more force with a nozzle. My only arguments are by analogy. In talking about a specific manuscript I would probably have emphasized the same things, because over a period of many years I have come to think point of view the most important basic problem in the writing of fiction. There we go back to Conrad, whom I encountered early. He was so much better when he used Marlowe; his best books are Marlowe books, through a voice, a mask. I taught Conrad a good deal and have always read and admired him. I suspect I have learned as much from him as from anybody else about fictional technique.

In some ways Angle of Repose *seems a major novel comparing the frontier and New Wests. Did you have this comparison in mind as you wrote the book?*

Oh yes, and it's more than that. It is not only a comparison of the frontier and the New West; it's a comparison of West and East. It attempts to be something relatively comprehensive about certain kinds of American experiences. Fortunately, again, a lot of the hints were there in Molly Foote. She was *quite* aware of the differences between East and West, much more aware than I would be, probably, though I had some notion, having lived in both. She felt it more because she felt the West for a long time as a place of exile. I suppose parts of the book look like a disparagement of the New West, because the ahistorical kids come out of it and there is some nutty seeking—pioneering in fields where I am not sympathetic to the pioneering. I was much more sympathetic to the kind of pioneering that the older Wards did. If the novel is in any sense judgmental it judges the New West as inferior to the Old, as being a deterioration from it, though that judgment is only glancing. If I were judging systematically I wouldn't do it quite that way.

So, in several ways the Mary Hallock Foote story gave you the horizontal story of East and West and the Lyman Ward one of the vertical line between the Old and New Wests?

Yes. Shelly, that product of the New West, is invented on the model of one of my students who finally wound up living in a commune. She seemed to me a nice girl, crazy in a peculiarly modern way and absolutely ahistorical; she had no sense whatever that time didn't begin yesterday.

Is Susan Burling Ward typical of many women who came west in the late nineteenth century, or is her story atypical?

I think atypical, though not so completely atypical as it might seem. You get used to the image of the pioneer woman in the poke bonnet, but a lot of people who came west in poke bonnets were not just housewives with a third-grade education. Tamsen Donner and others were perfectly well-educated people for their time. They botanized happily all across the West. In terms of her talent and her connections in the East and her personal career both as a writer and an illustrator, Susan Ward is quite atypical. There weren't many women like that. In fact, you can't think of any women artists in her time, except Mary Cassatt—who had to go to France to have a career. There were some writers, but there weren't any illustrators. In her art she was quite atypical; in her writing she was not unlike Helen Hunt Jackson and a lot of other women who came west, gifted and intelligent women.

In the kinds of life available to such a gifted woman in the West, I think she was typical. Anybody with her gifts would have had some of her difficulties. These were not pioneers in the plow-and-one-Shanghai-rooster sense; they were always people who had a household around them, who employed other people. There were always three or four people, a governess, people Ward employed in his surveys, hired men. Families like the Wards made a kind of economy for a whole bunch of satellite people. They would have to be considered the upper crust of pioneers—in this case, the upper crust in brains and talents rather than in money. There were plenty of people who came west and made a lot of money, but they didn't always have the dreams, and they didn't always have the gifts. Again, that makes the Wards special rather than typical. I had a strong feeling when I wrote them that this particular aspect of the westward migration hadn't been adequately told and that these were people who represented a phase of it more-or-less forgotten so far.

The sense of alienation, of being an alien in the West, does that seem typical of other women coming from the East, or is it more apparent in Mary Hallock Foote?

Well, what women can you compare her to? Josiah Royce's mother, for instance, or Mrs. Clappe, the author of the Shirley letters? Some women, particularly women with intelligence and a certain writing gift, found the West fascinating, but I think they found its life hard. Mrs. Royce is a sample. I'm not sure she felt exiled, but she had to live a relatively hard life. And Dame Shirley even more, dragged around by that husband-dentist, or whatever he was, a kind of incompetent. I am not sure how to answer your question because it seems to me that different people responded in different ways to the conditions they met; and the conditions themselves were various. It would depend to some extent, to a considerable extent, on how successful the family—that is to say, the husband—was; how many amenities could be gathered together to make a life. In those days, women were homemakers, essentially, primarily, first. Without ability to make a home, they would be frustrated, I suppose. If they had the facilities or the money to make a home, permanence and domestic satisfactions came pretty quickly after a matter of ten or fifteen years of hard times. It's hardly more than a lot of women graduate students, or married graduate students, go through by the time they get to be assistant professors. The mere adventure of starting a life is enough to carry you for a good way . . . . I don't think they were all unhappy.

I think the most negative comments by Mrs. Foote are when she is living up the Boise River canyon or when they have moved to the Mesa— her comments about Boise society; she hates it, she sees it as narrow and provincial.

Yes. Good society was what she missed most. She was not unhappy at all in the hardships; she could take those. She rode across Mexico on a mule, but . . . and she loved New Almaden because at that point she didn't need society. She was a bride. It's hard to tell. I don't frankly remember from the letters. Most of the complaints I remember occur in letters to Bessie or Helena about the army wives at the Boise Barracks. She certainly didn't, after the first while, like them. The Footes lived in Bessie's house in Boise for a while, right below the fort. They heard the bugle, and their son went riding with the cavalry. She thought that was all rather nice, as I remember; it was the ladies that oppressed her. And not only the army wives, but some of the wives of miners who had made it rich, who were really quite incompetent to deal on her level.

Maybe, too, part of it was that she was embarrassed. Her husband had not been able to do financially what she had wished, and it was difficult for her to accept the possibility that she did not fit in with Boise society.

Yes, it is a question, isn't it? When they opened the canal and the governor was there, obviously Arthur Foote was then a figure of some importance; I don't remember any bitterness about Boise society at that point. She had a feeling that they were on top of it momentarily. Later, when Coxey's Army comes through, she is a very rabid Republican; she's pretty harsh.

But at one time they may have voted for Grover Cleveland because they knew him—or maybe had met him. You are right, they were strong Republicans, but I think they were two of the handful of Idahoans who voted for Cleveland in one election. In this case, because of their ties to Helena Gilder . . .[3]

. . . and *her* friendship with Cleveland.

I am struck with the parallels between Elsa Mason in Big Rock Candy Mountain *and Susan Burling Ward. They seem gradually—but reluctantly—to accept their lives in the West. We see Elsa's acquiescence, but doesn't Susan come to a point of acceptance in the final years of her life in Grass Valley?*

I am sure Mary Hallock Foote did. Susan did not because I didn't let her. The situation I had given to her and her husband was a situation of virtual silence, virtual lack of communication. They were courteous and cool to one another. I may have borrowed that detail too from some place or other. I think maybe—you know the girl who wrote *One Day on Beetle Rock* and *One Day at Teton Marsh* . . . Sally Carrighar. A long time ago Sally told me about her grandparents, who were Quakers—rigid and relatively uneducated people. Some kind of difficulty arose between them, and they simply went on living together but stopped speaking. They didn't speak for the last twenty-five years of their lives. *Didn't speak*—just came out to breakfast. There may have been some echo of that in my notion of what could happen here. Likewise that bitter repudiation that my friend in Southern California had made when his wife took off and got unhorsed. Implacable repudiation I did want to make use of, and so that's the life Susan lives for the last years in Grass Valley *in the book*. Very *unlike* the

[3]Helena de Kay Gilder, wife of Richard Watson Gilder, editor of *Century Magazine* and publisher of much of Mary Hallock Foote's serial fiction, was Foote's closest friend and became the model for Augusta Drake Hudson in *Angle of Repose* (Garden City, N. Y.: Doubleday, 1971).

life that Mary Hallock Foote led in Grass Valley, which was happy and prosperous. Lots of Airedale dogs to walk and pick ticks off, lots of company coming through. She was a celebrity and the hostess of celebrities.

In the novel I think you use the image not of an angle of repose but one of two people standing together, beside one another, but who never reach an angle of repose.

I don't know whether you know the principle of the false arch. Do you? Agamemnon's tomb in Mycenae is based on the false arch; you just lean the rocks a little bit, overlap them a little bit inward until they meet at the top. A beehive tomb is not a real arch; there's no keystone, but the walls do support one another by leaning together. I thought: that was as good an image as the angle of repose. Another way of saying essentially the same things—an equilibrium of forces, at least.

Big Rock Candy Mountain *and* Angle of Repose *seem a quest for under-standing—in part an answer to the question of how are husbands and wives to reach their angles of repose in spite of such differing personalities and conflicting goals. The question seems to intrigue you, right?*

Yeah, it does intrigue me because I have been disturbed for the last twenty years by what the sexual revolution has done to marriage and family life. It has been a disaster for children, and it may even be—in the guise of freedom—a disaster for individuals, married individuals. There's always an escape hatch, there's never the necessity to bend yourself to make some kind of reconciliation of the unreconcilable, which is what a marriage is always having to do, a real one, that is. I suppose I was preaching a little bit from my stump about marriage. *Angle of Repose* is a book about a marriage, as somebody says somewhere in the book—I guess it is Lyman. Since his own marriage has collapsed he's interested in this one that didn't, even though it had all the provocations that his had to fall apart.

So there are three different kinds of marriages—that of the Wards, Lyman's, and the one between the young people of the sixties.

"Progressive decline," I would call it.

Does Lyman experience a moment of epiphany at the end of the novel? He seems to learn from history—something like the understanding Bruce Mason achieves at the end of Big Rock Candy Mountain.

I'll be frank with you. I am not sure whether he does or not. I wrote that whole last chapter—fifteen or twenty pages—in one night because my publisher was coming up to Vermont, and I was leaving for England the next day, and he wanted to take the manuscript back with him. I had to have something. What had been an ineffective realistic scene about people coming for Lyman—his wife and his son together, to get him—didn't seem to work. So it gradually just converted into that nightmare. I left him there in bed sweating and listening to the night sounds of traffic on the grade. I suppose it sounds as if he did have an epiphany. What I had meant him to have was something that Eisinger would probably protest—an ambiguous epiphany, a wondering rather than a decision . . . .

A question. He wonders if he'll be man enough.

Yeah, a question. I didn't really want to answer that question because it seems to me egregious to say all of a sudden: Well, now having thought it all through and having worked out this novel and finished understanding his grandmother's life and coming to the point of crisis in his own when he's scared he really can't make it any more by himself, he will have an epiphany and accept what up to now he hasn't accepted . . . . I think he might *wonder*, and that's as far as I wanted to take him. If that's an epiphany, all right, but it's got a question mark after it.

He's at least willing to ask that question now when he seems to have been running away from that question earlier.

Well, he's several months further along, and he has worked through a good many of his personal questions as well as most of his grandmother's. He's thought a good deal about all of this, and he's several months closer to the time when he'll be incapable of looking after himself. He's had the scare that Ada is laid out and won't be able to go on . . . he's lost his helper. I suppose the scare more than anything else would bring him to that question: Can I or can't I? Will I or won't I?

Some reviewers with a New Left bent thought you were too critical of young radicals in Angle of Repose, *but it seems to me that you were saying that too often youthful revolutionaries of the 1960s had little sense of history and were championing their revisionist ideas as if they were the first to think of these innovations. Is that correct, at least in part?*

That's correct. I would insist upon it, in fact. A lot of the young radicals of the sixties struck me as being hare-brained. They *didn't* have any sense of history, and so they had no notion that anybody had had those ideas before them. Their ideas of communes, for example. The whole history of the United States is full of them—full of their failures too. More than that, I knew quite a few of these young radicals, and it didn't seem to me that if the world were to be remade they were the people I would want remaking it. It's always very easy for young warriors to ride off to war and remake the world. They often end up scalps on somebody's spear. I am not at all sure about reformers. It does seem to me that when reformers set out to remake the world somebody has to say, "Are you the person designed for this; do you have the wisdom and the experience and the sense of history, the courage, the persistence, and the rest of it that it would take to make even the *smallest* improvement in this very hand-to-mouth kind of life that we live?"

You mention that when Benny DeVoto got into his pulpit you wanted to discount him ten percent. I suspect when these young radicals get into their pulpits you wanted to discount them more than that.

I wanted to discount them almost a hundred percent because all I respected was their emotions. Their minds I didn't respect; their minds weren't working. They were, as Benny used to say, "throbbing, not thinking." I don't think you remake the world with throbs. I was on the same side with them on a good many issues, but whenever they opened their mouths they alienated me. I was about ready to define a radical as a person who made a difficult situation impossible.

Although it is true that Angle of Repose *was atypical of much fiction written in the late sixties and early seventies, the novel won the Pulitzer Prize in 1972 and high praise from many reviewers. How do you account for this?*

Why it's easy to account for—it's a good book. It also should be said, though, that the *New York Times* never reviewed *Angle of Repose*. John Leonard, or somebody there, disliked it intensely. There was a whole kind of fiddle-around there. The publishers were upset; they kept calling him up to say, "When is it going to be reviewed?" Finally, as I heard it, he reported that the reviewer to whom it had been sent had so ripped it apart that he wouldn't publish the review. Later, when *Angle of Repose* instead of *Rabbit Redux* won the Pulitzer, Leonard wrote some kind of piece which people reported to me, blasting the choice. I didn't read his piece, since he obviously couldn't read mine. Shortly after that Leonard left the *Times Book Review*. He never did review *Angle of Repose*, but finally, having been forced by a lot of letters, queries, and publishers' pressures, he had somebody write a destructive piece on the back page—a kind of retrospective review— six months or so after the book came out. The *Times* did not treat the novel; it attempted to destroy it. I have forgotten who the Pulitzer Prize judges were in 1972. Those things, of course, make a profound difference. If you happen to get three judges who like it, your book can be absolutely unorthodox according to the fashions of the time and still win a prize. If the judges had happened to include John Leonard, then Updike would certainly have won the Pulitzer Prize that year. *Rabbit Redux* is a very different book from mine. Mine is old-fashioned by comparison—deliberately, conscientiously old-fashioned.

I raised that question because trends in American fiction in the late sixties and early seventies were so different from the setting, period, and point of view in Angle of Repose. *It dealt with a region and time and exhibited a tone quite different from much of the fiction of the late sixties. It certainly did not have the spirit of young liberals reacting to the counter-culture of those times.*

No, I wouldn't say it was a young liberal's or swinger's book. But it is also true that the *Times* didn't review *Spectator Bird.* So that they had a complete, one hundred percent record.

By that time was Leonard gone?

No, I think Leonard was still there. I haven't any idea what he has got against me, but he must have something because you can't skip over two books, both of which win prizes, without having a reason. It's a funny thing. *Spectator Bird* was even more a freak, I think, than *Angle of Repose. Angle* was a big novel and *Spectator Bird* was a relatively small one. But *Spectator Bird* didn't get a review in either the *New York Times* or the *Los Angeles Times*; it didn't sell quickly as a paperback. I don't understand things like that. I finally sold the paperback myself to Dave Gilbert at the University of Nebraska Press when it was obviously not going to be sold to anybody else.

And yet it won a National Book Award.

Yes. And I think, looking over the books that year, that it legitimately was among the book award candidates. I do know who the judges were. There, I suppose, I had the break of a couple of elderly judges who were judging books by something like the same standards I was writing them by. Otherwise, *Spectator Bird* could have easily dropped through the hole.

I have always had the feeling that it took the American reading public a year or two to catch up with Angle of Repose. *Since it didn't get all the publicity it deserved, readers found out about the novel through word of mouth, and so the work caught on more slowly than it should have.*

Well, it was a Literary Guild selection. Its advance sale was 30,000 or so. It wasn't completely ignored by any means. It sold about as well as any book I ever wrote, but it didn't have any particular appeal abroad. It was published in England and, I think, nowhere else. But that I understand. It's pretty colloquial American, western American. Everybody abroad gets his notions of what American literature is about by reading the *New York Times Book Review*, anyway. That gives you a very, very funny view. If you're a literary scholar and go by the *Times Book Review* you will have a very odd canon of American literature.

Or, since Angle of Repose *is about the West, many readers—here and abroad—would think it must be in the Zane Grey tradition of the popular Western.*

That's part of the problem—you have to escape from the taint. Touching pitch you might be defiled. It's not a fashionable stance to be in, to be writing serious novels about a country which is either ignored or can only be treated mythically. I've mentioned that dilemma before.

I agree with those who list Angle of Repose *as a first-rank novel and your most significant work to date. Do you think of it as one of your most important books, as a novel that reflects some of your most strongly held views?*

Oh, I think so, sure. I was guilty here and there of using Lyman Ward as a mouthpiece. I was certainly guilty of using him as a reflection of some of the preoccupations that I had. I didn't necessarily force him into the answers I would have made, but I certainly made him reflect some of the questions. The whole way in which the region, both past and present, is pushed between the covers of one book, along with attitudes both Victorian and contemporary—and both East and West. Yes, it is the most ambitious book I have done, and maybe technically the most expert. Just by plain brute force I had to do it because it was hard to do. By comparison, *Spectator Bird* is relatively simple. It may be just as good a book in its way, but it was much simpler to do. It took a lot less time too.

I asked you earlier if Big Rock Candy Mountain *wasn't a turning point in your career. Wasn't the publication of* Angle of Repose, *its acceptance, and its winning the Pulitzer Prize another pivotal point?*

Oh, sure. You go a long, long time and don't get any particular recognition. You don't find your name mentioned in the lists of the important writers, and that irritates you when you know you're as good as a lot of them, and better than some. I have a feeling that having left Harvard in 1945, I more or less withdrew from American literature. I was much more in it there, even though I didn't live in New York. My name got mentioned, I was visible, I had lunch with people now and again, people knew I was there. Coming out here, I had the feeling that I gradually receded over the horizon and disappeared. The books came out and were often respectfully received, but I was no longer a *presence* in any way. It went on and on until pretty late in life. I had a feeling that I had disappeared. In fact, I deliberately, just out of sheer rage, quit writing novels for ten years after 1950. What had I written? I guess the Joe Hill novel, which I had spent a lot of time on and which I thought was a respectable novel of a kind. It was

completely ignored. Again, I suppose I had chosen an unfashionable and
unorthodox way of doing it. I did a proletarian novel fifteen years after
the proletarian novel was dead as a doornail. And I didn't do it from the proletarian point of view. I did it from a more or less judicial stance. And that
was so ignored that I said, "Oh, the hell with it; I obviously have no public
out there. What I write doesn't interest anybody. I might as well quit trying
to write novels." And I didn't for ten years.

*Your career reminds me a bit of the problems Wright Morris has had.
A good writer accepted as a good writer, and yet there's not that public
out there to give the deserved response . . . .*

Wright's actually had more trouble than I have. He doesn't like to be
reminded that he's the most ignored good writer around. And I don't blame
him. It's not an enviable posture to be in because all it does is emphasize
the fact that you're ignored. The word "ignored" gets listened to more than
"good." He's been very busy producing a book every year or so. He hasn't
been able yet to crack the kind of stone wall against him. Publishers are
for him, and he goes back to Lincoln, Nebraska, and gets feted. University
of Nebraska Press has revived all his stuff, keeps it in print. But he still
doesn't have for his new books any eager and waiting public. I don't know
whether I do or not. In a way the opera of *Angle of Repose* was a curious
kind of break. As San Francisco's contribution to the Bicentennial, that had
a lot of publicity, and many people reacted as if I had written the opera—
as if I had done something new and special. I hadn't done anything; I was
just waiting around in the wings while other people did the transformation
from one medium to another. But it did get a lot of publicity and even
though it didn't wow a lot of people—the music was a little difficult for
most—it was still that kind of theatrical or entertainment publicity which is
often an indispensable element in a literary reputation. It shouldn't be, but
it often is. The more you stab your wife or throw big tantrums or big parties
the more your literary reputation seems to grow. It seems to me a frivolous
way to get a literary reputation. But I am *sure* the opera did something,
and the two prizes have done something. They are a kind of advertising
point. I am sure I am taken more seriously simply because I can be adver-
tised as the winner of the Pulitzer Prize and the National Book Award. It
does pay to have them, although there is a question as to how far they carry
you—what good they do for you ultimately. A little bit, I suspect.

*Does your publisher have any way of knowing where you have sold well?
The Bay Area sales versus the sales in New York City . . .*

I haven't the slightest idea, but I am perfectly aware that my reputation
in the Bay Area is probably stronger than anywhere else. That's not always

true. You can be known somewhere else and no particular hero in your own household. But my local audience is very responsive and loyal. Things like the Commonwealth Club awards. It turns out that I have won more Commonwealth Club medals than even John Steinbeck. If my national reputation were as good as my local reputation, I would obviously be selling a lot more copies.

Angle of Repose, *then, sold as well as any of your novels?*

Yes, it was, as I said, a Literary Guild selection . . . also a First Editions Club selection. So there were two editions besides the regular one, and the regular bookstore edition had an advance of, I think, 31,000. I don't know whether it sold many more than that. About 36,000, as I recall. But that's a good sale for me. I think *Recapitulation* didn't do more than 20,000, right around there, which is all right; it turns the corner, and the publisher gets his money back. *Recapitulation* was also an Alternate Book-of-the-Month and a First Editions Club choice. The book club things help the publisher past his difficulties and get me out of the red ink. I'm in the black at Doubleday now; I've earned all the advances they advanced me and something more. Occasionally I get a check. But to live I have to keep writing for magazines or giving lectures or doing stints at colleges. If we were living simply on my books we would live more meagerly. We might survive, but I wouldn't be as fat as I am and having to diet.

6. On the Mormons

Etulain: I suppose your first contact with the Latter-day Saints was during your high school years in Salt Lake City. What were your first impressions?

Stegner: I'm not sure I remember any first impressions that were in any sense religious. The first impression I had of the Mormon Church was of what the Mormons called Mutual, which you know about. Every Tuesday night, down in the ward amusement hall, youth activities go on, classes of one kind or other, Boy Scouts, Girl Scouts, all those other organizations that Mormons are very good at. I fell into that with great eagerness. The first thing of that kind that I had had at all was in Great Falls, where, though I was too young to be a Boy Scout, I was a Cub Scout, I guess, or something, and I liked uniforms, I liked uniformity, I liked belonging to things, and so when I got to Salt Lake I instantly was a Boy Scout. I've forgotten what ward, but . . . I liked it. That gave me a kind of hole to crawl in, and I liked it very much. It was good for me, but with no sense at all of any religious temptation. As a matter of fact, about the time when I began to have the usual adolescent religious questionings, I had already shifted from whatever Mormon ward I started in and gone over to an Episcopalian Boy Scout troop. There were two Episcopalian Boy Scout troops in Salt Lake which were, at least among our crowd, held to be the best outfits in town. I belonged to one, and we often went on camping trips with the other one for a week or two at a time up in the Uinta Mountains. We joined forces in a non-Mormon, even in some cases anti-Mormon, coalition. But certainly my first initiation into anything like that was through the local wardhouse where the neighbor kids around me went, and I just naturally went along.

You mention in The Gathering of Zion *[1964] that you "have a warm admiration" for "the everyday virtues of the Mormons." What characteristics did you have in mind when you made that statement?*

I suppose what I had in mind is precisely what people have in mind when they speak of the New England virtues. The old-fashioned virtues, the virtues that have to do with hospitality, with family life, with the sort of welcome that strays have in a big family. In Utah, then, you could fall in with a family which had nine kids. You probably still can there more than anywhere else. They were big families, and they were warm and open families. They had a lot of what I'd always missed; though our family was tight, it was not that kind of warm and open family. It was closed, closed against the world instead of open to it. These people were so confident of their family life that they just threw open the doors in every direction. It wasn't a desperation move, in other words, but part of living their religion. The family is so important in Mormon religion that without it the religion would hardly exist. And all of that meant a kind of welcome which I had never seen, which I tried to express in some way in *Recapitulation*. Though the Mulder family I created in *Recapitulation* was a Jack Mormon family, it was still part of the same sociology. The virtues are essentially virtues of hospitality and familial warmth, and also, quite commonly, a degree of community responsibility that, on a frontier, I hadn't seen much of. No, that was a society which, for better or for worse, was a developed society rather than a developing one. It had come developed. They traveled on the road like villages already developed, organized humanity instead of disorganized.

You also mention that you find Mormon women incredible. I suppose you mean the endurance, hard work, and patience on the overland trails, or did you have something . . .

I had been reading a lot of Mormon women's journals of the handcart companies and the early wagon trains, and also some of the journals of women who were part of the whole Nauvoo complex, and whose husbands sometime during that period took another wife, or two, or three—women who put up with that, who put up with the constant birth and death of children. Children died like flies along that route and sometimes had to be carried along for days before they could be buried. In the middle of horrors like that, the husband would get called on a misson and go off to England, and given the communications system of the time the wife might not hear from him for two years. He wouldn't hear of the death of his children until

eighteen months after they had died, that sort of thing. Women who put up with that kind of hardship had something, a good deal on the ball. Though I wouldn't have put up with it for a minute myself, I have to admire their stoicism and their faith and all the rest of it that let them do it.

And it seems to me that as I look at the church and the culture that surrounds it, there's been a continuation of that kind of commitment. Women right at the core of keeping the family alive.

Women are the sacrifice area of Mormonism. They were expected to sacrifice and they did. And they still, of course, not only sacrifice but go out and fight the church's battles for it against NOW groups and ERA. It's a very comic situation. What you would think of as these women's own best interest is precisely what they are most adamant to resist. Not all the women in Mormonism have been that way, but that's the kind that the church has been at some pains to develop. I remember in—the United Order down around Orderville by Zion Park. The thing really broke up over women's dress, because it was a very stoical, Spartan, homespun, linsey-woolsey kind of community, and all the women wore bags of clothes that they wove themselves out of the coarsest kinds of fiber. Eventually they just wouldn't do it. I'm sure that's why Orderville broke up. The women wanted to be pretty.

If some of the Mormon ideals have been eroded in the group's hundred-and-fifty-year history, what ideals have they been able to retain? You've mentioned one already, the family ideal.

That's at the very heart of it. Obedience, insofar as obedience is indeed a virtue, listening to counsel, hearkening to counsel. It's a very disciplined society, like Japan's. People do what they're told, most un-American really, and it's stimulating to see what that sort of society can do under certain circumstances, particularly under the circumstances of catastrophe or disaster. I guess the latest example of it was the rescue the church put on when the Teton Dam went out. Most of the people under the dam were Mormons, and it was the Mormon Church which did the best job of rescue and relief. They organize extraordinarily well for crises. They of course . . . Joseph was a wise man and put away enough during the seven rich years to feed people during the seven lean years. Mormons are forethoughted too—they always think that way. Those basements full of a year's food in case Armageddon comes are echoes of this strange kind of frontier belief in miracles and the end of the world, but also evidence of Mormon forethoughtedness.

Mormons in that part of the country saw the Teton Dam disaster as a kind of test.

I'm sure they did. Everything becomes a kind of test. It's almost Russian; it's not American. People love to suffer and see how much they can bear. I'm sure the harder you push the Russians, with their background and their general body of beliefs, the harder you would find them to push any further. The Mormons would be the same way. I would hate to get into a guerilla war with Mormons, they could be hard to dislodge.

When Frederick Jackson Turner wrote about the influence of the frontier on American life, he emphasized nationalism, democracy, and individualism as three results of the frontier experience. Has the Mormon experience differed from the picture that Turner painted?

Oh, absolutely. In place of nationalism, democracy, and individualism I suppose you'd have to put sectionalism, theocracy, and community. They really *are* un-American. You can understand exactly why unwashed frontier communities found them hard to live with and why they found it hard to live with the unwashed communities. They looked upon those people as without the true word. Nationalism, of course, came on later. Nowadays I suppose you'd find as many patriots among Utah youth as you do among southern youth. I think the enlistment rate and so on is very high and the kind of patriotism that rises in wartime is maybe more fervent in Utah than in most states of the Union, partly because of the habit of obedience. But it's

taken a long time for Utah to join the Union to that extent, as you know—
I don't have to tell you.

*That comment leads to another question. I once heard an LDS historian
suggest that Mormons were radicals in the nineteenth century but that
in the twentieth century they have become conservatives. How could
that be?*

Well, they were radicals *to* the society around them in the nineteenth
century. There weren't many radicals *within* their own society. Any radical
who failed to raise his hand when Brigham Young called for a vote would
find himself out of the Tabernacle very fast. They weren't radicals if by
radicals we mean dissenters. But Mormon beliefs, the groupiness, the polygamy, the habit of voting solid, and all the rest of it put them at odds with
gentile communities, particularly in Missouri and Illinois. I think they were
always conservative, in other words, and I don't think they've changed much
that way, though for a long time they voted Democratic because Joseph
Smith had aspired to run for the presidency on the Democratic ticket. Then
sometime, I think in the seventies or eighties, when prosperity began to come
to Utah, they were all advised and urged and counseled to turn Republican,
and they all dutifully did, and they've been—at least in national politics—
pretty Republican ever since. It's an up-and-down state like all the Rocky
Mountain states; you get variations, but generally speaking that's a conservative part of the world. The Reagan Republicans probably have as solid a
constituency there as anywhere.

*I suppose it would have been difficult to be a Mormon and a Republican
early on because the Republicans used the phrase the "twin relics of
barbarism" in referring to slavery and polygamy.*

Oh, sure. But when those hostilities were finally salved over, and when
the church itself became rich, it found that the Republican party was its
proper party. This may be part of the gradual joining of the Union by Utah,
and it certainly joined it on the conservative side.

*In their semiannual General Conferences, Mormon leaders often exhort
church members to learn from their heritage. What kinds of lessons can
(or could) Mormons learn from their history?*

The things they do learn from their history are ambiguous. One of them,
of course, is that paranoid lesson of persecution. Mormons always expect
to be persecuted. It's something they can learn from their heritage, but they
could also learn from the last eighty years that persecution doesn't exist
anymore—not in the ways they often envision it. I think they do learn the
lesson of stoical bearing of hardship and pain. It's a test of their faith, a test

of their solidarity. If they really learn from their heritage, I suppose they would learn some other lessons too that might not sit quite so well with the hierarchy. For instance, they could learn that the theocracy in Utah was a police state with a secret police and all the rest of it, which most Mormons won't grant. If they do grant, they just sort of wave it away, cover it over with dead leaves. But it's a very early example of a theocracy ruled by a priesthood. Existing on the frontier as it did, it had relative freedom of action for ten years or so in Utah, which gave it a pretty stiff and rigid form, and it was hard to resist. The gentile literature about the destroying angels and all the rest of it is lurid and exaggerated, but it's not based upon myth. It's based upon a fact. There *was* such a guy as Port Rockwell.

I was thinking of the first point you were making and the song, "Come, Come Ye Saints," in which the refrain says that they're going to come out West, be away from people, and be free to do what they wish. That song is still sung, and I'm sure that refrain has a great deal of meaning to them. Mormons wish to do what they desire, and yet they often feel that gentiles are after them.

Of course we can be mistaken about our heritage can't we? We have the same feeling about the Puritan fathers in New England—that they came to the United States in order to escape persecution, which was true enough. But they meant to be free in their own particular kind of worship, and immediately they began to hang Quakers and whip heretics of one kind or other and chase Roger Williams down to Rhode Island. Puritanism in New England was by no means an open religion, which is the way tradition would lead us to believe. Actually it went toward a sterner kind of repression than it had suffered itself in England. And the Mormons reproduced that particular aspect of the American tradition, almost verbatim.

Isn't there a paradox here? The Mormons plead their Americanism, and yet they emphasize community, cohesiveness, and a kind of theocracy in contrast to an American system said to be based on individualism, personal freedom, and separation of church and state.

Of course there's a paradox, but there are paradoxes like that all over the American tradition. It's true to a degree of Catholics; it's true to a degree of many religious sects which have on occasion been at odds with individualism, personal freedom, and separation of church and state. The Catholic Church has had that quarrel from the very beginning in this country. Individual Catholics have suffered also from all kinds of persecution from the democratic mass because of the Know-Nothing notion that they give their loyalty to the pope, or the Knights of Columbus, or something, instead of to the United States government. That paradox obtains wherever you have a disciplined subgroup within the whole group and where the subgroup itself has either invented a different kind of sociological and theological framework or has imported it. The ones that are imported tend to erode, little by little. I suspect that Mormonism on all its edges has eroded in the same way because the pressures of the loose and ad lib society outside are erosive.

Don't you think the change in status of blacks in the church, for example, illustrates some pressure that the church has felt from outside?

Of course, of course. The only revelation that I can remember any president of the church having practically since Brigham Young or Wilford Woodruff, until the revelation about blacks, was the one that had to do with the holy underwear. Heber J. Grant had it, and it came with the advent of silk stockings. It simply was true that you couldn't get Mormon women, the young women particularly, to wear the garments when there was a big wad showing underneath your silk stockings and when skirts got shorter and shorter. Mormon women were going to wear short skirts and silk stockings in spite of the church. In other words, fashion in that case was stronger than the church. Personal adornment was stronger. So Heber J. Grant had a revelation that the holy underwear could be just as holy if it ended above the knee. That isn't the way it was laid down first, but that's the way it came out, and a very timely revelation too—just like this one on the blacks. The next one will have to do with women, but it may take twenty-five or thirty years.

The noted American historian Daniel Boorstin, in comparing the Puritans and Quakers of the seventeenth and eighteenth centuries, praised Puritans for their willingness to compromise their ideals and in doing so to leaven a nascent American society; conversely, he criticized the Quakers for being too doctrinaire and unwilling to compromise. If one follows Boorstin's divisions, have the Mormons been more like the Puritans or the Quakers?

It depends on the Puritans at what time and the Quakers when, I suppose. The Quakers were always unreconstructed and unwilling to compromise, but so were the Puritans, in the beginning. All of those persecutions and hangings and drivings and whippings of Quakers were not the acts of compromisers. I'm not historian enough to debate Mr. Boorstin on that. It is certainly true that Puritanism broke down and degenerated into congregationalism and ultimately into Unitarianism. But I think that what broke down was Calvinist doctrine. In matters of personal integrity, the general notion of honesty as the best policy, a certain hard-mouthed integrity —really, those are still present in New England and the Puritan tradition. You see them more in New England, I think, than you do anywhere else, though you see some of them in Utah, too, probably derived from New England. Those things didn't get compromised, exactly, they just got de-theologized. They became, from a religious faith, something like a social ethic. I don't think the values were compromised. The faith itself may have been. When you hang and whip people, you don't do it out of ethical conviction, you do it out of religious conviction; and when the religious conviction breaks down you find yourself able to get on with people better. I don't know about Quakers; Quakers were notorious, or have been notorious, for doing very well in the business and financial world; I don't know whether that's a compromise or not. Doctrinally, I'm not very up on Quakers.

I was thinking of Woodruff's decision in the 1890s, the one on dress that you've just mentioned, and the one on the role of blacks. Here are pressures from the outside world on the church, and its decisions make it more like the world. The church becomes more like the world rather than moving in the opposite direction of separating itself from the world.

Maybe the difference is that the Quakers always represented the absolute dissidence of dissent. They were individualists in the way that Mormons and Puritans both were not. You did your own walk with God, and you sat in Meeting and you communed by yourself in silence . . .

And there was no prophet making a decision for you.

That's right, and the social structure of Quakerism was not a structure at all; it was just a collection, a mosaic of individuals, with the result that there was nothing there to compromise. There was only the individual; you came right down to him. What has compromised in Mormonism is, I think, social behavior, particularly polygamy and fashion. And of course in each case, in the case of the underwear, and in the case of the blacks, what gave way was something built absolutely into the theology. These were revelations by Joseph Smith in the first instance. I don't know where the holy underwear comes from. Perhaps from *The Pearl of Great Price* or the *Doctrine and Covenants*, one of those books of orders and laws, perhaps from temple ceremonials. In either case, it had sanctity. There isn't any question that it took a major operation to change it. The same goes for blacks, who of course are cursed of God in the Mormon story. And if you're cursed of God it's a little hard to figure out how you can come uncursed, particularly when it happens under social pressure like this. That act was absolutely necessary, for the church, but I think it begot a good deal of cynicism on the part of the church's critics.

You note in the opening pages of The Gathering of Zion *that Mormons have a "stylized memory of the trail" west. Isn't this a tendency in most Mormon history? Haven't the Mormons, like the Jewish writers in the*

Old Testament, produced "committed history"? Hasn't Mormon historiography often been an apology for the church's beliefs?

Oh, sure, absolutely—partly because it is a history of real persecution and in large part also because the paranoid memory of persecution begets a conviction of continued persecution, with the result that you can't see anything critical of the church that isn't a dagger aimed at your heart. The motivation for an awful lot of Mormon historians—very few, I think, escape it—has been precisely the defense of the faith. Not the impartial discovery of truth but the defense of the faith. The truth is given; it's there in the Mormon history and in Joseph's revelations, talks with God. You don't have to search for truth, the truth is there. What you do have to do is explain, I suppose, how everybody comes to hate you so.

Bernard DeVoto and Fawn Brodie, two well-known historians with Mormon backgrounds, have been sharply critical of early church leaders. Are their interpretations to be accepted, or should one make large allowances for their alienation from their upbringings?

One should make a good many allowances on Bernard DeVoto because he was only half Mormon to begin with; his mother was Mormon and not a very good one. His father was Catholic, and the training, the upbringing was all Catholic. Benny was never brought up a Mormon. He only lived in a Mormon community, and he was the only boy in a Catholic girls' school, and he was an altar boy and he assisted at the Mass. So far as he knew religion at all, he knew it as a Catholic, and he knew it with the kind of condescension that Catholics often feel toward Mormonism. The Mormons are Johnny-come-latelies and imitators and preposterous inventors, whereas the true tradition is ours. So Benny was always contemptuous of Mormonism. He grew infinitely more contemptuous of it in 1914–15 when he was a freshman at the University of Utah and that so-called Kingsbury scandal came about. You'll have to check it; my memory of it is imperfect—but in some way there was a conflict of roles between the Mormon and gentile faculty in the University and the pressures from above seemed to be strongly in favor of increasing the Mormon influence, with the result that I think about fifteen members of the faculty, mostly from the English department, quit all at once, and the whole thing was a terrific scandal. The AAUP investigated and blacklisted the University. President Kingsbury eventually resigned. This was the one year when Benny was at the University of Utah. He left Utah in a big cloud of scandal and controversy, full of contempt for the whole state.

Fawn Brodie, on the other hand, I think was very surprised to run into trouble with the church. In fact, I know she was—she has told me she was—

and so was Dean Brimhall, her uncle. She was terribly shocked when her book on Joseph Smith, *No Man Knows My History*, so offended the church fathers. She had gone off to school and in her innocent way studied to be a historian and assumed that a historian's job was to search for truth. She was interested in her own background, naturally enough, and got looking into Joseph Smith. I think she also had a singular interest in the sexual aberrations of people, because she did Richard Burton and she did Joseph Smith and she did Jefferson, all in something like the same terms, but that's for the critics to lay out. In any case, Fawn was perfectly innocent, I think, as a historian, and she was digging out facts hitherto unknown. She must have been aware that she was treading on ground that the church would consider sacred. But still she was shocked when her uncle excommunicated her. See, her uncle was in line to become and later did become the president of the church. She came to Dean Brimhall in tears, and Dean said she could hardly be comforted because she was so disrupted to be disfellowshiped. Every once in awhile when you're writing a book, the book itself can take hold of you so that you fail to look on both sides of it toward the consequences that it may bring about. I think she did that. She was—was she so sharply critical? I guess she was, in her way. On the other hand, she did something about Joseph Smith which I think is right. She reinstated him as a spoiled artist; he was a kind of untrained, spoiled novelist—somebody whose imagination worked in fictional ways. I suspect also that her picture of him as a person of great personal magnetism, somebody who was big and jovial, and whom everybody responded to, is an accurate one.

Benny DeVoto is rather contemptuous of Joseph Smith and very respectful of Brigham Young because Brigham was a hard man with a hard head. On the other hand, Brigham, it seems to me, is the one who is to be charged with all the secret police activities, with the destroying angels, possibly with the Mountain Meadows Massacre. A lot of things in Brigham's management of the Mormons after he got them to Utah don't stand too close examination. Admiration has to be tempered all the time, I think, by a certain scrupulousness, which doesn't . . . unless you can admire murder, and he was accused of being accessory to a good many. Maybe he carefully didn't know, but maybe he sent the Sons of Dan out. I don't think the Mormon historians have ever settled that one, and neither have the non-Mormon ones. They may never be able to. But it seems on the basis of Juanita Brooks's studies of the Mountain Meadows Massacre that in that particularly horrible mass murder Brigham was an accessory before the fact, and certainly after the fact. I don't suppose anyone will ever prove that he gave the orders. I doubt very much that he did, but he certainly contributed to the climate that encouraged hard feelings against the gentiles. So my admiration of Brigham Young is mixed, and my admiration for Joseph Smith is likewise mixed. But since I like bad writers better than ruthless politicians and colonizers, I'm more sympathetic to Joseph than to Brigham.

Will LDS and gentile historians ever be able to write full and balanced history of the Mormons if they are not allowed access to all the pertinent documents?

No, no, of course they won't be able to. Leonard Arrington assures me that now they are allowed access, and knowing Leonard, I think he believes that, and it may be absolutely true. I hope it is, because the restricted archives have always been a great difficulty. You can't have partial truth, you've got to have it all, and no historian can operate with some of the cards missing from the deck.

Did you experience any difficulties as you were writing about the Mormons?

I didn't experience any difficulties that really hampered me much. When I was writing . . . I guess *Beyond the Hundredth Meridian* [1954], a biography of Powell, I wanted to look at the Kanab Stake records because Powell had used Kanab as his base when he came off the river in 1870–'71, and his parties worked out of Kanab. So I wanted to find out the relationships between his group and the community. I thought there might be something in the Kanab Stake records, but the then church historian, who was Andrew Jensen, I guess, just sort of brushed me aside. Those records were not accessible. It didn't matter that much to me, so I never pursued it. I suspect that if I went to Leonard Arrington now and wanted to see the Kanab Stake records I could see them. And if I could, then any legitimate scholar probably could see almost anything. Unfortunately, scholars haven't been able to until recently, and so there's always been that little taint of the surreptitious and the underground about a lot of history written by non-Mormons. There is the suspicion that it might not wash. The Mormons get defensive and the non-Mormons blow it up into something more than it is, and controversy and dull prose are magnified again. The only way to get away from attack-and-defense history, it seems to me, is to throw the archives open to everybody. And I see signs that the church is finally ceasing to be quite such a closed society as it has been in the past. It's not stupid, you know; those are not stupid people, and I think they can understand their own best interest. By now it's safe too, even if it did turn out that Brigham was involved in the Mountain Meadows Massacre.[1] What harm does it do

---

[1] See Juanita Brooks, *The Mountain Meadows Massacre*, 2d ed. (Norman: University of Oklahoma Press, 1962).

the Mormon Church at the present time any more than the fact that some popes authorized the Inquisition? That history is pretty dead by now.

How is one to deal with such people as Joseph Smith and Brigham Young, whom the Mormons consider modern prophets and thus different from other men? Must gentile writers discount all supernatural incidents recorded in Mormon histories?

I think any gentile writer, any nonbeliever, is going to discount the supernatural incidents. When the quail fell on the poor camp beyond the Mississippi, I think they were exhausted quail that had flown across the river, a long flight for a quail. They had to come down, and they came down very opportunely for Mormons who were starving and in desperate straits. The supernatural probably doesn't have any place in either history or fiction. You have to deal with the supernatural as a motivation and a belief, but I don't think you have to believe the supernatural incidents. Even if you did believe them, I think you'd be wise to suppress your belief, for the purposes of history or fiction. I don't know what supernatural incidents you have in mind. The ones that spring to my mind are these episodes of the trail, the providential quail, the belief among Mormons that wolves didn't dig up Mormon bones, and that sort of thing. Probably the Mormons were better disciplined and buried their dead better. I would give them credit for making better graves.

I was going all the way back to the beginning. How does one deal with Joseph Smith and the supposed golden plates and these things?

Well, most gentiles find those events incredible, and some people find them preposterous. I find them incredible. But then I don't necessarily believe all I read in the Bible either, and the Bible has been the basis of at least two major religions, so you can't discount it. I doubt very much that I believe that the Lord appeared to Moses on Sinai and gave him the Ten Commandments, and I doubt very much that I believe a similar thing happened to Joseph Smith with the golden plates. What's striking to me in both of those things is the will of people to believe and the incredible lengths that belief will go to. You'll swallow almost anything if you want.

I suppose you could change words around and say it's the willing suspension of disbelief so you can believe.

Yeah, any theologian, I suppose, will admit that. You can't argue yourself into belief. You just have to believe. It's the act of faith. The giant leap. And I think that it's definitely true that no gentile, unless a very, very gullible one or one on the verge of conversion, is going to believe much of the Mormon story. For one thing, it's bad anthropology. The Book of

Mormon story is simply incompatible with what is known about the origins of the native Americans. I had a course in anthropology at the University of Utah in which I was taught that the Indians are the descendants of the Lost Tribes of Israel, that they came on up from South America as two tribes, the Nephites and the Lamanites, and that the Lamanites wiped out the Nephites in the final battle at the Hill Cumorah. I was also told by that same professor of anthropology that some marks in the granite in Little Cottonwood Canyon are the footprints of Christ, made when he visited North America. I don't know how college classes sat still for that, because that last detail not even the Mormon kids believed. But the professor was a man of great faith, one of those people who were put into the University through the actions of the church. There were one or two professorships which were church-endowed. Geology was one of them, significantly. Anthropology may have been another; I'm not sure. In any case, I remember being taught all that, and then going out and reading the reading list assigned for the class, and it's all about the land bridge from Siberia. Nobody except a true believer is going to accept the Lost Tribes story. You ask how should a historian deal with it. I think one has to deal according to his belief, sympathetically or otherwise, with the supernatural aspects; but one has to take very seriously the social and individual results of faith—what it does to people, and what it does to groups of people. That's the reality, it seems to me. It's just as effective as if it were true.

The power of myth, isn't it? It has its parallel in the western myth and how that myth has powered people's beliefs about the West, whether the idea is true or not.

Oh, sure, yeah. Whether it's true or not, it's equally effective.

On several occasions you've been asked why no great Mormon novel has ever been written. How have you usually answered this question?

Vaguely. I don't know why there hasn't been a good Mormon novel written, unless the constant attack and defense, the constant faith promotion from within the church in the face of what is, or is conceived to be, persecution, prejudice . . . [these feelings have not] permitted the kind of impartiality that a great Mormon novel would have to have. And anyway, I don't know what a great Mormon novel would be. I'm afraid for a good many Mormons it means a great novel justifying the Mormon faith. That isn't the way literary history would be likely to look upon a great Mormon novel.

What is a great Catholic novel, for instance? Heaven knows. There are a good many novels which are concerned with Catholic doubt and crises of faith and so on. I suppose Graham Greene is the contemporary example of somebody who writes from a definitely Catholic stance, but Huysmans and a number of others have written profoundly Catholic novels. They have many advantages because the Catholic faith is worldwide in a sense that Mormonism is not. Though Mormonism aspires to be. It's a faith of five million people against one of hundreds of millions, and it's a faith of a little over a hundred and fifty years as against two thousand. Its rituals don't reverberate in the same way. I don't think it's impossible that there might be a Mormon novel, but I would expect it to be a novel which took seriously Mormon society and Mormon sociology and was able to make within that context the kinds of dramatic character confrontations and pose the human dilemmas that one expects of a great novel. That would mean, I suppose, that the novel might be more about, shall we say, a father–son relationship than about Mormonism. Even if laid within the Mormon context, it's still a father–son relationship, and I'm sure that's much more likely to produce a great novel than one which limits itself to doctrinal matters.

I wouldn't think there's ever a chance of a Mormon novel which does limit itself to doctrinal matters. The best of the Mormon novels are such stories as Vardis Fisher's *Children of God*, which is simply the historical story told as novel, or Maurine Whipple's *Giant Joshua*, which is a settlement novel with Mormon context. It's the matter of the settlement that makes it an interesting novel. The kinds of crisis which the land itself produces interact with some others which doctrine, or political conflict, polygamy—the cohab difficulties—produce. You can get a good deal of mileage out of Mormon history. I don't think you can get much out of Mormon doctrine, because you can't make most readers believe in it or hold still for it. And we may be simply unlucky that Mormonism has not yet produced a good novelist, a really good one. There are some perfectly good novels of the standard passing kind, but if you're talking about a great tradition that will compete with the Conrads and the Henry Jameses, the Dickenses and the Dostoevskys, no, there isn't anything approaching that yet.

Although nearly all reviewers and commentators note differences between the hero of Big Rock Candy Mountain *and the Mormons, are there not some parallels one can draw between the dreams that fired the imagination of Bo Mason and those that inspired the Mormons?*

I don't think there's much difference between a dream of the Big Rock Candy Mountain and the dream of New Jerusalem. One of them is a purely material dream, but you can't say that the Mormon dream of New Jerusalem was entirely unmaterial. They inherit heaven in the flesh, you know, and with all their wives about them, and all their children and descendants and ancestors. It's a very material religion. Also, the church itself has set an example of busily making itself rich, and it doesn't discourage Mormon individuals from making themselves rich. Mormon individuals who become rich rise in power and influence in the hierarchy, generally speaking. As a matter of fact, wealth used to be one of the criteria by which the hierarchy would advise them to go and get extra wives. They could now join in some more, as it were, of the ordinances.

The dream of coming west toward New Jerusalem is of course a religious dream. That's Europe's oldest dream, but it's likewise a material dream, and the Mormon Church profited for years and years because it had an almost irresistible double combination to offer the poor of Europe— the black counties of England, the farm communities in Scandinavia, and so on. It offered them for one thing the hope of heaven, and for another free land, as well as the community of support which a lot of them took advantage of and needed. All that potential converts found hard to resist. Bo Mason is never satisfied with anything quite as pedestrian as the dream Mormons would settle for, but he's certainly motivated to keep on toward some ultimate Big Rock Candy Mountain which isn't very different from the streets of jasper and pearl of the New Jerusalem.

Among scholars of the American West, the work of leading Mormon historians like Leonard Arrington, Dale Morgan, and Juanita Brooks is well known. But novels of Mormon authors seem less well known. Why do you think this is?

I have said before that one of the temptations of western writers is to become historians rather than writers, because it's easier. It's almost basic. It's related to Hawthorne's notion that somehow or other in this country there were such lacks that the first job of a writer was to create a usable past. You remember in Henry James's *Life of Hawthorne* that list of things that this country lacks. The West is the latest example of a new country with a lot of lacks, a great shortage of cathedrals and royalty and tradition. It's harder to find in the West a society to write about, and fiction particularly comes out of social relationships, out of rich and varied and complex social relationships, more than anything else. Even when about individuals, it's more often than not about those individuals in conflict with or in relation to the complex society in which they are trapped, or with which they're in combat. That's all very difficult to find in a town as new as Rock Springs, Wyoming, say. You could hardly lay a major novel in Rock Springs. I can't imagine getting away with it. Fiction is far less likely about a town like Rock Springs than history is. The history of Rock Springs would be quite interesting, because the town has gone through several phases and it's been ripped off each time. I mean, it's been a hole getting deeper as history proceeds.

When you get to the specifically Mormon West, peculiar difficulties arise because in fiction you cannot explain, as you can in history, the social background and the sociological arrangements and structures in which your peculiar people function. You have to take them for granted, and it's very difficult because most of your audience won't be *able* to take them for granted. They will need explanation. Give them the explanation, and you become a bad novelist. The difficulties may cause you to become a historian, because you can explain things as a historian, where you can't as a novelist. Books like *Desert Saints*, for instance—you know that book by Nels Anderson; a good book, I think—and also Tom O'Dea's *The Mormons*, and Ray West's *Kingdom of the Saints*, explain the Mormon Commonwealth and the Kingdom, as it were. Fictionally, I can't think of anybody who's got away with it, very successfully, unless perhaps Maurine Whipple. Maybe Virginia Sorensen—one or two of hers, too. Those are both thoroughly competent writers, but I think their books would be less likely to catch an audience than historians' books on similar subjects.

It may be that having produced the usable past and having explained Mormon society sufficiently, the historians will have laid a basis for some later novels. Where are the novels of early New England? You don't really begin to get fiction out of New England until Hawthorne began to write it, and there had been quite a lot of history beforehand. That's partly because the Puritans didn't like novels and thought them frivolous and the work of the devil, but it's almost maybe because they couldn't have written them if they had wanted to.

Well, Hawthorne was able to take it right out of the history of his own family.

Sure. He had a past which he was busily engaged in making usable, but he had, after all, two hundred years of it to work with.

It seems to me that in the nearly forty years since you wrote your first book on the LDS, Mormon Country *[1942], until your recent essay in* Atlantic *[April 1978], you've retained much of your sympathy for the church and the people but at the same time have been willing to ask more wide-reaching and analytical questions about their heritage. In other words, you have become more analytical as time has moved along. Is that a fair conclusion?*

I think so. I wrote *Mormon Country*, as I guess I told you the other day (in Cambridge, though I came out for the summer to revisit Utah), out of sheer nostalgia. I wanted to get back west in flesh or in spirit, and the book gave me an excuse to come in both. *Mormon Country* was almost pure nostalgia, and there's nothing very analytical about it. It was simply reporting not only what I knew about Mormon history, which at that point wasn't a great deal, but also what I knew about Mormon sociology, about what living in Utah was like. People in Cambridge were likely to ask you such questions: "What's it like living out there in Utah?" and you began to think: "Well, what *was* it like?"; then I'd remember people like the postmaster from Manti, who used to come out of his shack next to ours at Fish Lake and dig a jug out from under the porch at six o'clock in the morning, or seven, and take a big, long swig, *Ah!* then go back in for breakfast. Relaxed Mormons—you couldn't make a Mormon like that credible without . . . sort of giving him a little space to expand.

Later, by the time I got around to writing *The Gathering of Zion*, I had read a great deal more, not only Mormon history, but history at large, and I'd written some more. I had done the biography of Powell which involved Mormon backgrounds to some extent, and the Joe Hill novel which likewise involved some Salt Lake background. I was altogether better prepared to ask some questions, though it doesn't seem to me yet that I'm very analytical or questioning. What I was trying to do in *The Gathering of Zion* was something very close to the Parkmanesque, Benny DeVoto thing—narrative history plus judgment. Well, I guess it was Bancroft who said it first, "Present a man in his own terms and judge him in yours," but I did want these people to present *themselves*. I was talking about a faith which I didn't happen to share, though it was perfectly plain in front of my eyes that thousands of these people were willing to die for it, so it couldn't be taken lightly. I therefore had to ask some questions about the nature of faith and the kinds of people who were recruited and the kinds of things that the Mormon Church offered. But I didn't ask very analytical questions about Mormon theology. It really doesn't interest me that much.

> *I was thinking that your parallel is a little bit like Perry Miller and the Puritans. Perry Miller was probably an agnostic, perhaps an atheist, and yet he dealt with the most religious of people and, I think, dealt with them in a very balanced fashion. No one would have come away from Perry Miller's books feeling that this man was anti-Puritan.*

Well, I hope nobody comes out of my books thinking I am anti-Mormon; I'm mixed about them. I suppose I have always made a distinction in my mind between the faith which I can't accept and the people whom I like as well as anybody—though politically I don't agree with the way they're going lately. Nevertheless, I'm sure that if I went to a door in Utah, I would get as warm a welcome as I would anywhere in the world. If I needed a crust of bread, it would probably be forthcoming. They'd probably sit me down and let me join a home evening hour and we'd end with prayer. I'd be singing with the children before the evening was over.

While historians of the nineteenth century rarely spoke in a positive or balanced fashion about the Mormons, recent historical accounts seem much more sympathetic. Why do you think this change has occurred?

Many reasons. One, they're no longer a threat to anybody, no longer conceived as a threat. They're no longer one of the twin relics of barbarism. Our view of polygamy itself, as a matter of fact, has changed. The more people have studied it, the more it's turned out to be a very Puritan institution. Mormon polygamy was not the sort of Susannah and the Elders kind of thing that it was conceived to be. It was clearly a sociological instrument for holding together a church which was composed pretty heavily of women, and converts who were largely female, and finding a place for them in a new country where survival was difficult enough for strong men. It could hardly have been done under any other terms. There would have been an awful lot of lost, helpless women. Polygamy is likewise, by almost any standard that I know, genetically a very good idea. The people who had many wives and who raised these massive families and whose family reunions now number six hundred or so were very likely to be the people who had come up through a very hard school and demonstrated staying power and capacity of one kind or other. To take only the most obvious example, the Young family has more than its share of distinction in contemporary times, in the descendants. I don't know how you judge that. I suppose by such things as entries in *Who's Who*. Dr. Russell Lee, the founder of the Palo Alto clinic, who comes from Spanish Fork and whose father was a Presbyterian missionary to the Mormons, gives them credit for being eugenically smart.

People do find out things about polygamy which make it seem far less fearsome than it did in the 1850s. As far as that goes, the sexual mores of the rest of the country have changed so much that now the Mormons can look upon the rest of the country as a depraved and lascivious lot. I remember a joke told by the late Heber J. Grant, a president of the church. He said, "You gentiles used to have polygamy too, but you called it stenography." Polygamy still exists as a fundamentalist underground, but it doesn't scare people the way it did in the nineteen forties, fifties, and sixties. The defiance of Utah as a kind of secessionist, semi-autonomous state doesn't mean anything anymore either. Secession was all settled in 'fifty-six and 'fifty-seven and again in 'sixty-one to 'sixty-five. Finally, there was a great deal of favorable publicity for the Mormons during the great Depression, when the rest of the country was paying out lots of tax money to support poor states, particularly the South, and the Mormon Church made a great thing about taking care of its own. It had all these bishops' warehouses full of canned vegetables and fruits put up by volunteers and distributed to the deserving. I don't think that system worked quite as well as eastern papers implied it did, but it certainly made Mormons look a whole lot better in the national eye. Moreover, our nation's wars have brought people together. In World War II there was a big surge of patriotism in Utah. I suppose in later wars, too— Korea and Vietnam.

But by and large, I think, they've just worn out the bad image; and the good image, or at least the better image, has now come to be that of a very successful, very slick, P.R.-conscious community, making a lot of money and going to make some more, allied to large corporations and corporate profits and not particularly careful of the environment that actually supports them. They've lost something in changing from a fully agricultural community to a potentially industrial one. They've lost something that Brigham would have had them keep. Still, they don't look so different from anybody else, and they do look, in some ways, more successful than anybody else, and so the history itself can be approached by the historians with far less foaming at the mouth.

You mentioned earlier that if Mormon fiction were to be written, and to be written at a high level, that such other topics as families, father-and-son relationships, or other aspects of Mormon sociology might be the subjects to be emphasized. What sorts of historical studies of the Mormons are needed? I heard Leonard Arrington say recently that the Mormons are planning something like a twenty- to twenty-five-volume history of Mormonism, along both chronological and topical lines. And he said, "It's going to satisfy—we're hoping that it will satisfy—two audiences: the church and the people who represent the leadership of the church, and scholars." Do you think that's possible?

I rather think that church leaders such as Ezra Taft Benson are not likely to be overjoyed at a completely unbiased, impartial history of any aspect of Mormonism. Some others, perhaps, might. It does seem that President Kimball has given Leonard Arrington a free hand as church librarian and historian—and that the liberated policies have his full approval. At least when I talked to him, he talked that way—and so did Leonard. I've never talked with Ezra Taft Benson. I have read him, and he doesn't seem to me to be likely that liberal. It can happen, since this is a hierarchy of old men, that Benson will be the next man in charge. The first presidency is very old, and any president of the church is almost certainly going to be seventy or more. And if Benson succeeds Kimball, who is by no means well, I would expect the liberalizing tendency of the last few years to be reversed, at least for a few years, until somebody succeeds Benson. You can't depend upon what amount of reform will last in that environment.

I don't know what historical studies the Mormons need; I don't know what twenty-five volumes Leonard has in mind . . . not being a historian and having played in the fields of the Lord only in limited ways, I'm not prepared to say what the essential studies should be. There are all kinds of possibilities. It might be very interesting to study the people who were converted, to make a study of Mormon converts in England, Scandinavia, and Wales, where a lot of them came from. And I've always been puzzled about Nathaniel Hawthorne, who was the American consul in Liverpool during the mid-fifties, when a third of all British emigrants to America were Mormon converts. They all came through Liverpool. So did the Scandinavians. Dickens visited those ships, and wrote about them, but Hawthorne, though he probably had to sign the papers for most of those ships as they went out, is silent about them. There's nothing in the *English Notebooks* to indicate that he understood what was going on, or had any interest in it. Nevertheless, if you studied the kinds of people from whom the Mormons gleaned their converts, I think you'd learn something about Mormonism.

The things that have been most dramatized are obviously such things as I've done myself. The trail, for one thing, the migration which has all the dramatic qualities of the exodus out of Egypt. That probably doesn't need to be studied much more, but I think all kinds of things—well, Leonard Arrington's own specialty of business history has great possibilities. A study of early Mormon economics would interest me. I would like to see where the church's money began to come from and how. That would take a lot of very deep digging into church papers that up to now have not been freely opened.[2]

We don't yet have a full and complete biography of Brigham Young, which I guess Leonard Arrington is working on.[3]

Well, that's good. Who else would you like to see try a biography of Brigham Young? Do you think Ray West could do it?

I suppose I would be interested in someone who understood religious and utopian ideas of the nineteenth century, who may or may not be a Mormon. It's been very interesting to me that in the last ten years or so there

---

[2]See Leonard J. Arrington, *Great Basin Kingdom: An Economic History of the Latter-day Saints* (Lincoln: University of Nebraska Press, 1966), and other titles. Dr. Arrington is presently (1983) Lemuel Redd Professor of Western History and Director of the Joseph Fielding Smith Institute for Church History of Brigham Young University.

[3]To be published by Alfred Knopf in 1984.

seems to be a tendency to send bright young Mormons, historians, to the very best graduate schools—to Berkeley, to Harvard, to Yale, to Chicago —and then to have them come back, either to teach at Brigham Young, or to work in the Church Historian's office. There's a coterie of bright young historians there in the Salt Lake–Provo area . . .

Well, I'd like to believe that actually, and it may well be true, but I have heard that the church still insists upon a degree of orthodoxy in the faculty of Brigham Young, which would seem to me to be a recipe for trouble. If people are trained in history the way Fawn Brodie was trained in history at Chicago, and then they go back to Brigham Young and find that they are going to be promoted on the strength of their faith rather than the quality of their intellectual life, it might make trouble. I don't know.

I'd like to ask you one final, personal, question. When I first met you in Logan, Utah, it was the first time I had heard you speak before a predominantly Mormon audience. I recollect the feeling that seemed to exist between the audience and you. They seemed to react in two ways. One, that they were delighted that you had written so much about the Mormons, and two, they almost thought of you as one of theirs. I wondered if you sensed that feeling, and if you did, how you reacted to it?

It's a case of regionalism, it seems to me, overriding religion. I was a local boy, and any region, I think, is delighted when some local boy does anything that gets his name in the papers. If this local boy has written something about the locality, that doubles it. A third element probably entered in, too—that I was a gentile who didn't turn out to be a Mormon-hater. So, I'm very happy to say that a lot of people in Utah seem to think well of me. That's fine. I think well of them, too. But I wouldn't think their approval is a very critical reaction. I think it's an emotional one—the same kind of reaction you could find now, for instance, all over Canada. If some Canadian writer writes a book that is reviewed on the first page of the *Times Book Review*, hurray!, you know, nationalistic feelings arise and people will be cheering one another with the notion that we can do it too. Leviathan has got one in the teeth, and we are not quite as provincial and second-rate as all those snobs back there think we are. There's an awful lot of that in any regional movement. Regionalists are almost as paranoid as the Mormons themselves, and we all think we're persecuted by New York. Maybe we are on occasion, but probably not to any great extent. We're ignored rather, and being ignored is worse than being persecuted. That really infuriates you. "Here I am," you think, "Notice me." I do think the Mormon audience, the Utah audience, Mormon and gentile, has been kind to me because it seems to them I'm a local boy who made good.

I can talk to Mormons, even though they know and I know that we don't talk exactly the same language. Many, many Mormons have sent me manuscripts on the theory that I know something about Mormon society and can judge the manuscript maybe better than some other people. I've read a lot of reminiscences of childhood in a polygamous household, for example. The authors, though they're perfectly good church members, are talking about an aspect of church life which has now passed, at least for the orthodox, and that they themselves disliked intensely. They expect that I, as a gentile, will be understanding of their feeling and sympathetic with it. Indeed I am, but I can't say that I've ever found a really good manuscript out of that kind of literature.

7. The American Literary West

Etulain: Is there a western regional literature? Do several western writers share a number of common characteristics?

Stegner: I think there is a sort of umbrella which covers most of the western region. But within that umbrella the regions are pretty disparate, sometimes as disparate as New England is from the Midwest. But I think there is a common denominator, a certain spaciousness for one thing—a sense of elbow room in people's minds and in what they write. A certain innocence, maybe. At least some western writers seem closer to the primitive beginnings, without the kinds of complications and corruptions that come with civilization. I guess I've talked about that in a number of essays which you know. Particularly in the one called "Born a Square," I was talking about a certain western innocence, even dewy innocence, in the teeth of the modern world.[1]

Modern literature and western literature are somehow irreconcilable, at least up to now. The kind of western writer who writes modern literature immediately abdicates as a Westerner, and the kind who sticks to the western attitudes is likely to be considered a little backward by the modernists. That dichotomy does persist. There are certain western writers who share common characteristics. I think you could tell, for instance, by reading Willa Cather, Walter Clark, Paul Horgan, H. L. Davis, or Benny DeVoto, that all of them are western. You could tell it partly by subject matter, of course,

---

[1] "Born a Square," *Atlantic* 213 (January 1964): 46–50; reprinted in *The Sound of Mountain Water*, pp. 170–85.

but also by manner and attitude. They would be different from Van Wyck Brooks; they would be different from other people comparable and contemporary. Not better, not necessarily worse, but different.

When Howard Mumford Jones was in his last years, as you know, he was trying to write a book about western literature, which he conceived to have been very badly overlooked by eastern critics. He thought that eastern critics concentrated upon a lot of secondary and tertiary figures because they were eastern, when something much more important was out here beyond the boundaries of their vision. I think Howard had a point. He never finished his book, and it's not a manuscript that's in any publishable shape; but he adduced a good deal of evidence to demonstrate that a lot of important writing was going on in the West from very early times. There were books written which somehow an American can't afford not to know. They were written in the West, and the East often didn't catch up with them, maybe is just beginning to catch up with them now. Their principal advocates have been students of western literature who, in turn, get checked off as being western regionalists and local patriots. I agree with Howard Jones that the establishment probably has never yet accepted a western literature, or many individuals in it, as being as important as they probably are.

We seem to be entering another era of increasing interest in things regional. Do you think that's a healthy trend?

It depends entirely on what you mean by regional. If you mean by regional that I am from the State of Utah, I write about the State of Utah, for the State of Utah, in the spirit of the State of Utah, and I don't care a damn about anything but Utah, then, no. That sort of regionalism is very unhealthy; it becomes a prison, a real prison. You can get stuck in the provincial; it's a very small hole. On the other hand, if you use the regional as a springboard or a launching pad instead of a prison, then you can be interested in the world; but you're interested in it from, somehow, the Western view, which is different from the East Coast view. The difference is probably instructive. It should be.

I think we all feel the lack, somehow, in a lot of our literary criticism— and to some extent in the literature as well—of the breadth of view that can come from a regionalism which is expanding and going out toward the world instead of closing away from it. The establishment has a tendency to be more parochial really than the regions. A Californian, for instance, gets around the world more, knows more about the United States, travels more, has more contacts with more different kinds of Americans, than any New Yorker I know. He's less parochial than the New Yorker, but the New Yorker lives at the literary center. He is limited in his perception of the country at large, and that limits people in other regions too, because most of

our literary commentary comes out of New York, and they feel they have to accept what New York says.

Well, put it back to the original answer. If regionalism is a launching pad, it's all to the good. If it's a prison, no. If it's just a matter of a local puff, praising something because a local boy wrote it—not because it's good —then it's no good either. I was telling you recently about the prizes that the *Los Angeles Times* is giving now. They're giving them *not* for West Coast books, but for books at large, combing the whole of America to find the prizewinners. But they're giving the prizes *from* Los Angeles and that makes the difference. Los Angeles is trying to be a launching pad and not a regional peekhole.

I remember one time saying to you it would be interesting to see a magazine like the Saturday Review *that would move west. We've both seen that. It did move west, and the move didn't work. Why? What happened?*

They blew it. They blew seven million dollars and then the chance. Yes. Because . . . I don't know, those particular owners had a wrong notion of the magazine. The *Saturday Review* when it was a literary review—which you probably don't remember because it was before your time—when it was the *Saturday Review of Literature*—was a limping marginal operation that never had a big readership. It was influential in its way, but it was not financially successful. The one who made it successful was Norman Cousins, who made it successful by adding Irving Kolodin's column on recordings, by adding a section on travel, by adding two or three things which made it a *general* magazine. Then all of a sudden it actually took off and was very successful and finally was sold, at great profit to Norman and to the other people who were involved in it. The people who bought it had made a success of *Psychology Today*, a single-interest magazine. They thought they should break the *Saturday Review* down again into its component parts, and did. There was a literary *Saturday Review*, a historical *Saturday Review*—four different kinds. They were published weekly, and the whole month finally came together as a general magazine. That move was a bust. I think what busted them was not moving to San Francisco, though some of their New York staff chafed at being that far from what they thought the center of the world. What busted them was a very bad notion of the marketing of a magazine and the market for the magazine. I would have gone on subscribing to the old kind of *Saturday Review* for quite a long time, but I got tired of that piecemeal *Saturday Review* fast; three out of four segments of it didn't interest me.[2]

That's about the only try in the last generation . . .

The only major try I know . . . well, the *Wall Street Journal*, of course, publishes a West Coast edition. The *New York Times* tried and failed—because they didn't have enough of a West Coast point of view, I think. You can't transplant an eastern magazine or an eastern newspaper here and go on publishing it with eastern attitudes, interests, and biases, and win a western audience. I think it's much better not to try to transplant eastern magazines here, but to grow our own. So far, no regional magazine has made a national place for itself, except *Sunset*.

I was thinking of some other attempts: for example, New West, West Coast Review of Books, San Francisco Review of Books. *They have tried, but I don't think they have reached a large number of readers.*

No, and it's unfortunate. A lot of western readers are bemused by the notion that these are regional operations, they aren't from headquarters. The headquarters are in New York. As long as you think New York is the headquarters, you're going to look upon everything else as second-rate, which is not necessarily so. *Sunset*, of course, is a special-interest kind of magazine. It's just wall-to-wall barbecues, how-to's, how to live in the West, but everybody in the West consults it, and it does some very good things. It is an

[2]*Saturday Review* ceased publication in July 1982.

extremely successful magazine, maybe the most successful magazine in the United States. I was involved in doing a movie on them last year, a movie that they will show to customers and advertisers. I went through the whole shop with Bill Lane, the publisher, and they came up here and shot some footage. We talked into microphones and made faces into the cameras, and it was kind of interesting. You can't look closely at *Sunset* without developing a considerable respect for the intelligence that goes into that operation, even though it's a kind of magazine which has no intellectual pretensions at all. It's about how people live; it's a continuing record of social history.

You have written recently, "there is a kind of provincialism, minus the aggressiveness and self-consciousness, that encompasses the most profound things a writer has to say."[3] Could you explain that statement?

Yeah, well that's related to what I was saying earlier about using provincialism as a springboard. The most personal reaction to landscape, to people, to ways of living, is that which is rooted in the local. So long as that local is not so absolutely eccentric, so completely out of the stream that it becomes merely local color, a strange picturesque kind of oddity, then the provincial basis is as good a basis as you can get. It's the kind of basis that Jane Austen had. She was talking about people in her world, a world of a particular kind, but they would be recognizable people in any world. One of the problems of Mormon fiction is precisely that Mormon society is so special that a Mormon writer can't project outside of it. He has to write his fiction from within, for a purely Mormon audience, or else he has to treat it as if he were a tourist, a foreign visitor coming to see the strange aberrations of the locals. But it's only among the Mormons, I think, that the problem occurs. The Northwest is recognizably a part of the United States, the Southwest is, the Great Plains, the Northern Rockies. The West Coast certainly is; it's one of the main ones. It may be the main one within ten years. It already is politically, and I suppose economically. The population flows from the Northeast and the Midwest toward the Southwest, the West, and the South.

So, I suspect those eastern seaboard biases, which are essentially the biases of power and influence, are changing already. In a short while we're going to find that opinion is made not in the Northeast, not necessarily, but in a lot of other places which are more in unison, and which together make a much bigger basis of power. Harvard is never going to shrink to a provincial university lost up in the northeast corner where nobody ever goes, but it could be that Berkeley will supplant Harvard as the major university center

---

[3]"The Provincial Consciousness," *University of Toronto Quarterly* 43 (Summer 1974): 307.

in the country. I think it's already true that Berkeley and Stanford between them probably are the equivalent of Harvard and Yale. They don't have quite the money, but they probably have the faculty and the students, and the plant, and maybe the advantage of youth and vigor. The young bulls with ambition come up against the competition of the old bulls of the herd. Anyway, the kind of provincialism that is aggressive, self-conscious, and limited to provincialism, I abhor. But the kind which says: "I am part of the world too, I see the world from my view, and it's just as good as your view, or at least is entitled to a hearing," that's another matter; I'm all for that.

I suspect that your essay "Born a Square" has been as widely read as any piece on western American literature. But that article was written nearly a generation ago—would you revise any of the ideas that you presented then?

I'm sure I would change it some, because events move on, and opinion with them. I doubt that the literature of the country is quite as sick as I thought it then, and the publishing situation has changed somewhat. But the basic stance from which I wrote the article remains the stance from which I still see things.

In the 1960s, when I wrote "Born a Square," we were more or less overwhelmed with freedom—we could say anything we wanted, and some writers got very aggressive about making use of their liberties and told us many things we didn't really want to know. There is still some of it. I was reading a review this morning about a new William Burroughs book, and I conclude from the review that it is precisely the kind of book I don't want to read—a form of literary poison. By now, though, most writers have suffered a reversion to sense and thoughtfulness and something beyond sensation.

As for publishing, we still don't have a publishing establishment of any real potency in the West, but what has been happening in trade publishing at large—the movie tie-ins, the paperback hype, authorial visits and appearances on the "Today Show," the effort to market books like pure commodities and milk the sensational ones of all their profitable possibilities— has driven out of many trade publishers' lists the good but unsensational books that used to sell a few thousand copies and hang around a long while and sometimes turn out to be enduring contributions to the literature. University presses such as Nebraska's, and a good many small regional presses, have been picking up some of that slack, because they can break even on a small press run, and at least the university presses are exempt from the IRS inventory tax, so that they can keep books in print. Eventually, that change will make a difference and perhaps bring about a solidly based western publishing industry. If it is smart, it will take on more than western books; it will take on good books of whatever coloration, for quality is a whole lot more lasting than regional piety. With luck, western publishers may ultimately publish books from western bases that are designed for reading by the whole country. If and when that happens, we will be over our regional agitation and growing pains.

In the other essay of yours that's so widely quoted, "History, Myth and the Western Writer," you state that the "typical western writer loves the past, despises the present of his native region." Why is that?

It's partly that the native writer is confused by the attitudes both of his own place and time and of other places and other times. He often accepts the evaluation of his present that other people make of it, and if, from an eastern point of view, or a midwestern point of view, or any other point of view, a western town is a place which is interesting only as a base for a vacation but a dull hole to live in, a place where you could give the world its enemas, you have a tendency to half-believe it. You shrink away from your present, but you do say to yourself: "Well, by God we had a really romantic past. Look at all those mountain men, look at all those arrowheads that Jim Bridger carried around in his back, look at those scalps he hung on his belt." You begin to romanticize. Benny DeVoto certainly did. The western past was a heroic age—that's quite simply what it was. The present never seems as heroic as the past, as Willa Cather pointed out in a number of books: it's there in *A Lost Lady*, it's there in *One of Ours*—the decline from the great past to the meager present. As Clarence King put it, the progress from savagery through barbarism to vulgarity; not to civilization, note, but to vulgarity. The kinds of little towns Willa Cather wrote about, in their meanness and their real estate mentality, are all some people find in western life. That's a leftover, a hangover from the twenties and the revolt from the village. I think most western people don't feel that way about their towns except in literary terms, but the stereotype persists.

I like the way that Lyman Ward puts it in Angle of Repose—*he didn't want to pan the gravel of Lola Montez anymore; too many others had already done that.*

Lola has been panned pretty thoroughly. You're not getting much more out of that old sterile rockpile. I was trying to justify my own approach in that novel. I didn't want to write a regional novel, I didn't want to write a historical novel. I wanted to write a novel which was written from local affairs, but which would echo or throw a shadow a whole lot further. I put my self-justification in Lyman's mouth.

One commentator on your writing cites a sentence in "Born a Square" as central to your career. He says: "we have [and he's referring to writers of regional fiction] all taken refuge in history, fictionalized or straight."

I've been resisting it. I put that idea into his head, of course, but I have been resisting it. In general I'm afraid it's true—again because of a lack of confidence in our own life as a legitimate basis for literature. It's new enough so we're still uncertain of it, and we're not at all sure that it's interesting enough to other people to warrant the effort of reporting it thoroughly and deeply. So we may fall back upon the thing which is by consequence much more salable: the past. You can always sell romantic western history. You can write from now till kingdom come about the mountain men and somebody will publish you. I'm not sure you could write successfully about modern Boise or similar places where the real life of the West goes on. The only way you're going to do it, as I think I said in that essay, is to do it the way Faulkner did Yoknapatawpha County. His were common people, living ordinary lives. He heightened them considerably, but there's enough violence in any ordinary life so that you can make use of it. There's certainly enough passion in any ordinary life. When Willa Cather said a novel is what happens today in this room, it's a passion within four walls, she was saying essentially what I'm saying in that essay: that you can make fiction out of anything if you have confidence that it's worth making. The problem has been, I'm sure, with most of us, a matter of confidence. We do fall back upon history, knowing we can sell it to *Holiday* or some place, instead of trying to render our real lives imaginatively.

Nearly every critic of your fiction has spoken of . . . and these are your words . . . "the middle ground" in your writings. What do you mean by those words?

You know, I've often wondered . . . . Forrest Robinson picked up that phrase, but where he picked it up from I'm not sure. I'm not quite sure of the context in which I said it. I thought I was talking about some middle ground between fiction and history, some business of the imaginative treatment of reality, but based on reality all the way. I'm not a fantasist, and I couldn't be if I tried, so that's for somebody else to do. I have to deal with the real world as I have known it. What I have known best is largely regional, provincial. Often it's limited in its geography to some extent. If that's what he means and what I meant by middle ground, then it is that middle ground in which we're using reality as the basis for fictional projections—what Mark Twain meant, I suppose, in his advice to young men: first get your facts and then do what you want with them. But first get the facts. I do think the real world exists.

The words "middle ground" are used in the title of a doctoral disserta-tion on your writings at the University of Utah, completed about ten years ago. That's where I'm taking the words from, although I know Forrest Robinson uses "middle ground" too.

What was that student's name?

Sidney Jensen.

Sidney Jensen, yes. I have a copy of his thesis around. I'm afraid I never read it carefully. It sounds as if I were talking about some kind of middle as between extreme liberalism or conservatism, or passion and restraint, or something like that. I'm sure I never meant that. I think I must have meant the middle ground between fiction and history, fact and imagination.

I was thinking of "middle ground" as a useful term for describing histori-cal fiction or artistic history—two possibilities of a mediating position.

In "On the Writing of History" I was talking about that particular opportunity that lies between the two extremes of absolutely objective factual history and the completely imaginary.[4] I do think that fiction ought to reflect the society out of which it arises—and I guess I like the kind that reflects the society more than the kind that reflects a personality, particularly an aberrant personality. That, again, is a kind of fiction I wouldn't try to write, and I don't know anything about. My kind derives from relationships among people rather than from the exposition of some anguish of soul in an individual—some private hell.

Have you ever felt isolated as a writer in the West, and has that isolation . . . if you have felt it . . . been a disadvantage?

Yeah, you feel isolated, you inevitably feel isolated because you're a long way from the engine room. You likewise get typed very rapidly. Book review editors, for instance, and editors at large—people who want literary jobs done—begin to think of who is there in the West to do something that they want written. They think Stegner, so they call me up. I swear, when Reagan was elected, or was about to be elected, the *New York Times*, the *Washington Post, New Republic, Atlantic, Harper's*—by a kind of backdoor —all came around asking me to do something on what kind of Westerner is Reagan and what does the new western surge mean politically to the country. They called me because they had all typed me as a western writer. I don't know anything about politics. I finally wrote a piece for the *Washington Post*, but only because I knew something about western history and western

---

[4]"On the Writing of History," *American West* 2 (Fall 1965): 6–13; reprinted in *The Sound of Mountain Water*, pp. 202–22.

character, and Mr. Reagan obviously didn't, so I pointed out what he didn't know. But I don't like to be labeled that way. I don't like, either, to be tagged as simply a conservationist and environmentalist writer. I would like now and again to be asked to review a novel instead of another book on western geography, geology, or water problems. But they don't take you as a literary man, you see. When they want a novel reviewed, they go somewhere else. A principal problem of living in the West is that you get labeled as a limited regionalist.

I notice that you prefer not to be called a western *writer. Is that because* western *writers are often thought of as purveyors of horse opera and formula fiction? But aren't you a* western *writer in the same way that Faulkner was a* southern *writer, or Frost a* New England *writer?*

I hope so; I would like to be. But I don't purvey horse opera and formula fiction. I also don't necessarily limit myself to subjects that are in turn limited by the geography in which I lay them. I'm trying to write about people. The people happen to be western because the West is all around me, and I see it all the time. Those images fill my head, but I would hope my characters would be people in London or Manchester or anywhere else. I don't like to be called a western writer, simply because it's a limiting term, a pejorative term like "local colorist." But I certainly am not objecting to being thought of as a person who comes from the West, as a writer who comes from the West, and who writes from the West. "Western writer" is likely to make you sound like Louis L'Amour.

I've always . . . and I suppose these are not very exact terms . . . I've always talked about the differences between western novelists *and persons who write* Westerns. *I have tried to make distinctions between the kind of writing you, A. B. Guthrie, or Wright Morris have done by calling your books novels about the West—in contrast to the popular* Westerns *written by such authors as Zane Grey, Max Brand, Ernest Haycox, or Luke Short.*

Yes. "Westerns" are examples of a good old American system: mass production with interchangeable parts. It began, I suppose, with the making of Winchester firearms and has spread to the making of western novels.

You comment that you don't enjoy the "liberated consciousness" of much contemporary American fiction. What do you mean by that?

Here's a partial answer to your question. It's a review of *Cities of Red Night* by William Burroughs, a review by John Rechy, which is a kind of suggestive name, I would think: "The effect of this work of radical art is not unlike a television set gone lucidly mad, splicing news clips, cartoons, commercials and movies into a nightmarish vision of a barbaric, doomed, hilarious world . . . ."

That review would not lead me to read that book. I guess I don't think of the world as doomed, not necessarily; and if I did I wouldn't think it hilarious. Neither do I think of the influence of Burroughs as being central or particularly important. I think of it as being exceptional and aberrational. I think of it as a sign of a sickness of the times which time may heal eventually, which we may recover from. When I disparaged some contemporary writing, it was people like Burroughs I was thinking of, the black comics and so on, who, out of understandable disgust with a good many manifestations of contemporary life, produce disgusting books. I think it's the wrong method. I understand the impulse, but there are better ways.

In commenting on Bret Harte's local-color writing, you use the term "synthetic" if I remember correctly, "the synthetic West." Do you imply that his fiction lacked the depth of good regional writing?

Yes, because he didn't know much about what he wrote about. He wrote a lot of stories about pre-Anglo Spanish California, which he didn't know anything about. He wrote a lot of stories about the Gold Rush country, in which he had been a very superficial tourist. He had never been a participant in the Gold Rush as MarkTwain was. His dialogue is not the dialogue of the camps. It's a synthetic dialogue with a flavor of colloquialism. His characters are made out of Dickens, generally by a process of juxtaposition of opposites. The strongest man is a man with only three fingers, the most dangerous man is a well-groomed gambler who never raises his voice, and so on. Yuba Bill, his stage driver, is the most profane man in the mines, but the gentlest soul among ladies and little children that you can possibly imagine. So it goes. "Tennessee's Partner," that story about a crook who was hanged and who was so beloved by his partner, is a sentimental intrusion into the realms of rough and criminal activity. I don't think that Harte matters much in the long run except that he was a skillful maker of stereotypes. I suppose he has a lot to do with Louis L'Amour and people like that. His descendants are all people like himself, who were not makers, not creators, but contrivers. My guess.

In another essay which appears back-to-back with the one on Bret Harte in Sound of Mountain Water *[1969] you call Willa Cather's works "authentic." I suppose you consider her fiction a model for writers who aspire to produce first-rate novels about the West.*

Yes, why not? She knew what she was talking about. She'd grown up through it. She had it in her bones and her blood. She was a much better novelist when she was writing about Nebraska than when she got off on other subjects. You don't have to go to the Avignon of the exiled popes to write a novel if you're trying to project yourself into the world. All you have to do is to make sure that the people you write about in Red Cloud, Nebraska, are people who would be recognized in the world. She did that in *My Ántonia*; those are indelible portraits of people. They're much better than the portraits she did in the Quebec novel, for instance, *Shadows on the Rock*, where they're all kind of . . . it's all in pastels, it's static, like a mural. There's no activity going on, there's no conflict, and there's not much depth of color or perspective. They pass like shadows on the rock. It's less virile. Maybe that's not quite the word for Willa Cather, but it is less virile than what she was doing when she wrote about people like Ántonia. *My Ántonia* is maybe the *best* novel about how people grew up in the frontier West and who absorbed its character. It is likewise, of course, because Willa Cather was an artist that *My Ántonia* is more cunningly made than a lot of western novels. It really is a beautifully made book.

> *How is it that another writer, Bernard DeVoto, who worked so hard to become a novelist, has never received much credit for his fiction, but has been recognized as a premier historian of the West?*

I tried to explain that in my biography of him. It seems to me that one of the big differences between fiction and history is that history always imposes the historian's point of view, which is a judgmental point of view from back in time, or up above. The historian reserves the right of judgment, the right of manipulating time, the right of doing things simultaneously, of being in all minds at once, of being, in other words, omniscient. I don't believe you could write history from any other stance. But a fictionist's point of view is very different indeed. You may often get the whole world as seen through one pair of eyes, and that pair of eyes may be cockeyed. You may be seeing events through the eyes of Humbert Humbert, who is quite mad but is eminently plausible in his way. The trick is to suck you in and show you an unexpected possibility—how different the world would look from another point of view.

A novelist these days is seldom judgmental or omniscient in the historical sense. Benny was much better at the historical judgment, holding a lot of facts in his head, seeing the whole picture, making these pieces fit the picture, and being a kind of god manipulating the machine, than he was at being a ventriloquist and speaking out of a single mouth, or, as he would have to, if he were a real fictionist, speaking serially out of many mouths. Faulkner could speak out of any mouth and still be absolutely right. That's a major difference between a Benny DeVoto and a Faulkner. That, I think, is why DeVoto's fiction failed. He never persuaded you about his people. He didn't quite have the capacity that Keats called "negative capability" of assuming another garb, another personality. He was just too damned intelligent. He wanted to judge, he wanted to denounce, he wanted to express his own ideas and his own feelings. He wasn't willing to suppress himself quite enough— or didn't know how.

On several occasions you have mentioned the necessity of western fiction linking the past and present of the West. Have western writers been able to do this? Hasn't that been a major goal of Angle of Repose *and your other recent novels?*

Oh sure, it was certainly a major goal of *Angle of Repose*, but there's a durational character to almost all the novels. *Big Rock Candy Mountain*, of course, goes through a couple of generations and covers quite a span of time. *A Shooting Star* [1961] goes back to pick up the Boston background of those migrants to California, those rich transferees. What else? There's not much background history in either *All the Little Live Things* [1967] or *The Spectator Bird*; those are essentially contemporary novels with just enough background to make characters seem to be coming from somewhere. But I was consciously trying to report time, growth, and change in *Wolf Willow*, which is of course not fiction but an essentially historical and reminiscent book. I've tried to deal with time in a lot of books. It's imperative that it be done, it seems to me. Western writers in general haven't been able to do it very well. I don't know anybody who has done it successfully except possibly Wright Morris, whose whole series of books about Lone Tree give readers a past and a present and the changes which have taken place.

Larry McMurtry tries to do some of that.

Larry's quit writing novels, hasn't he?

I heard him speak about a month ago, and he said he's working on a trail drive novel.

Good. That's something he could do. *The Last Picture Show* was certainly a record of change from past to present, a transitional book. Some of the others, *Moving On* and so on, I couldn't quite get into, but *Horseman, Pass By, Leaving Cheyenne*, those were good books, and intelligible books. I think when he gets into the present he's less persuasive, like so many other western writers. He's better in the past.

Guthrie tried to do it in his series of five novels rather than in one book.

Yes, and did you read the *Arfive*? Not one of Bud's best books.

Yes, he had artistic problems.

Artistic problems and character problems. His hero is a kind of dreams-of-glory macho. Funny fellow; I don't believe him, whereas I completely believe Boone Caudill in *The Big Sky*. His particular kind of savagery fitted his times, and he was at one with it.

As a historian I especially like Guthrie's attempt in Arfive *to deal with the ending of the frontier and the beginning of the West as a region. That's a difficult period of time to deal with.*

Oh yes, I agree.

You did it in Big Rock Candy Mountain. *The end of the frontier and the beginning of the regional West.*

Maybe, except that I wasn't limiting myself to a single place. The region got blurred, spread out, dispersed. I couldn't have done otherwise. Having started Bo Mason wandering, I had to keep him peripatetic, so I couldn't concentrate on a single region. The novel divides into sections, doesn't it? There's a midwestern section and a northwestern section and a Canada section and a Utah section. Each of them is a different kind of thing. But *he's* always the same thing, and it was Bo that I was trying to concentrate on.

The experiences in Big Rock Candy Mountain *remind me of the central concern of Kevin Starr's very good book on Californians and the American dream. He tries to depict the era from 1850 to 1915—what layers of experience had accumulated by 1915, what it meant to be a Californian as that state moved from a frontier toward becoming a separate region.*

Yeah, sure. Now you go to *Sunset* to get your clues, but a lot of people are beginning . . . there seem to be more people now who feel "Californian" than there were when we first came here. Right at the end of the war, in a great flood, a sudden burst, the population of this state went from about ten million to fifteen million almost overnight—and none of those people knew what they were getting into. They weren't used to the California seasons, they didn't know the California weather, they didn't know the smells, they didn't know the plants, the animals, the streets. They dumped their garbage everywhere because they had no community sense and no local roots. It was a bad as well as an exciting time. Growth was ugly as it happened then. But that seems to have calmed down a good deal. People have got roots now, they've lived in California fifteen or twenty or twenty-five years and have a stake in their communities. In spite of what you read, it's a stabler society.

Now I'm going to ask you to do something that you've told me you don't like to do. In the past you have praised such western writers as Willa Cather, H. L. Davis, Walter Van Tilburg Clark, A. B. Guthrie, Frederick

*Manfred, and Wright Morris. Which recent western writers deserve
our attention?*

That's a hard question to answer. What is a western writer? Is Joan
Didion a western writer? Is Tom McGuane? Is Evan Connell? Is Alice
Adams or Ernest Gaines or Robert Stone? Generally, the moment we segre-
gate a writer and put the tag "western" on him, we have implicitly down-
graded him into some secondary category. If he's a writer we truly admire,
we more often than not forget the regional limitation and think of him
simply as a contemporary American writer.

If you don't live within commuting distance of New York, you may see
things from a non–New York perspective and so get a regional label pinned
on you by reviewers and opinion-makers. I'm not sure it matters if you're
John Irving and somebody puts a New Hampshire label on you; but if you're
Joan Didion and live in Los Angeles, you never get discussed without refer-
ence to the Hollywood aura—and you invite it because that is what you
live in and write about. The fact is, many novels are rooted in *place*, and
the more different that place is from New York, the more likely it is that a
novel about it will be labeled regional. A Brooklyn novel is as regional to me
as one laid in Canyonlands would be to a Brooklynite. But his isn't called
regional, and mine is.

All of which is an elaborate way of evading your question. There are
many good writers who live in and write about the many Wests. I don't
want to diminish them by separating them out as "western" writers. They
can be read with pleasure even in Brooklyn.

*What about the three Native American writers N. Scott Momaday,
James Welch, and Leslie Silko? Are they authors who will have a lasting
reputation, or are we putting too much emphasis on our first well-known
Native American writers?*

No, I don't think we are. I think they have to be observed because this
is their day, they've got their hour in the sun coming. Momaday has written
two good books, especially *Way to Rainy Mountain*. I think Jimmy Welch's
Winter in the Blood is a splendid novel, and I like his poems too. Silko
I don't know, but I'd like to. What do you suggest?

Ceremony is her best-known book.

Ceremony. Well, I'll go get it. She's a poet too, isn't she?

Yes, she has written poetry and short stories.

Is she at New Mexico?

*She has been, but I'm told she's working . . . and this is only third-hand
. . . that she's working on a series of scripts for an Indian film series—
an Indian* Roots.[5]

I had seen that someplace too—documentaries of some sort on Indian
life. She sounds pretty good, and the other two are thoroughly good writers.
They appeal to me, perhaps, because they are western Indians and come
from my country. They're probably more intelligible to me than most black
novelists. I just don't react to Harlem as I do to the Rocky Boy Reservation
or the Jemez Pueblo. Also, Momaday and Welch write in very good, controlled English, and a lot of blacks write in black English, which I don't
respond to. I don't respond to dialects of any kind, really. Dialect seems
to me a mistake, another way of limiting yourself. Momaday and Welch
write English for anybody, for the world. They could be read in Singapore
or London and would make perfectly good sense. I'm not sure you can read
some of the most publicized black writers outside of the orbit of their own
special culture.

You touch me where I'm vulnerable and ill-informed on this Indian
business. There's a book by Storm called *Five Arrows* . . . which I have had
on the shelf for years and haven't read because I'm too preoccupied with
other things. There's also that big Sioux compilation, *Hanta Yo,* which I've
also got and haven't read. That isn't by an Indian, but it presumably has
the Indian imprimatur.

*That's the one there's so much controversy about. It was going to be
made into a film, but many Sioux who consider themselves traditional
Sioux feel that the book is not authentic.*

Well, I'll have to read it. I'm quite sure that I've got to read Silko, and
I probably have to read Storm, though Storm is pretty experimental, trying
to combine Indian forms with western American forms. The genres get kind
of mixed in him, so he'll take more reading than I've got time to give him
right away.

*During the 1960s Ken Kesey and Richard Brautigan and in the seventies
Brautigan and Tom Robbins have been cult writers on college campuses.
Can we call them western writers?*

Why, I suppose you have to. Brautigan comes from Oregon, doesn't he?
So does Kesey. They write about the West, *Trout Fishing in America,
Sometimes a Great Notion.* I think they are Westerners trying to be some-
thing else—I'm not quite sure what. Kesey got blown by the San Francisco

---

[5]Leslie Marmon Silko teaches at the University of Arizona. She was recently a
recipient of a MacArthur Fellowship.

hip scene when he came down from Oregon. Brautigan, God knows what blew him, but I'd guess his vogue is past. He was always more clever than profound, I think. He had a certain acid, satiric wit and a way of doing things in compressed little semipoetic paragraphs which appealed very greatly to the young. Students followed him around like little dogs. A kind of odd man. He didn't have much conversation, he didn't have many ideas. He had an attitude, essentially, a pose of the alienated and disoriented modern at odds with his society. A kind of freakish-looking figure. The last I heard of him, he was living up on the edge of Tom McGuane's Montana ranch in Paradise Valley on the Yellowstone. There's a whole cluster of former students and people from around here living up there.

We haven't said anything about poets. Many people who talk about western poets often begin with Robinson Jeffers and when mentioning recent poets they list Richard Hugo, Gary Snyder, or William Stafford.

I should know Hugo better than I do. A lot of people I know and respect like his stuff very much. But I am afraid that I haven't read more than scraps of it. William Stafford, on the other hand, I do know, and do like. I met him for the first time up in Banff in 1978. I liked the poems he read, and I like what I've seen of him since. I met him again down in San Diego last year and heard some more, and I've read him in between since. He seems to me a poet who is clearly western without being limited by his Westernness. I would put him very high. Who else have we got in hand here? Snyder . . . I don't know. I find it harder to swallow Snyder. Many of his poems, while authentically western in scene and feeling, strike me as a little pedestrian. I'm just afraid he didn't make any burning phrases that imprint themselves on my mind, and I expect that of a poet, perhaps wrongly.

Do you think it's more difficult to be a western poet than a western novelist? We've had many more novelists than poets in the West who have attracted national attention.

I suppose we have. I don't know that it's any more difficult to be a western poet than a western novelist. But it does seem to have worked that way, maybe because, again, the romantic story of the great migration, the westward movement, is something which these days commends itself to fiction rather than to poetry. Three thousand years ago it would have been made into an epic, but nowadays the drama and storytelling are taken over by prose. A poet has only the lyric left to him, and that is a limited area to work in. He has to be awfully good, as a matter of fact, to do it right. It's easy to write bad poetry, but very hard to write good poetry. Apart from Jeffers, on whom many people would disagree, I don't think of an early western poet of worth. There were a number of people in the San Francisco area in the early 1900s—George Sterling, Ina Coolbrith, and people like that—but they're not major poets by any definition. They just happened to be regionally interesting as part of ground out of which later things grew.

John Neihardt is the person who some people . . .

Well, John Neihardt—I knew John Neihardt a little bit; I met him once in Chicago, and we spent a day or two together. Little Bull Buffalo, the Sioux called him. Powerful little fellow. His writings, of course, are also in the general area of fiction and history, somewhere in that middle ground that we were talking about. *The Song of Hugh Glass, The Song of Jed Smith*, or any of those, are reasonably authentic history. They are also stories, so they blend several things together. Still, I suppose if you asked a normal college class about John G. Neihardt not one student out of two hundred, outside of Nebraska, would know who he was. I don't think he can be held to be a great influence, but he's good reading, and I have quoted him and used him.

When people applied for the Wallace Stegner writing fellowships, did more novelists or more poets apply?

We had a little bias in favor of fiction, partly because we had more people to teach fiction and partly because I was running the program and was more interested in fiction. We had two poets every year and four fiction writers. In terms of numbers, we had many more applications in fiction while I was still teaching. I think later that changed, during the time when Donald Davie was here. Donald, I think, had about as many applications in poetry as Dick Scowcroft had in fiction. But while I was doing it, in any given year we'd have maybe two hundred and fifty applicants, of whom two hundred would be fiction and fifty poetry. Out of those we would pick six. It was a kind of fine strainer.

I was just thinking about these other poets. Hugo I've got to read. I don't know whether you'd call Roethke a western poet or not. He spent a lot of time in Washington, but when I first knew him, he was in Pennsylvania. So I suspect his formative basis is eastern rather than western. He was, I guess, a teacher of Hugo, wasn't he?

Yes. Teacher of a lot of poets in the Pacific Northwest.

Well, he was a good one, a good poet. He *does* make phrases that stick in my head. There are some poets who just don't. I can't remember a line out of Robert Lowell, for example, though I've read him dutifully. And Gary Snyder, whom we were just speaking of. Maybe it's the Zen business that keeps me from fully appreciating him. He wrote me once that if civilization should come to an end, all human achievements could be reproduced by meditation, which I've been thinking about ever since, rolling it over in my head. It's a little bit like that monkey with the typewriter, who after a long period of time will eventually produce the works of Shakespeare by pecking randomly on the keys. It seems to me it would take a long time to reproduce all human achievement by meditation. Damn it, I don't think that's a very sensible statement.

You have commented on the lives and works of several western writers but have had little to say about John Steinbeck. Do you see him as a major figure in American literary history? Is he a western writer?

Sure, he's a western writer, though he got outside the West, to some certain extent, in *The Moon Is Down*, and things like that. But his whole upbringing and training and experience and everything else is western, and most of his books are. I don't suppose I do think Steinbeck is as important as Hemingway or Faulkner. But he probably is as important as Thomas Wolfe, say, and that's getting pretty high in the hierarchy. He was a very skillful writer, and he wrote some very good books. I think he has deceived a good many eastern critics by being more simple-seeming than he really is. A relatively lucid style, nothing difficult about it. He doesn't strain you, he doesn't put on any airs and manners that force you to readjust or put on your bifocals.

When he was given the Nobel Prize there were probably a half-dozen graduate students at Stanford, all from New York, who were literally livid. They thought it the greatest insult to intelligence that had ever happened, that Steinbeck should be given the Nobel Prize. I never did understand their prejudice. It was not merely dislike, it was actual hatred; they despised him. You remember a sketch called "Breakfast" in which some men are cooking coffee and bacon over a fire and warming themselves up on a cold morning, smelling the bacon and saying "Kee-rist." It's a perfectly realistic, evocative, heartfelt little scene. But these students were insulted by it as a fraudulent piece of juvenilia. I was too western to understand them. I don't feel that way about Steinbeck. I just don't return to him quite as much as I return to some other people, and there must be some significance in that, though I think *Grapes of Wrath* is a very interesting book, a landmark book, and I think some of the others, particularly *Tortilla Flat* and the strike novel, *In Dubious Battle*, are fairly good books. He got a little sentimental in *Cannery Row* and *Sweet Thursday*. He got really sentimental in *The Moon Is Down*, a piece of wartime patriotism. I think he did decline. The *Winter of Our Discontent* doesn't seem to me to be much, and I've never read *East of Eden*. I would think he has written at least three or four books that are bound to be around for quite a while—and that's a test, isn't it? Most of us go out of print; he hasn't gone out of print.

Several of your essays note that the eastern literary establishment has not paid much attention to the American literary West. Is this because they do not know about and understand western literature, or is it because Westerners have not produced a large body of notable literature? Both, or something else?

I think it's more of the first than the second. This was the thesis of Howard Jones's last book that I was telling you about—that the eastern establishment had simply never paid attention to what had actually been produced in the West. He was thinking of such books as Gregg's *Commerce of the Prairies*, which he took to be a book of great geographical and historical interest, and a record of the fascinating clash of two cultures. He thought *The Commerce of the Prairies* was a splendid book which most people in Cambridge, Massachusetts, or New York City had never heard of. Well, that's an opinion. He was trying to make a point. But it's the kind of book he was thinking of—not fiction and not poetry, but the reportorial, explorational, concerned with nature and action that were regional in fact and material in implication.

The tradition represented by Thoreau and John Burroughs, the *Walden–Wake Robin* tradition of nature writing, has persisted in the West well past its peak in the East, simply because the West has had more nature for people to go out into. The affection for nature has been more nurtured by that opportunity. You could make quite a list of major nature-writing works that have come out of the West. When you come to autobiography, that sort of thing, there are many equivalents to New England books of settlement and Indian captivities. Andy Adams's *Log of a Cowboy*, or Teddy Blue's *We Pointed Them North*, are books of historical, sociological, and literary interest. That's the kind of book Howard was thinking of. I don't think he would have been able to make a persuasive case for very many western fiction writers beyond Willa Cather, Steinbeck, and maybe Conrad Richter's *Sea of Grass*, and a few things like that. I know—and I say this with embarrassment—he was working up to me as being the peak and pinnacle of western literature. That would have embarrassed the hell out of me if he had written the book, because I don't think I am. But he was looking for somebody who was not limitedly regional and not limitedly literary. I think he had some of Benny DeVoto's suspicions of the merely literary, and he liked literary people who had a little history in them. He thought he saw it in me.

I do think that he had a point—that many eastern critics, historians of literature, the people who make the textbooks and create the curricula of classes, have ignored many good things in western literature. On this I think he would have the corroboration of people like Don Fehrenbacher, who has likewise had that feeling for a long time. There's more there than has been dug out. On the other hand, I must say I'm a little troubled by some of the students of western literature as I see them in *Western American Literature*. The things they choose to dig out and devote themselves to often seem to me selected for coterie reasons, or for the reason that they have not been studied to death. We'll have a solid western tradition sooner if we pay attention to its major achievements and bring them to general notice.

8. On Western History and Historians

Etulain: Western historians seem to be more interested in the Old West than in the modern West. Why do you think that is?

Stegner: I can think of some western historians who are interested in the modern West—Howard Lamar for one—and some people who go both ways, but I suppose that most of the people who have been writing about the modern West have been either reporters making some kind of travel or commentary book, or sociologists studying the Mormons or some other aspect of western life, or, perhaps, partisans in some cause like environmentalists—a lot of environmental writing has been about the West—but none of those involves too much history.

Historians, on the other hand, seem to have ignored the present and concentrated on the past, as we both noted, and I think it's partly because there is a dichotomy between the diverse present and the past of the settlement, which, even though there are many diverse areas in the West, has a certain single theme. Discovery, raid, settlement—those make an obvious, solid topic; the Westward Movement essentially. I suppose most historians like that because it's romantic, because it's encompassable, and because it makes a nice unified sort of theme. I'm sure that's what made it appealing to Benny DeVoto and to many others, including Turner. I don't know why they haven't carried on into the contemporary West as historians. Perhaps because the development of the West has been so broken and erratic. The Southwest is very different country from the Northwest, and Mormon country is very different from either. So it goes. You can hardly expect people to

[145]

be historians of the whole West. Moreover, when they deal with the present they tend to become sociologists, reporters, or partisans. Benny of course came into the present as a partisan, very strongly. That whole business of the proposed land grab in 1946. He spent a year and a half to two years doing nothing else practically but fighting that, bringing to bear his knowledge of history on it. He was a better reporter for being a historian, but he wasn't playing historian there, he was playing journalist.

Did he ever talk to you about his moving closer to the present in his historical work?

He was writing a book before he died, a book called "Western Star," in which he was trying to link the mythic western past with the real present and future. So far as I know, he published only one piece of that—a piece on the Johnson County War and the origins of *The Virginian*. The unfinished manuscript is down here at Stanford if you should want to look at it, but it wouldn't be worth your time. He always got the bite into his prose and the direction into his organization about the third time around. His first drafts were likely to be fast and therefore unpublishable. Avis DeVoto and I both looked at "Western Star" seriously, and we had Anne Barrett, an editor at Houghton Mifflin, read it over too. The three of us agreed that he had made his contribution and that it wouldn't do to put out a lame book as his last one. I think he did intend to build that one as a bridge between past and present, but he was burned out by the time he started it.

Historians of the frontier and West often argue over whether the frontier broke with or continued eastern customs and traditions. Would you, like Turner and his followers, stress innovation more than continuity?

I might stress them both serially. It seems to me the intention of settlers particularly, not necessarily of adventurers—mountain men, fur traders, miners, or whoever else—but of actual settlers who intended to make a home in the West, was to transplant the old one to the new place. That was true about my grandfather who came from Norway. What he did was to build a little piece of Norway in Iowa. He read Norwegian newspapers, he spoke Norwegian in the home, and he went to the Lutheran church. The whole bit. I spoke one time in Norway, at Ulvik, at the head of Hardanger fjord—where my grandfather came from—to his second cousin, a very, very old man. He must have been past ninety. My grandfather also lived to be past ninety, and he had been dead for fifteen years. But this second cousin had come to the United States, oh, way back when, about 1890, maybe before, and he worked around on farms as a hired man. He had worked, he said, on sixteen different farms during his five or six years in Minnesota, North Dakota, and Iowa, and he had never worked on the farm of anybody

but somebody from the town of Ulvik. That is concentrating your old life
in the new place with a vengeance. It seems to me (and I think Turner
would have agreed with this, maybe I got it from him) that innovation
happens when the edge of settlement strikes a new biological entity, a new
biome, a new kind of environment. When, for instance, they came out of
the oak openings and out onto the plains, it was a change, and it happened
not only to white settlers, but it happened to Indians. The Woods and
Swampy Crees in Canada came out onto the plains and within a couple
of generations were Plains Indians in everything, buffalo and horse Indians.
When white people came out they had to learn a plains craft, which was
different from woodcraft. When they got into the mountains they had to
learn a mountain craft in addition. Most of them were both plainsmen and
mountain people, as you know.

A big problem is of course the fact that west of the hundredth meridian
unaided agriculture wasn't possible in most places. Where there was water,
it was likely to be too high to raise anything but hay; and where there was
perfectly good arable land, there often wasn't water. That's going to come
up in later discussion, I'm sure; we're going to be talking about aridity when
we're talking about the West. Most of the changes in people's lives—which
I'm quite sure in most of their lives were unintended—were forced upon
them by the condition of aridity. They had to learn to be irrigators. They
had to learn a whole new attitude towards the environment because the
West doesn't heal the way Vermont, let us say, heals. You can tear the hell
out of Vermont woods and pretty soon, five years, you can't tell that the
loggers have been in there. It's all come back to woods. And you can do
almost anything to Vermont grass and it comes up grass again. But you
can't do that in the West. Changes happen because they have to happen
if you are going to stay there. And there is, of course, all that whole body
of law, institutional law, that both Powell and Walter Webb speak of. The
way in which riparian rights, for instance, turn into prior appropriation
rights in the West. The so-called Wyoming Doctrine that ties water rights
to the land. Those were arid-land developments.

So I think that there is both traditional preservation of the old as far as it
can be preserved and an inevitable development of the new. You simply
can't be the same people and live the same way in a new country. In our
town in Canada, when I was a kid, there were many Englishmen. They had
English habits, and they wanted to make an English life—being British in a
far land. They practically were like those spit-and-polish Mounties who
had brass bands and red coats and lived up to the tradition. These people
built a tennis court and played tennis, which got them laughed at by everybody in town. Tennis, my God! On that bald-assed frontier. And they

had tea parties. None of it has lasted. They don't drink tea up there any more, they probably drink beer or coffee. They don't play tennis, they play hockey.

I'm glad you mentioned your hometown, because that's the answer you give in Big Rock Candy Mountain *and* Wolf Willow. *Some continuity, some innovation.*

I would think so. You yearn for continuity, actually. I think somewhere in *Wolf Willow* I remark on how I wasn't sure who I was. I wasn't sure whether I was American or Canadian, so I decided I was a Norwegian; I took my grandfather's Old Country name and signed it in all my schoolbooks, which was quite preposterous, except that it probably indicated a desire for a continuity that wasn't there. I wouldn't be at all surprised if most people on the frontier are a little frightened by the lack of continuity.

Many commentators on the history of the Far West fail to realize that much of the Pacific Slope has been more urban than rural. Do you think this is because the myth of the Old West still colors our thinking when we write about the history of the region?

Yes, I'm quite sure it does. As a matter of fact it's not merely the Pacific Slope that's mainly urban, it's the whole West. I don't know where you come from—Idaho, I guess. But there is a lot of space between towns in Idaho, as you know. And the whole West—I don't know what the figure is now, but it must be eighty percent urban. It's an oasis civilization. And curiously, that little twenty percent of rural Westerners have put their stamp on very large parts of the West, probably because of the romance of the horseman. The horseman is always more romantic than the plowman or the townsman. Hence the developing myth of the cowboy, which I'm sure we'll be talking about. It's also true, I think, that ranching is the most natural way of life in large parts of the West; the future of that country ought to be grass. It may not be, but it ought to be. If ranching stays and becomes a viable economic enterprise, which it hardly is now, it would seem to me the best thing for the land and the best thing for a kind of continuous, forming life, and the best thing for the development of a local character, a local literature. All the things you would expect of a regional culture would be associated to some extent with the ranch and with those county market towns which serve the ranches. They are a unit after all, or should be. But when we think of the West, you're right, we do think of it as a lonesome horseman far off on some butte. And I haven't seen very many of those.

In my classes I sometimes give my students a kind of instant Rorschach test. I ask, what words do you think of when I use the word "West"?

Very seldom do they mention anything urban. It's almost always rural, cowboy, wide-open spaces.

Well, you see, it *is* urban; it's an oasis civilization, as Walter Webb said. And there's a lot of space keeping the oases apart, so that the *impression* is certainly not urban even though the population exists in clots. The impression that you get as you drive through is of a virtually empty country. Your students have a legitimate way of looking at the West, but it's not the only way, and sociologically it's kind of wrong.

You imply that one of the difficulties Westerners face is the conflict of living up to the myths and romantic notions of what they have been "officially taught" and the reality of what they know "through their pores." Is it that western history is quite different from what Owen Wister and Zane Grey wrote and what John Wayne depicted in western films?

Not necessarily different but infinitely more various. I suppose most horse operas, whether John Wayne's, Owen Wister's, or Zane Grey's, are built on a handful of places or episodes: Tombstone, Virginia City, Abilene, Dodge City, the Texas Rangers. Those are legitimate; they're part of western history, but there's a whole lot of other history to which those things really were attached as a kind of lurid fringe. When I was writing *Angle of Repose* I got into that because a friend of the family chased some horse thief or so down into Arizona, down towards the border, and got involved to some extent in Tombstone, which was a very wicked town—much wickeder than Leadville at that point. And so Molly Foote was commenting upon this excursion of her friend as a dreadful kind of development in the West. Even in Leadville, you see, she felt settled and civilized to a degree well above Tombstone. I suppose the lurid, the exciting, the romantic, the adventurous, the deadly, are always more interesting in fiction than the kinds of things that make a continuous society. I wouldn't necessarily take fiction as the best picture of life; it's a picture of some aspects of life, but it's very selective.

In other words, have we sometimes been nourished on the belief that the Far West was primarily settled by rugged individualists when many of us see little of that individualism in our urban western society?

Yes, I think so. You know Benny DeVoto's remark that the only true individualists in the West generally wound up at the end of a rope whose other end was in the hands of a bunch of cooperating citizens. That's an extreme way of putting it. But what made, for example, the Mormon country, was not rugged individualism at all; and that's a pretty big country, as you know. It includes Utah and chunks of Idaho, Nevada, Arizona, Colorado, and Wyoming. What made most of the ranching country in Montana and northwestern Wyoming was not rugged individualism, either. Most of the ranches that are still there were homestead ranches in the first place, and some of them had been built up into pretty big spreads; but all of the people who settled ranching country had to be cooperators. The weather was terrible, and there were communal obligations. They had to get together to build schools; they had to have some kind of community responsibility, figure a way to get the kids to school and back. Some of the ranchers that I know in Wyoming and Montana may think they're rugged individualists, but they're probably as helpful neighbors as you can find. That's really more to the point than rugged individualism. That's an illusion. We like to feel that way, but it isn't necessarily the way we act.

I was talking with a sagebrush rebel up in Jackson Hole last week. He was violently anti-government, but an interesting man, one I could talk to. I asked him about the economics of ranching. He had a big ranch down by Pinedale on the upper Green River. He inherited it, unfortunately, with all of its encumbrances and debts, and he was having a hard time—and just when he was having a hard time the government was beginning to put a little more pinch on the grazing leases. So he blew up and got mad. I asked him why there weren't any beef subsidies the way there were tobacco subsidies and milk subsidies. Wasn't cattle raising just as legitimate a farming industry as sugar or hogs or dairy cows, and just as worthy of being kept alive by the government? "Christ," he said, "we wouldn't *take* a beef subsidy. We'd cut off our noses to spite our faces first." That sort of rugged individualism still exists, but my Pinedale friend may have to cooperate in order to stay a rancher. He may even have to cooperate with the federal government, which has always been a partner in the West.

I was thinking of the story "Genesis," where you picture a lot of rugged individualism, but it is the group that keeps men alive—that marvelous section where one man keeps the other person alive by his interest in the group, in others, rather than in himself.

Yes, oh yes. I had never been in that kind of storm; or rather, I've been in that kind of storm, but not in those circumstances. I was inventing to some extent, but I've been dragged home from school, for instance, in a sixty-mile wind at fifty-five below, with everything pulled down over my face, and tied to my father by a lariat and a whole string of kids tied on behind. Three or four men in the line helping along; it would have been impossible to move without them. And there's a sample of western cooperative enterprise. Kids get marooned in the schoolhouse; you have to get up a kind of posse to go get them. I don't think rugged individualism exists in the West, or ever did, except in the persons of people like Adolph Coors, corporation bosses, people who have built up something big and very personal like Coors beer. Corporation executives sometimes act as if they were rugged individualists, but actually they are all company men, and the rugged individualism may belong all to one person at the top of the pyramid.

Why is it that the mythical Old West, as you say, "is the West that everybody knows"?*

It's the one that's been sold to the public ever since the first Currier and Ives prints, I suppose.

You mention in Wolf Willow *that you grew up reading Zane Grey, and you read other popular fiction . . .*

Hardly anything else.

And you were experiencing a different kind of West than what they portrayed.

I think I made a fairly specific point about that somewhere in *Wolf Willow*—the fact that we were reading all about Blackfoot Indians and all that stuff that James Willard Schultz used to write. He had been a whiskey trader among the Blackfeet, lived with them, had a Blackfoot wife and all the rest, and later he was writing these things in *The American Boy*. It never occurred to us that he was writing about our country. A lot of what he wrote about had happened right there in the hills within five miles of us. I always thought of history, fiction—and everything else I read—as being somewhere off both in time and space, off at the edges. I don't know what I thought reality was, but it wasn't anything that you read about.

Do you think historians of other American regions have had to wrestle with as many myths or romantic notions as those writing about the West?

Maybe not as many, but they certainly have had to wrestle with some. I think for instance of the Jeffersonian yeoman, who was largely a myth. He was a kind of Jeffersonian hope more than he was a Jeffersonian fact, though he existed and though the fact of free land had meant that a great many people acquired freeholds in the New World. Nevertheless, it was doubtful even by Jefferson's time that the future was going that way. That well-educated, civically responsible Jeffersonian yeoman was a kind of myth that has haunted us since. It haunts the Democratic National Convention every time they meet. That's one. Another, I suppose, is the myth of the extreme physical, masculine competence of the frontiersman, which maybe began at Bunker Hill or Concord Bridge where the irregulars with their virtue routed the regulars with their red coats.

---

*The Sound of Mountain Water, p. 30.

The Revolution was full of delusions like that. Americans had a notion that one American could whip ten British redcoats, and they often came to grief because of that democratic arrogance. In the War of 1812, as a matter of fact, those frontiersmen, most of them from the Ohio, Kentucky, Michigan wilderness, were both badly led and very spooky in battle . . . by no means the resolute, unconquerable kind of American that frontier myth generated. I suppose the first literary expression of that frontier competence is Natty Bumppo in *The Pioneers*, but it came also in William Byrd and all kinds of people. The mythic figures, as they recede in the past, begin to look like Hercules, and all of the labors credited to them could only have been performed by superhuman people. Most people, past or present, couldn't possibly live up to that kind of image. And yet we fool ourselves that that somehow is a basic part of our character and our inheritance.

It seems to me that if western historians could spill a little bit past the 1890s, they might be able to show some continuities in our history that would get us away from some of these romantic stories that we continually get about the nineteenth century.

Yes, but they aren't interesting. Irrigation congresses are not nearly as interesting as lynching parties, or shoot-outs. I'm afraid that the romantic imagination has taken the West, and it's probably never going to let it go. You're always swimming upstream when you try to write something serious about the West. Even some good writers fall into the sensational. I think of Oakley Hall, for instance, who did the libretto for the opera of *Angle of Repose*. He wrote one book called *Warlock* about Tombstone, and one called *Bad Lands*, in which he has a character who is very like Theodore Roosevelt and another like that French baron, whatever his name was. Oakley made him a Scotch baron, but it was the same principle. And he threw in Granville Stuart, who was a leader of the Vigilantes in the Missouri Breaks. In those two books he was picking out of all the western past two lurid periods when the most heightened and sensational events took place.

I was thinking of a person like Charlie Russell who surely would have seen a great deal of change in Montana from 1890 to the early 1920s, but chose to continue to paint about, to comment on, those things he had known much earlier.

Well, he hated plowmen, he hated nesters of one kind or another. He had a cowman's prejudice. Plowing turned all the god-damned country upside down, he said. In all his attitudes and his history, though not in his gifts, he was characteristic. He was a youngster who ran away from home in St. Louis, and at the age of seventeen or eighteen was out in wide open, exhilarating, adventurous space.

Was he in Great Falls when you were there?

I used to mow his lawn. My brother tended his furnace. We lived on Fourth Avenue North, near where the Russell Museum is now—just about half a block down—and he lived there where the museum is. His log cabin is still there. I never got into his log cabin. That was for special people from The Mint.

You have noted that Owen Wister and Frederic Remington helped create the mythic cowboy, who is certainly a significant figure in western popular culture. Why has the cowboy been so important to Westerners, and for that matter for Americans and I suppose people internationally?

Oh, he's everybody's fantasy for one thing. He's a continuation of an earlier kind of fantasy, the frontiersman fantasy, but he is more romantic because he is mounted. He suddenly acquires trappings, dress, mannerisms, a set of instruments like lariats, spurs, chaps, the big hat, the whole bit, which came from Spain via Mexico and gave cow herding an exotic quality. People are not only out in this big wide open West, but they are people such as we haven't seen before, and they live romantically on horseback. As you are no doubt aware, Mrs. Gene Manlove Rhodes wrote a book called *Hired Man on Horseback*, which is a somewhat more realistic picture of a cowboy's life. Actually a cowboy was not in the beginning as romantic as he later became, and his life was never romantic. It was hard, killing work for thirty a month and found. Most cowboys didn't live very long, as a matter of fact, not because they got shot up in saloons but because they got busted by horses. Almost all the old cowboys I know are crippled in one way or another and go to a chiropractor twice a week to get their spines kinked. It was a rough life, and I suppose the very roughness of it, if you didn't have to experience it, made it even more romantic to readers. The thing that Remington, and particularly Wister, did to the cowboy was to make him into a kind of knight errant. You know that book called *My Dear Wister*, letters between Remington and Wister?

Yes, yes I do. That's the book I've just quoted from.

A very interesting book, because you can see these two people making a myth before your very eyes. Wister's whole excitement about the cowboy was based upon the fact that he saw him as a knight errant, as a chivalric kind of figure. He *was* errant, I suppose; he wandered in the same way, he may have been chivalrous to women in the same way, rescuing maidens in distress from dragons. That's the way the myth developed, and it's curious how much of it is actually out of the imagination of Owen Wister. Remington was more realistic; he drew what he saw. I know the horse, he said; that's all he would admit to knowing. Wister imposed all the chivalric trappings on the cowboy, and quite calculatedly—almost like Poe writing "The Raven"—created the cowboy vehicle in *The Virginian*.

I was thinking in conjunction with this of the five books A. B. Guthrie has written in his western historical series. People have differing opinions about the literary value of the novels, but critics have usually said that These Thousand Hills *is too romanticized. I suppose this comes from the difficulty of trying to write good fiction about cowboy and cattleman experiences.*

It is difficult, and it has its own forms of cliché, which Oakley Hall falls into in *Bad Lands* too. The whorehouse madam who is a real pal to all the boys, an essential part of society. In most cowtowns that I knew, there would have been such a whorehouse, but she wouldn't have been that kind of character. She would have been a pretty brassy old character, and she would have been ostracized by the town. She would have lived on the fringes of it.

In several of your essays you mention aridity as a determining factor in shaping the American West. How specifically has this happened, and is aridity more important than other factors?

We were talking about that earlier in connection with the question of innovation and perpetuation. It does seem to me that the kind of innovation which was enforced was the kind most likely to happen; it took generally a couple of generations. No *individual* was likely to be able to innovate in a new country because he had to find his way. He had no feel of the land. Aridity is certainly of the essence, and it made people irrigators rather than just plowers of the land; it should have made them learn how to take care of the range, but they didn't—perhaps because so much of it was public. They didn't learn in time, so they turned most of the ranges into sagebrush and shad scale and rabbitbrush. There's hardly a range in the West that isn't fifty percent deteriorated from what it was in the beginning. Even down in southern Utah, where some of that country won't carry any animals at all now, there used to be stirrup-high grass. It was sparse, but it was stirrup-high. Most of the grass reproduced from seed; when it was overgrazed it was gone. In some areas such as the Escalante Basin you've got not even shad scale and sagebrush but bare rock. Grass and soil just blew away.

Such things have to be learned. There's a whole lore of blizzards, for instance, in North Dakota. Swedes and Norwegians and Bohemians knew something about snowy weather, but they didn't know about it on the high plains, in wide-open spaces where the exposure is so complete. Compare, for instance, Beret in *Giants in the Earth* with the Norwegian wife in Ibsen's *Brand*. In *Brand* the woman's problem is not exposure to all the thirty-six winds and empty open sky, but quite the reverse. She's down in the bottom of a fjord where the sun never shines, as if living in a cave. She's a neurotic too, she's just as crazy as Beret, but it's a very different thing. The one is a Norwegian experience and the other one is a North Dakota experience. They both drive women crazy, but they're different experiences.

Webb really emphasizes women and the wind, doesn't he, in The Great Plains?

Yes, he makes a big point of that. And it *is* important. You feel terribly exposed. I don't know if you've ever lived in a flat country. It's both exhilarating and ultimately frightening. We were in Africa about six weeks ago, on the Serengeti Plain, which reminded me of Saskatchewan, except that it was full of animals—an absolute, sea-bottom flat which stretches clear to the horizon. I was reminded of a remark by Castañeda in his history of the Coronado expedition. They were out in the Staked Plains, which he said were so flat that when you looked at the "cattle" (the buffalo) you could see the sky between their legs. We saw that every place we looked in the Serengeti. And the feel was just right. It was like coming home. Same kind of big clouds going over—big, fair-weather cumuli.

I wonder if novelists, creative writers, haven't done a better job of showing this than historians have. Do you know Dorothy Scarborough's novel The Wind? *It deals with a woman who is driven mad by the winds in west Texas. Conrad Richter's* The Sea of Grass. *These books depict characters having to learn about the terrain . . .*

And about the wind. Bill Mitchell, in Alberta, has one called *Listen, the Wind*. That wind comes right off the North Pole sometimes, and sometimes it's like a furnace, but you always have wind on the plains. There's hardly any time when you aren't being blown and your hair on end. Your eyes wobble. That's again something which people used to the protection of woods would have to learn to get used to, and it probably does something to the psyche. Looking a long way probably does something to the psyche, too. Looking a long way where there's nothing much to see, which is a curious kind of situation. You're aware of a big geometry, but what you notice is ants in the grass. It's an awareness on the one hand and an enforced observation on the other.

In The Sound of Mountain Water *you note that the West lacks a coherent culture. Why is that, and do you think this lack of coherency is more evident in the West than in other regions of the United States?*

Yes, I think it is. Again because of the diversity of the West. New England is pretty much of a piece. The South is essentially of a piece. The Middle West is there from the eastern edge of Indiana clear to the Rocky

Mountains, practically—at least clear to the Missouri—all one homogenous thing, and it does one thing primarily, or it did in the beginning, which is grow grains. But the West is several different regions. The Southwest is one, very different ethnically, historically, religiously—and in the way the Indian cultures have interpenetrated with the Spanish—from the Northwest, where Indian cultures were shoved off to one side on reservations, and where the ethnic mix includes a considerable Scandinavian element which stretched from Minnesota and the Dakotas to Alaska.

We were speaking of continuity. One of the continuities is that people from the Old Country tended to find the kind of country here that they knew. The Swedes and Icelanders and Norwegians all found cold country, very much like Sweden or inland Norway. The Icelanders settled on places like Washington Island in Lake Superior, looking for water around them, having the feel of islands. The Italians found California and began raising wine or fishing off the coast. There's so much variety, even within the state of California; it's at least two states, maybe three. Maybe it would be better if it were at least two. But the Mormon country, the Northwest, the Southwest, the plains cattle country—North Dakota, Montana, Wyoming— they're so different as regions, and they are also so different in their history and ethnic compositions, that I think trying to make a unanimous culture out of them would be a hopeless job. It would be like wrapping five watermelons. As a writer, you have to do it by subregions if you're going to do it really intensely, and in personal terms. Or you can do it serially, which I was doing to some extent in *Angle of Repose* and even in *The Big Rock Candy Mountain*. I was doing two or three kinds of regions, leaving one and going on to the next. It's like a curtain coming down. To try to do in historians' terms a book about western culture would be a much harder job, because you couldn't confine yourself to the piece, you couldn't let yourself go with just one sample. You'd have to try to encompass the whole works, and that would be very hard. Maybe that's why western history sort of stopped at 1890.

> *You imply in the historical sections of* Wolf Willow *that the West has been more Mild than Wild, in some cases. Would this have been truer for the Canadian West than the United States?*

Considerably, I think. I was making the point (I *think* that's where I made that point) that in the American West there was no law before people came in. The whole California Gold Rush, and every gold rush after it, was simply mass trespass. They had no right to that gold or the land that they filed claims on. There was no law by which they filed them. They made their own law and justified it among themselves and later got it accepted. In the Canadian West the Mounties were there from 1870 or so on, before any settlers, except a few whiskey traders, were in the country at all. It's interesting to note that most of the Canadian prairie provinces were settled not by covered wagon but by train. The railroad, like the law, came through ahead of most settlement. Canada was not mild in terms of its weather and the ruggedness of the life, but it was certainly mild in terms of the shoot-'em-up, self-enforced, side-arm law, which did apply to some extent in the United States, and which influenced a great many people who never practiced it.

I'd like to move in another direction. Few western historians have paid much attention to history as a literary art. Might that be a reason why so little western historiography has gained a large readership among professional audiences? I'm excepting Bernard DeVoto when I . . .

Would you except Paul Horgan?

I would say he is an exception too.

Because *Great River* seems to me a good book in the literary sense as well as the historical. The one on Father Lamy is not so good. It doesn't have the same excitement for me.

Both of those writers, if I remember correctly, had training in literature.

They were both novelists to begin with, or wanted to be. Paul has written, I don't know, books of short stories and eight to ten novels. Actually he was trained as a musician, so that he's spread over a tripod. But apart from those two, I wouldn't think of most western history as literary art. And that's odd, too. History as literary art begins with Bancroft, Parkman, Prescott, and Motley in New England. They all had the same romantic notion of history, of taking a great subject, a big tragic subject with a tragic hero like La Salle, and doing it like a great romantic drama coming down to a catastrophe at the end. Nobody, to my knowledge, has done that kind of book about any aspect of western history. A lot of people have done their best with their little blow pumps to blow up western history and make it sound romantic and exciting. But the result often has a sense of strain about it, and nobody has really been swept up as Parkman was by La Salle, or the way Benny DeVoto was about the western movement. There's no question that he got most of his cues from Parkman; that's where he learned the most about writing history. . . . I'm trying to think of some other western historians.

Let me suggest some that I think have tried to do this. I think David Lavender has tried.

Yes. He's a good historian, and he writes well, but I don't think he has the unmistakable gift. I've enjoyed his books and learned a lot from him, but I wouldn't put him quite in that top category. There are a lot of other people, like Dale Morgan, who were superb historians and knew enormous amounts but didn't write quite well enough to rival Parkman or DeVoto. They weren't Samuel Eliot Morison, any of them.

Those are the people I'm thinking of; they don't belong in that category.

No, it's a different kind of history.

We talk about Bernard DeVoto, and we talk about Paul Horgan, and we talk about Wallace Stegner. Their beginnings were in literature, and they also have written history.

Yes, although I suspect you would have a hard time getting most historians to grant that the history we write is legitimate. Quite.

I think you would be surprised.

I think there is a prejudice against the fact that a thing can be readable; it has to be a little hard, or it isn't legitimate for some historians. Or if it isn't about white papers, diplomatics, wars, and so on. The kind of history that Benny liked, not the kind he wrote, but the kind he added to Parkman, more or less, was the kind of thing that Arthur Schlesinger, Senior, introduced to Harvard in the 1920s—social history of the humble kind, an account of the way in which people actually lived. Benny was putting together two traditions, but he was romanticizing even the humble. *Mark Twain's America*, for instance, is a sort of social history book; it's about how people lived. But a lot of people wouldn't recognize themselves in there because, even there, where social history's his intention, he had the other impulse. Do you prefer Thucydides or Xenophon? Thucydides is marvelous, but he isn't the storyteller that Xenophon was.

Repeatedly you have written about Bernard DeVoto as a major historian —a major western historian as well as an American historian. What is it about his historical writings that appeals most to you?

Among other things, his choice of subject. I'm interested in the western movement as much as he was, and I was as much born to it, so that I couldn't escape it. Also, I like a storytelling historian, and he always was trying to tell stories. He managed to—I think I said this in the *Uneasy Chair*—he managed to tell better stories in history than he did in fiction. His invention wasn't up to his capacity to seize upon a historical incident of great dramatic value, or a historical character, or real, prickly individuality, and put them into his history. It is as if he trusted history but he didn't trust his own imagination, quite. There's always a little bit of shrillness in the fiction, but I don't hear it at all in the histories. He had some qualities that many historians don't like. For instance, he was very judgmental; he didn't hesitate to judge historical characters as if he were judging the man next door who just burned down his chicken coop. John Charles Frémont—Captain Jinks of the Horse Marines—he's scornful of all the way up and down, and I don't imagine that Allan Nevins particularly responded to that. But DeVoto combined the quality of judgment with a very large amount of historical knowledge. He was loaded, he was a learned man. At least that one subject he knew inside out. And when you combine the storytelling impulse and the kinds of simultaneity and other literary tricks that he played, with the romantic choice of a big subject . . . the result is Parkmanesque. He always tried to do it as Parkman had done it, in terms of personal experience, so that it was constantly evocative in the way fiction is. So far as I'm concerned, that's good. I like history like that.

What other western histories have been useful to you in writing your historical and fictional works?

Oh, all sorts. I suppose every history I ever read has had some effect on me because it taught me something, and I had to get my education in public and by myself. I never was trained as a historian, and I don't know anything about the trade. So I've learned it from reading other historians, insofar as I've learned it at all. There are people scattered all up and down the historical spectrum who have taught me something. William Byrd's *History of the Dividing Line* taught me something. Castañeda taught me quite a lot. There are people who have dealt with Mormon history or western history, people like Dale Morgan and Juanita Brooks, who have taught me plenty. Ross Toole, in Montana, his histories of Montana. Paul Horgan. Chittenden on the fur trade and Yellowstone Park.

You cite Webb an awfully lot, too . . .

And Webb—I should certainly not have forgotten Webb. And that's not by any means all the historians I admire. Certainly Sam Morison can't be left out of any major list.

Do you remember when you first encountered Turner and his ideas?

Yes. I was writing *The Big Rock Candy Mountain* and trying to figure out what it was I was writing about. I was at Wisconsin then, right in Turner's backyard. And I guess I got the feeling there of something meaningful to my work in Turner: the importance of the impact of the frontier upon human character and upon human lives. I could braid that in with my own family's experience so that it seemed to have a particular meaning. Also I'd been reading a lot of Norwegian literature for some reason, I don't know why, including a lot of saga novels and three-deckers and things.

Didn't you tell me at one time that you had planned your Big Rock Candy Mountain *as a three-decker . . .*

As a three-decker, yes. I told Stephen Vincent Benét that. He said, "I'd try to get it into one."

But you did tell me that you had cut out long sections.

Oh yes, I threw away hundreds of pages of North Dakota. I was just spinning my wheels in the sand; I wasn't getting started. In *The Big Rock Candy Mountain* there's a point at which somebody brings some gold dust into Grand Forks, North Dakota, and Bo Mason gets excited by it. Then the novel skips a year or two and jumps to a tent in the Washington woods. That gap represents about three to four hundred pages of cutting. I resorted to the quick cut because I couldn't see any other way of getting around that material. I knew too much in that book about what I was doing, and I hadn't learned yet how to leave things out. So I had to write them first and *then* leave them out, which is time-wasting.

In such works as One Nation, Beyond the Hundredth Meridian, *your biography of DeVoto, and your Mormon books, have you consciously "shaped" history? Isn't history-writing a literary art for you?*

Oh, it certainly is. I think we have to make some distinctions about how you shape history, though. You shape it to some extent simply by choosing a subject. If you choose it in Parkman's terms, you have carved a big T-bone out of the meat of history, and that's where you're going to concentrate. You also, I suppose, make some changes in history simply by the treatment you choose to give it. If you are absolutely, coldly, objective that's one thing. But if you are going to see the Oregon Trail in Tamsen Donner's terms, or Narcissa Whitman's, that's different. DeVoto was constantly seeing things through the eyes of participants, utilizing their journals and staying close to their perceptions with a lot of quotations. That's the most evocative way of doing it, it seems to me, but the treatment does change the whole tone and character of the history.

And you shape it by selection, by the fact that you choose to play up one scene because of its dramatic or thematic value and tone down others. I was doing that all the time in *Gathering of Zion* because a lot of those journals were dull, but you had to get through the days. So I was concentrating on the days when something drastic happened to some individual and lumping a lot of other things into a summary paragraph. You do emphasize some things and play down others, according to the conception that you have. But I don't . . . let me think this one out. . . . It seems to me there are several kinds of history. If you're writing a history of events that might be called public events, historical events that are almost everybody's property—conspiracy of Pontiac, Montcalm and Wolfe—then I think you had better be very, very careful about changing anything or inserting anything which is too personal or speculative. A lot of the history that I have written in novelistic terms, or have used in fiction, is the history of a small, relatively unnoticed individual within some large context of events. I think you have a legitimate right to take such a character and make him into a fictional character, whether the fiction conforms to the actual biographical fact or not. What you're doing is using history as the raw material of fiction, and you can't use it unless you can use it flexibly. It just won't work.

> *I noticed in your biography of DeVoto that you made use of synecdoche. You praise DeVoto for utilizing it, and you use that method in your biography of him. What you say about the writing of the* Gathering of Zion *is another example, isn't it? You select a part to show something larger.*

Yes. I guess I was using a quotation from Robert Frost, too, that "all an artist needs is samples." All art is synecdoche, according to Frost. I don't know who thought that up first, whether Benny did or Frost did. It could have been either one. They were constantly goading one another. But it does mean a marked difference of approach when you use it in history—or biography. Nowadays you can't write the old-fashioned, two-volume life-and-times. What you can do is comparable to a modern novel as against a novel by Dreiser, let us say. If you compare two novels of practically the same year—Dreiser's *American Tragedy* and Scott Fitzgerald's *Great Gatsby* —you find a very great difference. They're both biographical novels; they're both novels of a life and a death. But the treatment is different. Something similar happens in biography.

> *Dos Passos does this a little, doesn't he, in those sections of* U.S.A. *where he picks a figure to illustrate something larger?*

Oh sure, yes. The biographies, the newsreels.

> *In writing about the Oregon Trail you speak of the "feel" of trail experiences. Has that been a major purpose of your historical writing—to give a "feel" of the past?*

Yes. The first thing I wrote that was at all historical was *Mormon Country*. It isn't much historical, it's just a kind of reporter's book mixed with reminiscence. When I got to *Wolf Willow*, which is, I think, true history of a kind, there wasn't much history to work from, because nobody had written much about that country. A little bit in the *Jesuit Relations*, a book like *The Company of Adventurers*, reminiscences of two or three old cowpunchers, newspaper accounts of certain episodes, were all I had to work with. So I did interweave a lot of my personal experiences as well as my personal feelings and made reminiscence serve history much more directly.

In the Powell biography there is no reminiscence, but some echoes of personal experience. I took the trouble to know the country, for instance. I wasn't really writing a biography of Powell in the sense of personality, I was writing a career, and the career dealt with the plateau province. I wouldn't have felt comfortable writing that book if I hadn't gone down the Colorado River in two or three different installments and if I hadn't spent a half dozen years when I was an adolescent in the southern Utah plateaus; I knew the succession of strata, and I could have drawn you the profile of Table Cliff. That kind of familiarity seems to me useful; at least it was reassuring to me while I was writing.

> *I think I sense this familiarity as much as any other time in the opening sections of* Wolf Willow, *when you're finding your steps back until finally you smell the wolf willow. Then you know that's what it was that led you back through time.*

That's absolute autobiography. My wife and I drove up through from Medicine Hat, driving east, and I hunted around that old hometown incognito, trying to find out how it felt, and I smelled that smell at once. It all came back. I couldn't figure out what the smell was. It took me two days to find out. I ate leaves of every shrub in the valley, I think, before I found the right one. Well, sure, that's a very personal piece of history. The Powell is maybe a better example of how most history would be written. Actually, I took the same kind of pains with *Joe Hill*. I could have written a history of the IWW, but I chose to write a novel. In certain episodes that are part of the fabric of history, like the hop field riots in Northern California, I was going by eyewitness accounts; I wasn't inventing. But when I had Joe Hill working for a rancher in Goleta picking lemons and sleeping in a culvert, I was inventing out of whole cloth. I had him hold up the ranch. Pure invention. It's the kind of thing that might have happened, since he was a migrant, and the kind of place he would have come to, and it was a place I knew. So, I was inventing there, but where it came close to the surface of history I didn't feel I could, or should.

> *When you have written such novels as* Joe Hill *and* Angle of Repose *you have made extensive use of historical documents, yet you mention in both cases that you have "warped," to use your word, history to meet your fictional needs. Are there dangers in this process? How do you react to people who say you have misused or abused history?*

Some people did say I abused it in *Angle of Repose*. I was just following my usual procedure, and it never occurred to me that I was abusing it. And I wasn't warping any of the history which people know; I was warping the biography of the woman on whom I was drawing as a model, but I wasn't warping her life. If I had been writing her life, I wouldn't have done any such thing. But in writing fiction you have to keep a character flexible. You can't freeze her, and historical events have a tendency to freeze; they get inflexible and won't move. I don't know what I meant by "warping" history. I suppose I meant I use history as a plastic, malleable material out of which fiction is made. And as I was explaining earlier, it would only be a certain kind of history that I would feel justified in doing that to. I wouldn't warp anything in the life of George Washington, for instance, if I was writing a book about the Revolutionary War. Any time Washington appears there, he would have to appear as history would justify. That was true in *Angle of Repose* where Clarence King or any historical figure came in. Those meetings in the Leadville log cabin authentically happened. Howard Jones swore I made them up, but he was wrong—I didn't. I was just making use of history.

On several occasions you mention that novelists and historians should see the continuities between the frontier and the modern West. What legacies has the frontier left us?

Several—not always desirable, I think. One of them is that cowboy myth, that myth of rugged individualism, freedom, adventure, everybody's fantasy of being out alone with nature in wild colorful places. Most western lives are not like that, though most western lives have a real legacy from the frontier which is useful; it is all the open space that has been saved by the United States government. It surrounds every western town, and there is hardly a western town that doesn't have good country within walking distance, certainly easy driving distance. And that's the thing about western life, which, it seems to me, Westerners could least spare, would be least ready to give up. In fact, they abuse the privilege. Witness the off-road vehicle guys who want to take their jeeps up into the wilderness where they don't belong. Without invading wilderness areas, we all have free use of eminently desirable country. So the double, contradictory, legacy is a continuing legacy of spaciousness and an illusion of independence and rugged individualism. I suppose the one is fed by the other. It's hard to see how you can eliminate the myth, or the illusion, of independence and individualism when you have all that country against which to test yourself individually from childhood up.

Maybe it isn't absolutely a myth—it's only a myth as it applies to delusions of grandeur, dreams of glory. You have a feeling that if you're from Wyoming, you can lick anybody—contemptuous of sheepherders and potato farmers from Idaho. Wyoming has this myth very bad. I remember a couple of Mormon cowboys who worked on Struthers Burt's ranch in Jackson Hole in the summertime. Handsome, robust, effective guys full of macho feelings. Always getting into fist fights with potato eaters from

I-DE-HO. They came from Idaho themselves but, having moved to Wyoming, they were superior. Blacked the eye of a hired man from Wisconsin. Living up to the local traditions.

Several people have mentioned to me that they think if there's a place in the United States where the Old West is still alive, it's in Wyoming or in Montana.

I think so. For one thing, that country heals a little better than further south. Utah, Arizona, and New Mexico are pretty badly depleted ranges; as cattle and sheep country they're diminished a good deal. I think of the Escalante Basin, which used to carry twelve thousand sheep and four thousand cattle. It carries nothing now; it's just bare stone. But cow country is still preserved in Montana and Wyoming—northwestern Wyoming particularly—and out on the plains. The ranching life in Montana and Wyoming is now a hundred years or more old; it's sometimes the fourth generation on a single piece of ground. It begins to be a culture if you stay that long in one place. Ranching is the only continuing culture I know in that country. The mining towns like Butte are up and then down again in decay, and the new places like Colstrip are just company towns, ephemeral blisters on the landscape. The enduring towns exist for the ranches. In the Yellowstone Valley, say, it's in towns like Billings, Livingston, Big Timber. The ranching country has these little clustered towns for market places. That's a good life, I think, and it could go on forever if it were intelligently done.

Thanks in large part to the federal government, people are learning to do more for range protection than they used to know. There was a thing called the Mizpah–Pumpkin Creek experiment in Montana during the Dust Bowl years which convinced a lot of old hard-nosed guys who thought they knew more than the professors. That experiment increased the carrying capacity of that range from two thousand animals to five thousand in six years. Big leasing outfits are often careless of the range, but many ranchers I know in Montana are careful of their grass and shrewd about it, and a lot of them have degrees in range management, which is more than most of the Sagebrush Rebels have. That country has just enough water on it so that it heals; even if it's overgrazed some, it'll come back to a considerable extent.

We've been talking about the kind of western history that's been written. Many people say that the romanticizers have western history in their hands. If that's true, what kind of history is going to have to be written, history that tells what the West is really like? How are we going to overcome an excessive fascination with the Old West?

It would be a hard job to get that out of the path. I think it is true that many good western historians have been romanticizers, including Benny

DeVoto and Paul Horgan. I don't know—perhaps Earl Pomeroy is a person who could handle the West in its realistic aspects. Billington, who just died—I don't know, would you call him a romanticizer?

I think he was a healthy combination.

Yes, it seems to me he was not an objectionable kind of romanticizer certainly. He knew a lot. Hawgood, I guess, is a romanticizer. Who else is there? To some extent David Lavender is too.

I guess I wasn't thinking so much of those people as I was of the kinds one finds in—and I suppose they've replaced the old pulp magazines— True West, Real Frontier.

The kind the cowpunchers used to read out behind the bunkhouse. Reading their own myth. Life imitated art there, for sure. I don't know if they still do. Where do they get those pulps? Do they still sell such things? Or has Louis L'Amour cornered the market?

There is still a series of them coming out of Texas.

Well, that's where it would have to be. That's where the myth is still nine feet tall.

I'd like to ask a final question. You've written about numerous facets of western history—for example, about explorers, about Mormons, about surveyors, and on several recent topics—but you've not written an overview summary of the history of the West. Why not? Have you ever thought of doing one?

No, I haven't, to tell you the truth. I don't think I know enough, for one thing. My education is spotty. I learn a few little areas, but I don't know what comes in between. It's like knowing Billings and Livingston but not knowing anything of the Yellowstone Valley in between. You have to know it. Also, I'm not that much of a professional historian. I used to write history when I was teaching because it was possible to write history—I must have told you this—while I was teaching. I could do a little research here, a day's work or a weekend or an evening there, around other work. Fiction can't be written that way, not by me. So I got into the habit of working on history. I wrote *Mormon Country* that way at Harvard, and I wrote *The Gathering of Zion*, the Powell book, and the DeVoto book, all while I was teaching at Stanford. I was luckier with *Wolf Willow*, which I wrote during a year at the Center for Advanced Study in the Behavioral Sciences. Fiction demands longer submergence. You have to take time off, or else you just write in the summer, which means that a novel can take a long time.

If I contemplated writing a whole history of the West, I would be looking ahead fifteen years. I don't have fifteen years. There are other things

I probably would rather do, too. Such a history would be a major work, and it ought to be done by somebody who could start doing it at the age of twenty instead of coming by it accidentally and sidelong, the way I did. My involvement in history is personal, not scholarly. I wouldn't have got into Mormon history if I'd never lived in Salt Lake and lived at the ward-house on Tuesday nights. I wouldn't have written Powell if I hadn't known the Southern Utah plateaus, and I wouldn't have written Benny DeVoto's biography unless I had known him. All the history and biography that I've done has been an offshoot of personal experiences and personal acquaintances.

9. The Wilderness West

Etulain: In some of your nonfictional writing, you speak of growing up without qualms about killing wildlife. How do you explain the change to becoming an advocate of conservation?

Stegner: Oh, that's just a function of growing up. When you grow up on the frontier, you're more or less encouraged—in fact, you're urged, driven—to go out and kill gophers, for instance, because they're eating all the wheat. When you're given a .22 at the age of eight or nine, as I was, you just shoot at things. We always had a kind of half-Indian notion of living off the land too. We'd catch some unsuspecting wood duck sitting on the river, shoot his head off, and roast him by a fire—terrible. We didn't like it at all, I'm sure, but killing and eating him gave us the satisfaction of being self-sufficient. I quit hunting ducks a long time ago. I just don't get the thrill out of killing anything that I used to. When you're young, it's a matter of skill, partly; the fact that you've hit him is a satisfaction. But . . . I don't know . . . it wears out, and at a certain point I decided I wasn't doing that anymore. One way to get to know a good deal about wildlife is to hunt it. Obviously that's one of the reasons why hunters and fishermen have very often been close to the conservation movement. They've been saving ducks and duck habitats because they want to shoot ducks, but at least they've been saving them from other kinds of things which would have done them in. Hunters know ducks. They can tell a scaup from a red-eye just by the way he flies, and a lot of other things. They often know the animals better than the people who are trying hard to save them from hunters.

[167]

Hemingway, evidently, never made the transition that you did. He seems to have wanted to hunt till his last days.

Yes, he did. I don't understand that. He was a sort of congenital killer. Even Mary Hemingway's book, which you may have read—*How It Was*—shows her as a hunter too, and a killer of a sort. She grew up with a father who was in that same backwoods mold. I guess one of the things that endeared her to Hemingway was the fact that she liked to go on safaris and shoot.

What kind of wildlife was there in Saskatchewan as you were growing up? Coyotes? Wolves?

No wolves. Coyotes, lynxes, wildcats, no deer, very occasionally ante-lope, but most of those were gone. Very occasionally out from the hills a bear, but mostly it was small fur-bearers—mink, otter, muskrat, beavers, and weasels. All of those I trapped along the river and out on the prairie. Quite a few badgers, some black-footed ferrets which are now virtually extinct. And millions of Richardson's ground squirrels, which we called gophers. We greatly encouraged those by planting wheat fields. We created the best environment a gopher had ever seen in his life, and he came in from miles around. I had to kill them all off.

Some of your first writings on wilderness appeared about the time you returned west in the 1940s. Did your move to California have anything to do with your early statements on conservation?

Not really, I think. I'd been interested in conservation—because I was interested in Powell—long before I came to California. I started being interested in Powell when I was still teaching at the University of Utah, way back in the 1930s. I had read Dutton and all of those people because we lived down in the plateaus in the summer. But I didn't get to writing anything on conservation until sometime about—just about the year we came out here, I think. I guess I was doing a piece for *The Reporter* on the whole question of public lands. It's essentially the Sagebrush Rebellion in an earlier version. I wrote this piece called "Public Lands and Itchy Fingers," or something like that, and I got an instant telegram from Benny DeVoto, saying "Do it some more," because he was just—it was about 1946—he was just revving up to take on Senator Robertson and Congressman Barrett from Wyoming in that big land grab of 'forty-six. I wrote a couple of pieces at Benny's urging, then, and that got Dave Brower on to me. Dave was and is a very alert and effective propagandist and partisan. In 1955, when I had written three or four random conservation pieces in no particular pattern, he came down and got me to edit a Sierra Club book on the Dinosaur National Monument problem, dams in the national parks and monuments.

So I edited the book. I wrote a couple of chapters in it, and we got other chapters from Alfred Knopf, Martin Litton, Dock Marston, and others. It was published by Knopf and distributed to all congressmen and senators. That was the first real hardening into unity of the whole conservation movement. Previously these had been little special interests—the Izaak Walton League, the Audubon Society, the Sierra Club—one of them fishing, one of them birds, one of them hiking. But they all got together on this one, and we really whipped the Upper Colorado River project. We could have strangled it to death. We had it down completely. They took the dams out of Dinosaur in a desperate conviction that if they didn't they were going to lose the whole thing. Maybe we should have been harder-nosed than we were, but that's hindsight. Having saved Dinosaur, we accepted the ruin of Glen Canyon, which was not very smart of us. Dave has regretted that all his life. Nobody knew Glen Canyon then except me; I'd been down it a couple of times, and I told him it was better than Echo Park. He didn't believe it, and I didn't push it. But anyway, that first book got me into the thing. It was the first real fighting book that the Sierra Club published. Previously they'd published guides to the Sierra, and backpacking. . . . That was also the beginning of Dave Brower's meteoric career as an effective conservationist. For my own part, moving back to California had something to do with it because it brought me more in touch with the activist movements, particularly with regard to the public domain. In Massachusetts, the public domain seemed a long way off. But once we got back here it was perfectly clear it was something that interested me, and I kept getting mad.

What do you mean when you write that your early essays on the West began "in innocence"—"a simple-minded love of western landscape and western experience"?[1]

I mean that I had no real notion of the threats against the West. I was innocent enough so that the first time I saw Hoover Dam, I was really very impressed with it. I said so in one of those essays in *Sound of Mountain Water*. When I was beginning to work on Powell—I suppose because reclamation was a kind of fulfillment of his ideas—I looked upon the Reclamation Bureau as being really a big savior in the West. A lot of the modern West would have been impossible without it. But I think the West is going to be short-lived, too, partly on account of it. Innocence, I suppose, is just a response to landscape and weather and familiar images and the kiss of the wind. There are many things that make me like living in the West, but I didn't at first *know* anything about it; I didn't know too much about its history, and I didn't know anything about the threats against it. I began to understand the threats the more I wrote on conservation subjects, and the more I got wound up in the Sierra Club—and with Benny.

Would you refer to yourself as something of a local-colorist at that point?

I don't think I was a local-colorist. I wasn't thinking about the writing, I was thinking about my response to landscape or the whole livingscape. It was not a critical response, it was merely appreciative. The more you learn about what people have done and continue to do to the environment in the West, the less you can go around cheering, saying, "God, isn't that great country," which is the way I began.

You praise Bernard DeVoto's efforts in the field of conservation in several of your books. What impact did his ideas and actions have on you?

He galvanized me. The minute I showed signs of being a potential activist in his direction, he was behind me with the cattle prod, because he was looking for allies all over the place. He was almost single-handedly fighting a whole swarm of bees. He and Struthers Burt in Jackson Hole, and Arthur Carhart in Denver, and a fellow from Dubois who was head of the Wyoming Dude Ranchers Association, fed each other information. Carhart wrote a lot of articles himself, made a lot of speeches. Also, William Vogt, who was another of Benny's informants. Vogt published a book, fairly

---

[1]*The Sound of Mountain Water*, pp. 10–11.

recently, on the public domain. Those were the people who were working with DeVoto. I've seen all that correspondence, and it was constant—back and forth. Benny was getting the dope from informants in the West, and he was the spearhead of publicity in Washington and the East. He had a lot of influence on me. He was very persuasive. He knew a lot. He was from the same part of the country as I was, we had a lot in common. And, I suppose, he looked upon me as a kind of protégé, so he felt justified in kicking and boosting me.

He'd already encouraged you in fiction writing, and now he was encouraging you in this field, right?

Well, encouraged me in fiction writing, I don't know. I had written before I met Benny—I met him after one book, at a Chicago Modern Language Association meeting. After that, I didn't meet him again for two years, and in the meantime I wrote two more books. I'd written maybe three books and quite a lot of stories by the time I got to know him well, and didn't need encouragement in writing stories or novels. I would have done that no matter who told me to. But Benny did take me into his confidence once, into his study, and got out all his files and showed me all his *Collier's* and *Saturday Evening Post* stories. I kept on saying: "God, it's hard to live in Cambridge, Mass., on my half-time salary," and he said: "Well, my boy, write for the magazines. Anybody can learn to do it in two years. You ought to be able to learn to do it in less than that." So I tried. I wrote one-part serials, two-part serials, for *Redbook*, and I published stories in *Collier's*. But I found that I didn't really want to do that. I found I would rather teach than write hack stories, so I just quit it. But he *tried* to teach me. He was an old pro. He knew the ropes.

I find it notable that few of your fictional characters have become spokesmen for ecological causes although some of them seem to speak for other ideas that you espouse.

That begets another question. Which ideas do they speak for that I espouse?

It seems to me that some of the ideas that, for example, Joe Allston or Lyman Ward suggest—I'm not saying that they are spokesmen for you, but that some of the themes they illustrate are ideas that you've also spoken for.

I think that if you look carefully, you'll see that they speak often more intemperately than I would. I sometimes let a character take some of my own tendencies to an extreme. Joe Allston, for instance, on the young, represents at a hundred percent what my own attitude would be at about forty. Yeah, I'm in that direction, but I'm not that far in that direction. As for Conservation, it's a cause. It means joining, it means activism, and I don't think fiction should really have proselytizing as its purpose. Fiction ought to be concerned with the perception of truth, the attempt to get at the concerns of the human heart. It has to do with human relations, and human feelings, and human character, and not with things that you could join and get a card in. That's probably why I haven't put any outright conservationists into my fiction, because they would then begin to speak from a soapbox, inevitably. They wouldn't be real characters; they would be characters that I created to do some particular limited job. I would prefer to keep those things separate. I think I have, mainly. There's a little leakage of conservationist, anti-development sentiment in *A Shooting Star*, where the woman's brother—I've forgotten what his name is, Oliver, I guess—is going to subdivide the old mansion and grounds and make a mint of money out of it. Out of unformulated, inchoate feelings, both she and her mother resist that—sentimental reasons maybe. But he's the kind of bulldozer who makes that kind of thing come about, and I didn't present him very sympathetically, or intend to.

But in another way, your characters do front the wilderness, in that many of them have to adjust to their natural settings. Right?

Sure. I suppose Bo Mason is a perfectly good case in point, somebody who is shaped by the wilderness, by the frontiers, by several generations of frontiering. One of his problems is that he's like an Eskimo culture, he can't change enough when the conditions change. He would have been a perfectly sound man in 1840, but he wasn't in 1890 or 1920.

I was thinking of the difference of the two characters in Angle of Repose. *The man and the woman, the ways they react to the natural setting.*

You mean Oliver Ward and Susan . . . yeah, well, he is also a kind of frontier type. To some extent that book presents an absolutely standard, almost cliché, situation: the wandering man and the nesting woman—the woman representative of stability and stasis and civilization, and the man a restless, creative creature in a wide-open environment. But they both, I would say, were definitely on the side of the environment; they just had, shall we say, a masculine and feminine response to it. I don't know that there was much difference between those two in the matter of defacement or marring of the landscape. He was one of those who really did mar the landscape—digging shafts and tunnels in it and building dams and canals—on the theory that this was a way of improving life in the West. It is an almost admirable delusion, but I think it's a delusion. She looked upon everything for its possibilities as an exemplification of the picturesque,

I think. She was an artist and a writer, and she was always looking for copy. She saw the picturesque stances of things. Some of her best pictures are of people loading up a string of packhorses to head up into the hills, or people unsaddling and saddling horses. She had the eye to catch those details, and she loved them, obviously. She loved a lot of the places she lived in, even while she felt like an exile. I wouldn't say either of those people was anti-environment. They were simply too early to understand what they were doing.

> *On one occasion you said that the western past "is a history of resources mismanaged and of compelling conditions often misunderstood and disregarded." Do you think this occurred more often in the trans-Mississippi West than elsewhere?*[2]

Not necessarily. The woods of Michigan and Wisconsin were certainly mismanaged; they were simply devastated, cut down; most of the broad-leaf forests the same way. Trees were just weeds to be got out of the road. Most primitive farmers in Ohio and Indiana spent their time cutting down forests and burning the stumps; rooting the trees out of the earth. So certainly we wasted plenty of resources in other places. The trouble with the situation in the West is that the West doesn't heal. The Midwest has finally come up to second growth, and it *looks* like a forest. It isn't anything like the forest it was, but it begins to look halfway passable. But if you cut down a forest on Lemhi Pass in Montana, the growth rate is so slow there that you're going to wait a hundred years before you see anything like a forest again. What happened in the West was a series of raids. The raids on gold and silver left some rather picturesque ruins around, and some holes in the ground that were dangerous to wandering children, but actually didn't do that much serious damage to the whole country. Towns mouldered away and died in their dry gulches, except the few that were retrofitted and made over as tourist traps. But the raids on timber, mostly for mine timbers, deforested whole mountainsides. In Utah, for instance, a lot of floods and erosion resulted from Mormons cutting timber on the slopes. In Colorado the same. There have been drastic and serious results on those steep slopes, in country of severe storms, which didn't happen in the Midwest on flatter ground.

Likewise, the raids on the grass left all of the ranges of the West about fifty percent deteriorated. Some of them have been partly brought back, some of them have been changed, some of them have been through a stage of going to sagebrush; they're now dragging the sagebrush with chains to sow it to crested wheat grass and creating an altogether different range from the one that was originally there. Not as good a one either, but better than

---

[2]*The Sound of Mountain Water*, p. 19.

sagebrush. Anyway, the raids on resources have been more damaging in the West, partly because it is arid and steep, and you get a lot more scars on the land and slower healing. Even visual scars take forever to heal. Down in the Escalante Desert and in the San Rafael Swell, during the uranium boom of early World War II and the fifties, all kinds of prospectors were running around, and oil crews were doing a lot of seismic exploration. The tracks of their vehicles are still there. It's hardly rained three times since. It never heals. If it does rain, the ruts generally create little erosion gullies that wash away topsoil. It's a much more fragile environment than any well-watered country.

DeVoto called the West a plundered province, and others have referred to it as a colony of the East. Who's plundered the West, and who's caused it to be a colony?

Most of the plundering of the West has been collaborated in by certain interests within the West. For instance, Huntington and Stanford and the others of the Big Four produced in California a body of capital which in turn became, as it were, predatory on the rest of the West. Big, big companies— Union Pacific, let us say—got so big on land grants from Congress that an enormous amount of money was set to working upon a relatively unresisting or helpless section of the country, in the same way that big oil conglomerates now work on the mountain states. There's so much money that it's almost impossible to resist them. They buy up everything. Another example: Anaconda Copper is now owned by Atlantic Richfield, and Atlantic Richfield and Anaconda are involved in platinum mining and manganese mining in the Beartooth-Absaroka country. What they are after has nothing to do, really, with the continuing life of the West. What mining corporations are there for is to get the copper out of Butte Hill or the gold or the platinum out of the Mouat tunnel, or the oil out of the ground. Then they go away again, leaving their ghost towns and little scatterings of survivors who cling to the shacks and make use of the remaining, dwindling facilities, and maybe grow a few vegetables, or go back to the subsistence ranching that may be all that's possible there. The plundering was done mainly with eastern capital, in spite of the example of Stanford and Huntington. It comes from California now, quite a lot of it, but in earlier times it came from the East; a lot of it came with the railroads. Jim Hill, for instance, practically settled the dry plains of Montana and North Dakota, places that shouldn't have been settled in those terms. But he had to sell land in order to pay his railroad bills and get his railroad built. So as an empire-builder, he built the lives of an awful lot of people into his empire; a lot of them, like *my* family, went places where we shouldn't have gone, trying to make a living where we couldn't make one. All thanks to Jim Hill. We were all plundered to make Jim Hill's success.

The rugged individualists often turn out to be the tycoons and the economic tyrants. Other people have to sing smaller tunes.

In the twentieth century the West has been closely tied to the policies of the federal government. Does this continuing policy bode well for the future of the region?

As you know, I have some pretty pronounced ideas on that subject. I think the West would have been impossible without federal intervention. In the first place, that land that was left public (what became the Bureau of Land Management lands) was left because the government couldn't sell or give it away. Nobody wanted it. Hoover tried to give it to the states in 1930, and the states just laughed. "Who wants more of that desert?" they asked. Now, of course, it's another matter, because the desert seems to be loaded with resources, and the technocratic power of companies to go into the most unfriendly environments and get stuff out is greater now than it was then. But not only land. Water. The federal government has produced . . . no, that's not the right word . . . it has dammed up, redirected, diverted, stored, all the water in the West—the water that the whole West lives on. No state has any substantial water system except California, and even California's is based ultimately on federal dams. The water's federal, the management of the open range is federal. Without the federal management, it would be much worse off than it is; it would be a disaster. Federal management had to get really acute about 1934 with the Taylor Grazing Act, because in the Dust Bowl years western soil was blowing clear to Washington. Even the cowboys got wise for a while. Yes, I think the federal government is largely responsible for the fact that the West is habitable by anywhere near as many people as it is, and I think it will be necessary for the federal government to stay right there as a collaborator and partner if the West is going to avoid the bust after its boom. What the West has always done—what states like Utah, at least, have always done—is to cry like hell about the absentee landlords and the soulless bureaucrats in Washington, and fight them every bit of the way. But when a Dust Bowl comes on, when a cyclic drought comes on, when a depression comes on, when resources run out, when water is needed, they cry for help to the same old Feds that they've been knocking. It's a wildly schizophrenic position they assume, and they irritate me when they do it. All right, be independent if you want, but don't be independent with your hand out, which is the way most of the western states have been—or at least certain interests in the western states.

Now I should instantly qualify that. It isn't the whole West that thinks that way; it's what you might call the Republican economic West, the development-minded corporate West. Most people on the street would give you perfectly sane answers on questions like the public domain. Anybody who has all his life enjoyed the use of the public domain for hunting, or fishing, or backpacking, or mountain-climbing is not going to be very friendly to the notion of turning it over to the states, who would by constitutional requirement close it or sell it to private owners who would put up "No Trespassing" signs. Most of the freedom of the West is federal freedom.

What do you think about the Sagebrush Rebellion?

I've just been talking about it. I think it's another grab by the same old people. Governor Babbitt of Arizona said, "If you pull off the mask they are the same old special interests who have been grabbing for the public lands ever since Teddy Roosevelt." That's who they are, augmented by certain greedy state officials who think that now with all these natural resources revealed to be in the public domain (if those could get into the hands of the state, and they could sell them to Exxon, or Peabody Coal, or somebody), the state could realize a big rise in income. I think they're deluded. They get more income out of it as it is, because they get half the leasing fees—eighty-seven-and-a-half percent of some kinds of leasing. They also get a lot of things taken care of. They get extra money for roads, highways, freeways, interstates through the public land. They get every sort of subsidy, which they forget. They think, though—some of them do—that they could make a killing. They probably have some personal reasons for thinking so, too, because there is a local élite in almost every state which actually realizes most of the economic opportunities and reaps most of the profits from them. Those are the people who are for the Sagebrush Rebellion. The ranchers themselves, I think, are deluded, and to some extent they're being maneuvered by mining companies. The entire mining industry is absolutely solid for the Sagebrush Rebellion because it's got an interest in getting those public lands opened to mineral and oil exploration. The United States Chamber of Commerce, the *Wall Street Journal*, the Sagebrush Rebels, they're all of one economic complexion. It's the party of privilege; essentially it wants the lands given to the states. I have been sort of crossly resisting that tendency.

You have been playing Father Mapple and climbing up into your pulpit, have you?

Well, I wrote a piece in the *Washington Post*, and I've written two others for *The Living Wilderness*, and I've given a speech and seminar in Jackson Hole, and I'll give another one in San Diego, on essentially the same subject. I've helped other people who were working on the same things, and been helped by them; I even worked the subject into the Tanner Lecture at Utah last year. Any time I get a chance to open my mouth, I air that topic. But not in fiction.[3]

Do you think that some of the people who are backing the Sagebrush Rebellion were encouraged by the kind of revenue that Alaska and Texas . . .

Oh, I'm sure. But Alaska is backward and magnificently endowed, and Texas, of course, never had a public domain. Texas was a self-owned republic when it was annexed. But even Texas, without a public domain, hollers for help to Uncle Fed if it comes to drought, or heat wave, or many other kinds of things. To some extent, every state is entitled to look to the federal government for help in catastrophe, but it's a little less than becoming in the public land states for them to lambaste the poor Feds in between times. I fear the states as potential owners of all this public land because I don't trust them not to be manipulated by the élites which run local government. Also, I don't trust them not to be manipulated by that local empire of the Bureau of Reclamation, which is hand-in-glove with the water users—and in places like Salt Lake and Denver is a very potent political force. It's a federal force, but it's on the states' side because it gets its political backing from the states' side, from the local élites, and from the water users. The Bureau of Reclamation becomes, in effect, one of the enemies that the federal government has to resist. All of those forces work for private interests as against the public interest, I think. That's what I find wrong with them.

Isn't there a conflict here that lies at the center of western history? We have emphasized individualism, every person speaking for himself or herself, and yet many people have come to realize that we're going to have to plan and cooperate more if we're going to preserve the West.

I wish more had realized that. I think the environmentalist movement does realize it. There is among environmentalists a sentimental fringe, people who respond, as you say some of your students do, with a blind preservationism in all circumstances. But you can't do that. You manifestly can't go that far, though it would be nice, visually and in other ways; people do have to live, too. Some kind of compromise has to be made. Individualism I've already expressed myself on. I don't think you see it too much in the life of the ordinary, garden-variety Westerner who is urban, by-and-large, and who works for some company, by-and-large, not for himself. I don't think there are any more small businessmen in the West than in any other place

---

[3]"The Twilight of Self-Reliance: Frontier Values and Contemporary America," in Sterling M. McMurrin, ed., *The Tanner Lectures on Human Values, Volume II* (Salt Lake City: University of Utah Press, and Cambridge: Cambridge University Press, 1981).

in the country. So the West isn't any different in that respect. Most people work at jobs. As a matter of fact, in the West I suspect there is a heavier-than-elsewhere proportion of people in federal jobs. If you took all the federal employees out of Denver, you'd depopulate the town. Salt Lake, every regional capital, has them; all of those bureaus maintain regional offices, and that's another thing that states forget. They get an awful lot in federal payrolls and an awful lot of jobs and homes and everything else from the federal involvement. I'm sure we're going to have to plan more and cooperate more, and I think the first stage of that is to acknowledge the fact that the federal government is not only a permanent partner in that collaboration, but a very essential one, absolutely essential. We may get talking about water later on, but in case we don't, let me say that the future of the West is built on running water, and that's not a very stable foundation.

When you speak of wilderness as the "geography of hope," might you not imply that a shrinking wilderness would bring disillusionment and despair?

Well, it brings at least dissatisfaction and anxiety. It hasn't, fortunately, shrunk as much as it might have. We haven't really busted the whole continent. There are, what, a few million acres in wilderness that are permanently set aside unless Mr. Watt succeeds in undoing them. Just a few million acres is not by any means enough, but they do give you some sense of a line beyond which you don't have to fall back. That's, of course, speaking of wilderness in its purest form. There are also all the national parks, national monuments, and national historical sites, lakeshores, seashores, and recreational areas. There's quite a lot of federal land, besides all of the state land put aside in parks. Having really gutted the place in the nineteenth century, we've been doing much better in the twentieth, up to 1980. There's still a chance, in spite of Watt, that some more land will go into wilderness. Some BLM land, the southern California deserts, for instance, and certain areas that have been under study for a long time. If the Forest Service had really cooperated in this, the RARE II program would be a lot further along. There would be better planning coming out of it. The Forest Service has been dragging its heels; it really wants to cut wood more than anything else.

How can you be hopeful, then, when so many recent events suggest a lessening commitment to ecological concerns?

These certainly are not very encouraging signs. I hope and pray that they are ephemeral. I wouldn't be at all surprised if Mr. Reagan's attack upon all of these things, not piecemeal, but across the board—the Clean Air Act, the relaxing of emissions regulations on automobiles, the loosening of constraints on chemical companies, the dumping of toxic wastes—all kinds of things—will eventually bring him a terrific public kickback.

I saw in the paper this morning some figures, polls of how well Reagan is doing. Fifty-nine percent of the people polled thought he was doing fine. But at the same stage in his administration, Jimmy Carter had seventy-five percent of the people in favor of him. John F. Kennedy had sixty-seven percent. Every recent president has been higher at this stage than Reagan is now. Moreover, the number of people who have gone from undecided to definite opposition has gone up from fourteen to twenty-four percent. The number of nays is increasing fairly steeply. I think that trend will continue. I don't think the party of privilege can ram its privilege down people's throats very long without getting very obstreperous public resistance. It'll take a while for it to get into Congress, because the Reaganite folks elected their own people last time, but the 1982 Congress is going to show some changes. There won't be enough senators up for reelection to change the balance; probably some of the bad ones will be safe for six years. Some of the good ones will be up for reelection, and that's going to be a dog fight. But I would expect that in the House, where a change of heart is most immediately apparent, you're going to see an off-election change and a heavier Democratic representation. That Democratic representation is going to be environmental, it's going to be consumer-oriented, it's going to be minority-oriented, it's going to be oriented toward all of the areas where Reagan is clamping down. So, I'm not that hopeless, I'm just annoyed that there has to be even a two-year interruption in what was beginning to be some very sensible environmental legislation. The seventies produced quite a lot of volume.[4]

Has the physical proximity of large wilderness areas and the knowledge of their existence made a difference in the outlook of Westerners?

Oh, I think so, I think so. You know a book by Bernard Malamud called *A New Life*? A very irritating book to a Westerner. He takes trout fishing, for instance, as a strange, aberrant, cockeyed kind of Boy Scout activity. You get the impression that a much more adult activity is sneaking into other people's files and reading their private mail. I really wanted to kick Malamud around the block for that book—it presents such an obtuse city-view of the West. But the West that he's talking about—Corvallis, Oregon—*is* much more outdoorish than anything Malamud's characters stand for. It's much more physical. It actually is a good deal more cheerful and less neurotic,

---

[4]In the 97th Congress the Senate had 46 Democrats and 54 Republicans, with 241 Democrats to 192 Republicans in the House; in the 98th Congress the Senate proportions remained the same, with 270 Democrats to 165 Republicans in the House.

which is one of the things he can't bear, but he thinks it's a bunch of Boy Scouts. If it is healthier and more outdoorish, what's to be mad at? Anyway, here is a discernible difference between Westerners and people from more urban environments. It involves the effects of smaller population, as against the effects of larger population. You can't get "Good Morning" out of a lot of Easterners when they come out into other areas. They're used to protecting themselves by keeping their distance. On the farm, we used to look with great eagerness upon anybody who came down the road. He represented excitement, something new. That's true in most rural areas, small towns, and even small cities in the West. The degree of public friendliness, openness, a sort of extroverted good nature, is considerably greater than it is in places which have been, for one thing, polarized by successive waves of immigration, so that you get mutually suspicious ethnic neighborhoods, as in Boston.

> *I think you made some of these differences clear, perhaps, when you were commenting about Leslie Fiedler's reaction to Montana in your* Atlantic *article.[5] You mentioned Fiedler's background, his seeing and experiencing novel things in the West, and his not knowing quite how to react to the region.*

Oh yes. Well, he saw some guy in a big hat, with, as he said, a stern, vacant face, stalking down the platform on high heels, and he thought— I think I'm paraphrasing—he thought to himself: "Healthy, I thought in contempt." Fiedler seems to me to have left a bad legacy in Missoula. There's a taint of him that lingers, a Mephistophelian smell of sulphur. I don't think he should have been teaching in Missoula, ever. He's probably better off where he is now, Buffalo, or wherever he wound up. We've had a few people in Stanford, too, who have come out from the East, particularly from New York, and have been unhappy living in Squaresville. It's that square connotation which I think comes close to answering your question. I think Westerners are a lot squarer than Easterners, which is why Easterners don't understand them and why Westerners are sometimes a little bit irritated at being misunderstood. They think they're better off than the people who are misunderstanding them, and I wouldn't be surprised if they are.

> *It's in A. B. Guthrie's* The Big Sky, *too, isn't it? Where he talks so much about the western sky, where Boone Caudill says he can see and think the whole world is the sky. The sense of space and openness.*

Space and openness and thin population do make differences in people's living. They even make differences in human cooperativeness—the coopera-

---

[5]Wallace Stegner and Page Stegner, "Rocky Mountain Country," *Atlantic* 241 (April 1978): 44–91.

tiveness of neighbors in a cold and difficult and even dangerous country. But on Fifty-Seventh Street, some woman being murdered can scream, and within hearing distance of her screams thirty thousand people lock their doors. That's not Eastern or Western, it's a big-city versus a more human scale. The human scale still persists in the West, but in some parts of the East and Midwest it's pretty well gone by. If you look at the picture of Detroit in Joyce Carol Oates, that's not a place you would choose to live, is it?

Her works are not western novels in any way, shape, or form, are they?

No, they're not.

I gathered from your sympathetic treatment of John Wesley Powell in Beyond the Hundredth Meridian *that you find his attitudes toward land and water and conservation still very useful for our generation.*

Oh yes, and still being resisted by a good many forces in this generation. Powell said, at the 1893 Irrigation Congress in Los Angeles, that the West was being endangered by the boosters and their dream: millions of acres irrigated, millions of people flooding in, prosperity for everybody. He warned the delegates that there was only water for about twenty percent of the land in the entire West. You can't make it; you can only hold it back and store it, divert and redirect it, and maybe—this would have been added since his time—recycle it. But you can't make it. If you can't make it for agriculture, you can't make it for industry either, and you can't make it for the cities. If Billings is going to grow to be the size of Denver, it's going to drain the Yellowstone River, and the Yellowstone River is already being used by a lot of other people. The Indians, moreover, have a claim on it under the Winters Doctrine which they haven't yet been able to collect on. I would say there's a very definite constraint upon western growth, and Powell knew why. Aridity is something that you simply cannot fake out. You can only make the maximum use of what water you've got. Beyond that, there isn't any, unless you resort to what the boosters call augmentation. That means bring it in from the Columbia, the Yukon, or somewhere else. Augmentation is, for one thing, enormously expensive. It might cost a hundred billion dollars to bring water into California from the Columbia.

Northwesterners are very much afraid of that kind of project.

Oh sure, and it's not the expense that scares them. Engineers say, "Oh, gee," their eyes light up, they would love to do that job. But there's a political difficulty as well as a financial one, which I think will prevent it. The Northwest doesn't want anything happening to the Columbia such as has happened to the Colorado. The Colorado now just runs into the sand, miles from the Gulf of California. It's used up; its water has been used over and over again. Finally, in order to deliver the million and a half acre feet of usable water we have, by treaty, agreed to deliver to Mexico, we have had to put in a big desalinization plant on the border. The Colorado River is a sample and symbol of the West. It's quite appropriate that it was the river that Powell knew best. He got his information at headquarters, and it was right. A lot of people haven't yet granted that there are these limitations. Oh, they say, I suppose, that the doctrine of prior appropriation shouldn't apply to them. If ranchers in the Yellowstone Valley are already using *x* acre feet of the Yellowstone, for what Peabody Coal or Exxon thinks is a sort of sub-economic activity, these companies would happily take it away from them and use it for slurry lines or power plants. Companies are buying up ranches one by one and just holding them for the water rights on them. That's going to get to be a tight little fight between the traditional ranching and farming life and the very disruptive and damaging industrial life. You could make Billings into Bayonne, New Jersey, as Ross Toole said, without too much trouble, if you had the water.

I was thinking of that controversial article that W. P. Webb wrote; I think it was in the 1950s. In many ways, all he was doing was restating what Powell had said earlier, but people just hadn't heard it.

The one about the West being an oasis civilization, a semidesert with a desert heart? He was absolutely right, though I'm not sure that I agree with his spatial metaphor. It doesn't seem to me to be a semidesert with a desert heart. It seems to me to be strips of desert with well-watered high land, uncultivatable but essential as watershed, between them. It goes in waves, rather than in circles. But that's a quibble. I don't quarrel with the general principle. Certainly Powell taught Webb that; and Powell and Webb, between them, taught Benny DeVoto; and they all taught me. The more you know about the West, I think, the more basic the fact of limited water seems. Regional planners trying to reclaim the Dust Bowl of the 1930s swore by Powell. The closer you get to the facts in the case, the more you have to admire him, I think.

Isn't Powell the ideal western conservationist? He sees through the romantic, distorted notions about the West; he discards them, and moves toward a hard-headed, well-organized plan for conserving the frontier's resources . . .

That's certainly my view of him, and I think the evidence supports that all the way. In fact, I began his biography with a comparison between Powell, on the one hand, and William Gilpin on the other—Gilpin being the standard Manifest Destinarian, the western booster with the most fantastic notions. If people asked him, "Well, but what are people going to do for wood in this treeless country?" he replied, "They dig for it; the ground underneath there is full of roots." "What are they going to do for water?" "They dig for water too. Artesian water wells up all over." Actually there's one little section of the Dakotas where it does, but you could dig a long way without finding artesian water in a lot of the West. To Gilpin, South Pass was going to be a gateway "more thronging than Gibraltar." The Mountain West was going to house more people than the Roman Empire under the Antonines. I used Gilpin, with all his hyperbole, as a sample of the individual who lives by mythology, as against Powell, who was dealing from observed fact.

Much of your time seems to be taken up right now with writing and speaking for conservation measures. Do you really enjoy this kind of activity?

Not really, no. But I feel obligated, since I think I know something about it, to say how I think it is, because so often the people speaking for the other side are misleading. They try to persuade people who don't know, and have no means of knowing, that their mythology is fact. If you know anything at all it's your obligation to try to keep the record straight. No, I don't enjoy it, and I don't suppose I'm going to do it very long, but I did have a certain obligation, I thought, and people told me I did. William Vogt, one of Benny's old henchmen, wrote to me saying somebody had to do some of the things that Benny used to do—somebody who was a good enough writer to be noticed. Then the Natural Resources Defense Council called and wrote me with the same burden. You begin to think that if people are depending on you, maybe you do have an obligation. I'm certainly not Benny DeVoto. I haven't the capacity or the temperament to do what he did. I likewise don't have the forum he did: the Easy Chair was a very good pulpit. He was known as the personality in that place, and a lot of people read him religiously and what he said had a great effect. I can't do that, but I can at least publish articles and make some speeches. I can toss my pebbles onto what I wish were an avalanche of protest.

10. What's Left of the West?

Etulain: Are you optimistic about the future of the West? We've made some mistakes, but haven't we done some things right, too?

Stegner: A few things right, maybe, belatedly, inadequately, too little, too late. But I'm not very optimistic about the future of the West. Particularly in the Southwest—Utah, Nevada, the desert areas of the West—something that has to be called "desertification" is going on. And that's a product to some extent of drought, but to an even greater extent of irrigation—a ground water table which rises, alkalization of fields, salinization of water, and so on. Take the Colorado as a sample river of the West. The Colorado is already over-utilized. A good many places in the Colorado basin are already on the way to desertification. It depends on what you mean by "the future of the West"—but one future of the West is to be a great big overpopulated, urbanized, industrial area pouring out coal and oil and uranium and sending its stuff in slurry lines and high-tension lines to the rest of the country. I wish the West would come back to what it can support, which is a very minimal population based ultimately upon minimal water and minimal grass. I don't think the utilization of water through the Reclamation Service has done anything but promote what will before too long be irrigation ghost towns. That's a gloomy view, I admit, but I don't see any plausible alternative.

Do you see anything in the way of planning or cooperation at this point that you would vote for?

Oh, all kinds of things I would vote for, but I don't think I'm going to get the chance to vote for them—for instance, Mono Lake, which Los

[185]

Angeles has been bleeding and has now drawn down thirty or forty feet. The gulls there are exposed to raiding through coons and coyotes, and a quarter of the world's population of California gulls are in Mono Lake. Pretty soon, within a very few years, there's going to be no place for gulls to breed except Great Salt Lake, and that I suppose is safe. But Mono Lake is a much bigger and more important breeding ground. Likewise, a stopping place for all kinds of traveling wild fowl, especially ducks and geese, flying on the Pacific flyway north and south. In the Great Basin there are very few places for a duck or goose to land, you know. Mono Lake is one of them. What would I vote for? My goodness, I would vote for a thousand things, but one of the things I wouldn't vote for is the heavy industrialization of any part of the West, because all of it has to be based upon water, and the water isn't there. The water will operate about twenty percent of what all the boosters think it will operate, and there's no way of making it. As we were saying earlier, the only alternative to shortage is augmentation, as they call it. We could bring water in from the Columbia or Yukon, which could make waterworks you could see from the moon and which would cost so many billions of dollars. Ultimately it isn't worth it. You might as well raise your crops in Georgia or somewhere where it rains. It's ridiculous to try to promote the West as what it is not—a great growing area where millions of people can live. I don't think they can. Well, those are pessimistic views.

In the April 1978 Atlantic, *you and your son speak about the destructive raids made on Rocky Mountain resources. Won't these raids become even more destructive and numerous if our energy needs increase?*

Oh, absolutely. They're already becoming much more destructive, and the energy companies—Exxon, Peabody, Westmoreland Coal, Atlantic-Richfield, all of those big conglomerates with oil money behind them and oil money to spend—have begun to engross other kinds of energy resources and also water resources. And, as I told you the other day, these companies are buying up ranches in the Jackson Hole area, and in Pinedale and Farson on the west slope of the Wind River Mountains, headwaters of the Green River —buying them up simply to have their water rights available for future industrial development, whatever that might be. Industrialization is a threat to any kind of continuing life in the West. Industry is part of the economics of liquidation. It has a tendency to take those resources which cannot be reproduced or renewed, and gut them, and go. It could use up western water and much of the western landscape, and leave a desert. We've had deserts before, man-made. This is going to be one.

Will the West be able to withstand national pressures to use up the region's natural resources?

That depends on who's in power in Washington, doesn't it? Mr. Reagan is certainly not going to help us do that, or Mr. Watt or Mr. Watt's appointees. Now, as you know, it begins to be the House of Representatives backed up against the final barricade. The Senate is obviously going to go the way the Reagan Administration wants it to, and the House is the only chance of holding the line on a lot of the environmental legislation which evolved in the seventies. That legislation was based on the primal realization of things which for a hundred years have been getting worse and worse and finally began to be adjusted and fixed. If the Reagan administration persists in going through with what it proposes, then the only chance of saving the clean air act, the surface mining act—all of the protections of wilderness and national forest areas and national park areas and BLM land—will depend finally on a very slim majority in the House of Representatives. Between now and the 1982 elections it's very grim, I think.

It's clear in several respects that the West is still a colony, economically, of the rest of the nation. Is that true of its culture also?

Oh, I suppose so, sure, although that's an attitude mainly. It's not a question of culture, it's a question of self-confidence. Its self-confidence is subordinate and colonial. Its culture is something else, and it has a certain stubborn integrity of its own, which is going to insist upon itself in the face of all kinds of intrusions from world, nation, or other regions which seem to want to absorb and swallow it. No, I think the culture itself is safe enough, assuming that it doesn't get overwhelmed by industry, which is a big danger at the moment. But I don't think the self-confidence of the region is at present quite enough to let it make the most of its own essential and integral regional culture.

It seems to me as I look at the subregions of the West that people living in California and perhaps in Texas, in Austin, here in the Bay area, perhaps in Los Angeles . . . these are the places, the subregions in the West where Westerners believe they can compete with cultural influences coming from the East. They seem to believe this more than other Westerners.

There are always attempts to compete; they are regional by definition and by the natural limitations of circumstances. But I would add Dallas to Austin; Dallas–Austin, I suppose, operate together. For example, *The Texas Monthly* is a very vigorous provincial or regional magazine, and it serves a real need in its area, and it probably gets outside of its area to communicate something of that culture to a nationwide audience. The more local magazines in California, *New West* for instance (now *California Magazine*), have seemed to me to be tentative in a way that the *Texas*

Monthly is not. The *Texas Monthly* is a lively magazine which has some of the confidence of its own capacities. *California Magazine* is trying hard. It remains to be seen if there is a statewide and nationwide audience for it.

I think a new thing has happened too in the last generation. Some of the other regions of the West have begun to compete more with California than they do with the East Coast.

Oh sure, and by the same token, California has become one of the raiders upon the Mountain West. It used to be that the West was raided by the East and then controlled by eastern capital. A lot of that capital now comes from California, and a lot of the branch plants that make a colonial economy of the Rocky Mountain states—Hewlett-Packard, Lockheed—they're California capital, California corporations, California energy. I don't think the rest of the West looks upon California as a part of the West, really. It's part of the East; it's just the other end of the dumbbell, and the West is in-between on the handle.

My colleague Jerry Nash has written a book about the twentieth-century West in which he argues that in the period after World War II California has become in several ways a pacesetter for American culture.[1]

I think California is away ahead of a lot of the United States in all kinds of things. In legislation, for instance—even such rudimentary business as automobile emissions—the laws of California are more stringent than the federal laws. And California has learned more about the dangers of uncontrolled growth, simply because it's been through it. It has done all of the things that the rest of the United States may be doing very shortly, but hasn't done quite yet, and has come out the other side. It has even begun to lose population to the areas outside which are less populated and dense, as if by some variant of the second law of thermodynamics. Modern California has been bleeding away into the Rocky Mountains, as it did after the gold rush. They used up the gold in California, and then they hit for Colorado, Utah, Nevada, Idaho, Montana, and from there to the Caribou in British Columbia. The big boom comes to California first and then spreads out to the other areas.

You mentioned that the Rockies are undeveloped culturally. Is that region likely to produce any notable literature? I ask this wondering if anyone would have predicted a major novelist out of East End, Saskatchewan.

---

[1]Gerald D. Nash, *The American West in the Twentieth Century: A Short History of an Urban Oasis* (Englewood Cliffs, N. J.: Prentice-Hall, 1973; rpt. ed., Albuquerque: University of New Mexico Press, 1977).

Major, I don't suppose. But novelists can come out of anywhere. They can come out of Oxford, Mississippi, they can come out of Salinas, California, they can come out of Asheville, North Carolina. Why not? There's no bar against the development of a major talent in any particular area, though I do think that every town developing within a regional setting has to have some kind of base. It's a pyramid, and a major writer is the peak of the pyramid, but there's got to be a support of local interest and local talent, a local storytelling tradition or something else which supports it, as in Faulkner's case. Southern storytelling, oral storytelling, is a platform on which Faulkner built. As it also was for Mark Twain—the whole business of the Mississippi. Insofar as region is concerned, there's no reason why major writing can't come from anywhere, except that in some regions things are a little further along, there's a little better audience, there's a little more enthusiasm, the local historians have managed to sustain the local place and get some of its history. I just had a letter the other day from a fellow named Henri Le Bastard. Henri is a French native of East End, Saskatchewan, and he is the chairman of the local historical society, and they're doing a history of the town of East End, the town in which I grew up. They want me to write an introduction to their book, which I probably will do. Henri represents the kind of tradition which every little local region—Los Altos Hills, East End, Saskatchewan, wherever—begins to develop, and to nourish, and to cherish, put in the museums, and write up as history. The extension of that over larger regional areas begins to produce the sort of tradition out of which Faulkners, Mark Twains, and Wolfes come.

I suspect that you would agree with Josiah Royce that it's acceptable for the West to be guilty of a healthy provincialism—a regionalism that understands itself and its relationships with other regions. Have we Westerners ever had this sense of community that Royce approves of?

Very imperfectly and spottily, I would say. I agree with him entirely. As we were saying the other day, I approve of regionalism if it is a platform from which you take off. If it's an imprisonment—something that you can't escape from—it's quite different. I do think that a kind of acknowledgment of who you are and what you come from and what you mean and how you relate to your immediate surroundings is an absolute essential for the kind of identity that any effective art comes from. But most American and most western cities have been frequently disrupted. The whole history of the West is a series of consecutive raids. The Beaver West gives way to the Gold West, gives way to the Grass West, gives way to the Irrigation West. Everything has to be readjusted about once a generation. It's not quite the same as being a cotton farmer in Mississippi, where the same kind of cropping goes on for three or four or five generations. It's difficult to establish a sense of community when everything changes so fast, as it has in the West, which was developed and settled pretty much after the development of swift communications—railroads and the telegraph especially—with the result that the isolation that produces local cultures didn't quite happen. The West was generally in contact and always moving on. And it takes a longer time to develop arts in a place that has never had a chance to become a region, to develop a kind of context. I expect the West will do it sooner or later, but I don't think it's done it very effectively yet. I don't think of any western state with the healthy provincialism of Iowa, say, unless maybe Utah, and that's not very communicable because it's a separate theological and sociological island in the middle of the West. The rest of the West is still amorphous, still forming.

What is it that western writers will have to do to produce a crop of distinguished novels? I know that . . .

Write good books.

In "Born a Square" you dealt some with this.

Sure. I think all it takes is to write a good book, and partly what it takes to write a good book is to have confidence in what you're doing; and partly what it means to be colonial, and provincial, is *not* having that confidence. I suppose what I'm talking about is confidence—a sort of boldness about utilizing what you've got, what you know. If you utilize it well, somebody's going to come and listen.

I think you quote Josiah Royce in one of the headnotes of Wolf Willow *and . . .*

I do. I like that book of Josiah Royce's about the great community.[2] He spoke to me very personally when he was talking about growing up in Grass Valley and seeing these decaying log cabins that had been built, as far as he knew, away back in prehistoric times. They were probably ten years old. Royce's notion of time as a youngster in Grass Valley was like mine in East End, Saskatchewan. The chimneys up on Chimney Coulee were, as far as I was concerned, absolutely archeological; but they went back, I suppose, at the very earliest to 1869. They were the chimneys of the métis cabins of the Hudson Bay post that went in there. The perception of time by children as they grow up is a very flexible and unreliable thing. You can grow up in Greece, I suppose, in Tríkkala or some such town in the middle of Thrace, where what you see is three thousand years old, and have no more sense of

---

[2]*The Hope of the Great Community* (New York: Macmillan Co., 1916), cited in *Wolf Willow*, p. 239.

the past than if you grew up in Grass Valley, where what you're seeing is ten years old. It's all the same somehow to each generation as it comes on, and yet in the long run the generation does absorb some sense of its past. A Greek has a sense of his past that somebody from Grass Valley can't have; there is the clang of bronze in it, it echoes of Homer. Nothing in Grass Valley echoes of Homer, it only echoes of Lola Montez.

Perhaps by now the real West is a blend, for example, of Billy the Kids, Buffalo Bills, and romantic cowboy-heroes on one side, and on the other side, pioneer women, Mormons, and John Wesley Powells. Maybe the myths and the realities have been so congealed that the Westerner is a marriage of both.

I'm not sure it's a marriage. I wish it were. It's much more likely an alternative—several alternatives between which people, particularly writers, and to some extent painters, pick. If you're going to be a Borein, let us say, you're going to do cowboys, you're going to be an artist in the tradition of Remington and Russell; and if you're going to do contemporary western life, you're going to be in an absolutely other tradition. One kind of tradition is represented by the Russell Museum in Great Falls, Montana, and the Buffalo Bill in Cody, Wyoming. But there's another kind of western art which it seems to me is developing as an alternative, or a much enlarged possibility from the original horse and cowboy and soldier and Indian tradition.

I've always thought it intriguing that Jackson Pollock came from Buffalo, Wyoming.

Well, isn't it intriguing also that Hemingway went back to die in Ketchum, Idaho, about five miles from Hailey, Idaho, where Ezra Pound was born? That's a curious concatenation, that two of the greatest figures of modernism in contemporary literature should either have come from or ended up in a little jerk town on the Big Wood River. It's a strange accident.

I was thinking when I raised this question that some writers realize that their audiences are so accustomed to a romanticized, stereotyped West that when they write about the region they satirize or play with this romantic tradition. The Owen Wister–Zane Grey tradition. I am just reading Ed Abbey's The Brave Cowboy, a novel which uses the tradition of the tough cowboy.

One way to escape from it, of course, is to parody it, and it has been parodied plenty. It's been parodied all the way from *Little Big Man* up and down. That's all right. That's fairly legitimate, but it's not the ultimate reaction or the final solution to that particular problem, because sooner or later some of the worth of that original tradition is going to have to be incorporated in some other tradition, and repudiation or parody seems to me to go too far. They cut out something that's valuable; they throw out the baby with the bath water.

And yet when Lyman Ward tells us he's tired of seeing and hearing so much about the romantic West, he has his audience with him because they know what he's talking about. He's not parodying, but he's talking about this being a vein he really doesn't want to pursue; he doesn't want to write in this tradition.

Yet it's part—a very strong part—of the American tradition. It's mythology, most of it; it doesn't exist in fact, never did exist in fact or only very briefly existed in fact. But it's something that is part of everybody's fantasy, that business of perfect freedom in an absolutely new continent. It's arcadian, but instead of going backward in time to Arcadia and the perfect society, or Eden or wherever else, it goes forward in time to the American wilderness.

Will Westerners generally—like the writers you mention in "Born a Square"—have to go away for a period and look at themselves, and then return, before they will be able to realize what kind of region they want the West to be?

It depends entirely on how much the West grows up. If they can get their education at home they might as well stay at home, but if they have to go abroad to get it, then they'll have to go abroad to get it. The only way to get perspective on your own culture is to step outside of it. It's like the anthropologist who wants to study New Guinea headhunters, or whatever; he has to step out of his own culture and into theirs, and in this case you're stepping out of your own culture and into some culture which is vaguely a world culture, or a national culture, and learning to look upon your narrower provincial culture with some kind of perspective. If you can't get perspective at home, you've got to go abroad. Generally, people have gone abroad. Think of all the American artists who went to study in Paris and then came back home to become American artists of some integrity: Grant Wood, John Steuart Curry, the whole Ashcan School. All of them learned their art abroad to some extent, but came back to apply it at home. I think writers are like that. A lot of American writers have done time in Paris, in Rome, in London, or somewhere else, and got distance upon their own perceptions and their own lives.

One commentator, after reviewing your career, concludes that "it is region and personal experience within that region that have been the crucial determinants in the development" of your art.³ Do you agree with that statement?

I suppose. I've got an exaggerated sense of place. I also have a feeling that my personal experiences are all I surely know, and those experiences are very likely to be rooted in places. I wouldn't ever have the nerve to write about something I didn't know, that I hadn't somehow experienced, and particularly about places I don't know. Maybe that's a weakness. Saul Bellow wrote *Henderson the Rain King* without ever having been to Africa. I couldn't possibly do that. That's beyond me. I'd just give up in front of a situation like that, because I couldn't conceive of making scenes without knowing the kinds of trees that were looking in the window, or the kind of house my characters were living in, or the kinds of people who were coming in the house. Though I could invent, I'm sure I would invent very woodenly. I wouldn't have any confidence in what I was inventing, whereas Saul invents with enormous facility and élan. It's a brilliant book—maybe better because he hasn't been to Africa—but not the kind of book I could write.

I was thinking of comparing you with two other recent western writers, Walter Van Tilburg Clark and A. B. Guthrie. Both write a great deal about the region. They have a strong sense of place, but most of what they write about does not seem to come out of personal experience. Certainly the City of Trembling Leaves *does, but I was thinking of . . .*

City of Trembling Leaves I was about to cite as the most personal of experiences. It's almost too personal; it's like the first novel of a sensitive young man in a western environment. Also, I think there's a lot of personal experience represented in the background—the brute detail, the corroborative detail—of both the *Track of the Cat* and *The Ox-Bow Incident*. In a lot of the short stories, too, though by and large, Walt was fairly objective. He kept himself out of his stories, except in *The City of Trembling Leaves*. Bud Guthrie keeps himself out of his pretty completely. He's always projecting himself one step beyond himself and into objectively observed characters, and yet I can't imagine that Guthrie would have been able to write any of his books without having grown up in Choteau, Montana, on the edge of the Bob Marshall wilderness. He grew up in country that he has now gone back to, to realize himself in. Personal experience is important to me, even when I'm disguising it and modifying it and projecting it into some kind of fictional character. It may not have been as important to them. It doesn't seem to have been.

---

³Forrest G. Robinson and Margaret G. Robinson, *Wallace Stegner*, p. 160.

I've been thinking recently about your experiences growing up on the tail end of the frontier and the similar experiences of another western writer, Louis L'Amour. You're about the same age, you've both written numerous books about the West; and yet the kinds of novels the two of you have written are so different. I know that L'Amour feels that he's been true to the history of the frontier West, and I'm certain you feel the same. Do we then have two literary traditions that have approached the western past differently in the last century or so, traditions that are likely to continue?

I'm afraid they're likely to continue, yes. The difference between L'Amour and me is that he's made two or three million dollars more than I have by writing the kind of western books he writes. It's not the kind of book I would want to write, but it's obviously a book with a very large public. I think he's writing western myths, not writing western realities. And he's true to the myths, which in turn derive to some extent from historical fact. I don't think that six-gun West amounts to much, really. It never did amount to much when it was current. It involved a very brief time and a relatively small segment of the population.

Perhaps it is something like the difference between a Frank Yerby and a William Faulkner in the southern tradition. The Frank Yerby mode— a sort of formula fiction based on the expected ingredients—and the fiction of Faulkner, who knows how to take those materials and work with them.

Sure. Faulkner is away above any of the standard southern traditions. He does them all, as you say, but he does them in terms which absolutely surround them and encompass them and melt them down and make them into something else. He's not the slave of his tradition, somebody who is aping and imitating and mouthing the conventions of his time and place. He transcends and transforms his tradition.

What projects, what books about the West have you once thought of doing, but for one reason or another not done? I remember your telling me that you had at least thought of doing a book about John Muir, for example.

I did think about that. Now it's been sensibly done by a gentleman named Fox.[4] I'm reading it right now; it's there on the dining room table. He had access to some new papers which hadn't been utilized before, and he uses Muir as a kind of kick-off for a history of the whole conservation-

---

[4]Stephen R. Fox, *John Muir and His Legacy: The American Conservation Movement* (Boston: Little, Brown, 1981).

environmental movement. It's a good book, but it would have been for me merely a job, I guess. I never was drawn that much to Muir. Even though I respect him and admire him and read his books with great interest, I somehow never could get next to him; I could only respect him. I also thought once, and I haven't absolutely given up the idea yet, of writing a novel about Clarence King, who seems to me to represent another variant of *The Big Rock Candy Mountain* theme—the big, quick, easy splurge of fortune-making and ultimately the way in which that fortune-making subverts and ruins a considerable talent. A potentially great man goes down on the basis of the profiteering of his place and time. It seems to me a nice moral fable, the reverse of the Powell story. I touched on it a little bit in *Angle of Repose*, when I had Oliver Ward comment on his disappointment in Clarence King because King had given up his principles in order to get rich. Those are two books that I haven't ever started to write. I haven't written a line on either one, and I may never do so. If I do either one, it will certainly be the King and not the Muir, because there's more dramatic conflict in it. Muir never had a doubt in his life as far as I can tell. He's right down one line, and therefore doesn't provide anything very dramatic to write about.

What projects are you working on now and plan for the near future?

God knows . . . I have to finish a lot of little pieces, articles, speeches, things like that. And I have to write an introduction to Leo Holub's book, which is not a little piece.[5] When I get around to finding some time and getting myself straightened around, getting the desk cleared. . . . There are constant opportunities to serve the Audubon Society, the Sierra Club, or the Committee for Green Foothills, or Hidden Villa, Inc., or some other good cause, local or national. I could spend my whole time doing volunteer work for them. They all need help, and they're all good causes, and they all look upon me as an ally, which I am. But I've got to quit that, if I'm going to write any more books. I've got to quit it. And I may quit it about the first of May.

You've turned out now two or three full shelves of books, you've won numerous major prizes, and you've established a reputation as a leading man of American letters. Yet something keeps you working at new projects, facing new deadlines, and accepting new assignments. Why?

It's like a beaver's teeth—he has to chew or else his jaws lock shut. A talent is a kind of imprisonment. You're stuck in it, you have to keep using it, or else you get ruined by it; done in by it. It *is* like a beaver's teeth. You keep doing it because that's really what you're made to do, that's what

---

[5]*Leo Holub/Photographer* (Stanford: Stanford Alumni Association, 1982).

you want to do, and everything that you do projects you one stone further—like the Giant's Causeway in Ireland, where giants were supposed to have thrown rocks ahead of them and stepped from rock to rock as they proceeded. Every rock you throw moves you one step forward, so you throw another rock, until you just wear out. I don't think there's any way out of it, and I don't really mind the imprisonment. I was never a very good consumer, or a very good tourist or traveler. I begin to get very, very restive when I begin to kill time.

You mentioned in a recent interview in U.S. News and World Report *that in some way your salvation is work.*[6]

I wouldn't know what to do if I didn't work. And actually work is most of my pleasure. It's not anything I take credit for. I'm unhappy doing anything else. To play for very long—I like to play a little while—but to play for very long begins to make me very uneasy. To go, for instance, for three weeks to Africa and have nothing to do, no notes to make, no books to read, no plans to move forward. On safari there was no problem—I loved it. But we spent the last week in a couple of game lodges on the edge of Mount Meru, with nothing to do and nothing to read but a book about Evita Perón. I wasn't that interested in Evita Perón, and it was the only book to read, so I read it. There wasn't anything else, not even a magazine. No news, no anything. I had too much of a sense of impermanence to sit down and actually make notes for, or to write anything, so I just waited and marked time and began to chew on my own fingernails.

I have one final question for you, Wally. What has Wallace Stegner attempted to leave for his readers?

Oh boy! You're now looking for a philosophical residue, the sludge in the bottom of the cup. All right, I'll try. To some extent, Hemingway's intention—to say how it was. That's the personal experience aspect of it. The human response to a set of environmental and temporal circumstances. To some extent, also, I suppose, a sort of hangover from Presbyterian Sunday School. When I was young, I got little badges and then little wreaths around wreaths for never having missed Sunday School for seven years. I suppose that must have marked me in some curious and unpleasant way. It probably leads me to take a moralistic view of writing—to think of it not only as an art, but also as a kind of cultural function. I suppose I'm constantly trying to bear in mind that having been very lucky, I also am very responsible, and that the only thing that makes civilization go forward is the

---

[6]"A Conversation with Wallace Stegner," September 22, 1980, pp. 53–54.

responsibility of individuals, whether gifted or otherwise, small or large. All of us have the obligation somehow to have some kind of concern for the species, for the culture, for the larger thing outside of ourselves. I'm sure that's buried not too deeply in most of the books I've written.

I would gather that was something your mother felt strongly too.

I think so. I probably got it from her. My father was notably irresponsible, but she was notably the other way, and I obviously reacted against him and toward her. But it's—I see it all the time, and I'm quite sure that what I least like about some kinds of people is irresponsibility. I don't give a damn what their morals are or anything else, but their irresponsibility to something larger than themselves, to some kind of social stability or common tradition and standard, does seem to me a kind of delinquency. All kinds of people usually called immoral are moral in that sense, and that's the only sense in which I think morality matters very much. It's the sense in which literary morality matters. The sense in which, just incidentally, I think Hemingway was delinquent, as Maupassant was delinquent. We were talking the other day about how Hemingway's stories contain no parents and no children. He's always involved solely with the present—a present-tense life. That's a limitation; it ignores the bonds that make individuals into a society.

You mentioned a couple of times that you felt—you didn't use these words—yes, you did—one time you said something about feeling as if you were an old-fashioned novelist. Do you feel . . .

I said I felt like a nineteenth-century anachronism, and I still feel a little that way. I really don't belong in the twentieth century; I grew up in the nineteenth century, even though it was technically on the calendar as the twentieth. What I was growing up in was 1914 Saskatchewan, but in its development it was about like 1860 Kansas. I never literally—you won't believe this, Dick—but I never saw a water closet or a bathtub till I was twelve years old. I never saw a lawn until I was twelve years old. It never occurred to me that people lived with such grace. It was Great Falls, Montana, the great mecca of civilization, where I first ran into those things. I was really from way down under, from below the grassroots. In some ways that belatedness was probably useful, because it gave me some sense of the whole course of human development, from the baldest frontier up into something like Stanford University, which is a long way from any frontier. On the other hand, it left me, I'm sure, permanently behind in certain ways, behind in my attitudes and expectations. My demands upon life are nineteenth-century demands rather than twentieth. There's nothing I can do about that. I have long since given up trying to.

So you would probably agree, then, with Faulkner's Nobel Prize speech that man will endure, but he will endure especially if he perseveres, if he's responsible, if he keeps up with his duties.

Of course. Nothing that blunt and direct, but in that direction. Some kind of responsibility in a social way—to family, to community, to nation, to whatever else—is absolutely essential. You don't get enough out of leather and chains, S and M groups, or Hell's Angels. That is too limited, too hedonistic, too selfish, for the making of a life. Anyone who goes that route is as irresponsible as a wandering feudal baron whacking off heads. That kind will always be around. I don't think you can get rid of them. But they are not what civilization grows by, or what the good life is made of. Aldous Huxley asked a question once with regard to whether all souls are equal in the sight of God. Were Cicero or Aristotle equal in the sight of God to the spearmen who did them in? I'm not sure they were. I think the spearmen were something a good deal less. They were the equivalent to Hell's Angels. The world proceeds by the Aristotles and the Ciceros and not by the spearmen. I try to remember that. It sounds pretentious, and I'm incapable of working at it all the time. Nevertheless there is some such conviction behind every writer who takes his writing seriously. I'd like to think I have a small place in the development of the civilization of western America, and hence, in a much smaller way, in the furthering of civilization in the world.

Afterword

By RICHARD W. ETULAIN

Early in 1978 I asked Wallace Stegner to collaborate in these interviews because I believed he was a major figure in American letters and perhaps *the* leading western writer. Within the previous decade he had capped a full and very successful career with a Pulitzer Prize and a National Book Award for fiction and had narrowly missed another Pulitzer for his biography of Bernard DeVoto. In addition, his authoritative comments on conservation and on western American culture had been widely cited for many years.

Before we began the conversations, Stegner warned me that he had "probably said more than once . . . everything [he] knew about the West and its history and literature." But, as I suspected, the interviews proved to be much more than repetitions of earlier observations. Indeed, as readers of this volume will soon discover, he had many new things to say about the West, about his life and career, and a good deal about the culture of the American West, past and present.

Few, if any, of my previous experiences can match the stimulation I received in talking with Stegner for two hours a day for two weeks. I experienced firsthand what so many observers have been saying recently: no one speaks with more persuasion, with more humane insight about the American West than Wallace Stegner. Working closely with him on this project has been a challenging and memorable experience.

Five interviews were conducted in August of 1980 at Stegner's attractive home in the Los Altos Hills west of Palo Alto and Stanford University. The second set of five also took place there eight months later, in March of

1981. After the conversations were transcribed, Stegner and I made minor changes in wording and punctuation, but the interviews are essentially as they were recorded. Above all, we have tried to retain the mood and format of informal conversations.

For their help in preparing this book for publication I wish to thank several people. Ellen K. Foppes helped with transcription, and Marion Honhart typed drafts of several interviews. Most of all, Annabelle Oczon did yeoman service in transcribing most of the conversations, typing drafts of several conversations, and helping prepare the index. I would like to thank Pat Devejian for her help with the 1989 conversation with Wallace Stegner that follows Norman Cousin's Foreword.

I am also indebted to the Research Allocations Committee of the University of New Mexico, which provided funds to conduct the interviews and a second grant to help cover some of the costs of typing the manuscript.

Finally, I owe a great deal to Trudy McMurrin, editor-in-chief of the University of Utah Press, who remained enthusiastic and helpful from the project's inception to its conclusion.

BOOKS BY RICHARD W. ETULAIN

Interpretive Approaches to Western American Literature, 1972 (coeditor)

Owen Wister, 1973

The Popular Western, 1974 (editor, with Michael T. Marsden)

The Idaho Heritage, 1974 (editor, with Bert Marley)

Idaho History: A Bibliography, 1974 (editor, with Merwin R. Swanson)

The Frontier and American West, 1977 (editor, with Rodman W. Paul)

Anglo-American Contributions to Basque Studies, 1977 (coeditor)

Jack London on the Road, 1979 (editor)

The American Literary West, 1980 (editor)

Basque Americans, 1981 (editor, with William A. Douglass)

Fifty Western Writers, 1982 (editor, with Fred Erisman)

A Bibliographical Guide to the Study of Western American Literature, 1982 (editor)

Western Films: A Short History, 1983 (editor)

Faith and Imagination: Essays on Evangelicals and Literature, 1985 (editor)

Ernest Haycox, 1988

The Twentieth-Century West: Historical Interpretations, 1989 (coeditor)

The American West: A Twentieth-Century History, 1989 (coauthor)

Index

NOTE: Boldface numerals indicate full-chapter treatment of a subject. The 1989 conversation added to this revised edition is not indexed.